SOVIET MILITARY POWER

SOVIET MILITARY POWER

William Koenig

Peter Scofield

Brompton

Published by
Brompton Books Corp.
15 Sherwood Place
Greenwich
CT 06830, USA

ISBN 0 86124 127 4
Printed in Hong Kong

Reprinted 1989

Page 1: Soviet tanks and
helicopter gunships on
winter maneuvers.
Page 2-3: Close-up of the
forward part of a Tu-95
Bear-D showing the
massive propeller blades of
the Kuznetsov turboprop
engines.
This page: Port bow view of
a Kashin class destroyer at
sea.

CONTENTS

WAR & SOVIET HISTORY 6

THE NUCLEAR SUPERPOWER 30

LAND POWER 54

AIR POWER 98

NAVAL POWER 142

THE SOVIET FIGHTING MAN 190

INDEX 222

WAR & SOVIET

In the early days of the
revolution, the Red Guards
were a motley lot of factory
workers, disaffected
soldiers, and sailors

As the Imperial Army suffered on the Eastern Front, Imperial Russia crumbled from war weariness and discontent on the home front. Here machine guns, unseen at the left, sweep rioters from the streets of St Petersburg.

Military power and its concomitant, military weakness, have always played a role in Russian and Soviet history. Both histories reflect a long record of painful foreign invasions and an equally long record of imperial expansion by force of arms, weakness and vulnerability balanced with raw military conquest. The military power built by Peter the Great in the late seventeenth and early eighteenth centuries was the basis of Russia as a European power in the eighteenth and nineteenth centuries, the Russia that alone of the European powers defeated Napoleon and established a hegemony over Eastern Europe. Military power has also been a vehicle for the rise of the USSR from extreme weakness through regional dominance to global superpower. As the Russian philosopher Nikolai Berdyaev observed, 'Bolshevism entered Russian life as a highly militarized force' and the Soviet state has maintained this military focus. Indeed, some western observers have described it as a warfare state in a condition of semi-permanent mobilization.

To a greater extent than their Russian forbears, the Soviets have seen military power as the main guarantor of the survival of their state and its revolutionary mission in the world. The Soviets define their security primarily as a function of military power. The early Soviet state was extremely weak and saw itself surrounded by hostile capitalist states, some of which had actively participated in the Russian civil war. The Bolsheviks, having barely subdued their internal opposition in the formation of their revolutionary state, were also very sensitive to internal security. Beset by enemies within and without, the Soviets developed a 'siege mentality' which they maintain to a surprising extent to the present. Over the years, the Soviets have come to define their security requirements as extending well beyond protection of the homeland and communist rule to control of adjacent regions and subsequently, with the advent of long range nuclear weapons, to regions far removed such as the United States.

The Soviets have also fixed on military power as the main means of encouraging conditions in which they can realize their foreign goals. Their massive investment in military forces since World War II, and especially under Brezhnev from the mid-1960s to early 1980s, gave them dominance, if not outright control, over the key regions adjacent to Soviet borders but the real dividend on this huge and long term investment came in the late 1960s. As a result of the growth of Soviet strategic nuclear forces, the United States implicitly acknowledged Soviet arrival as a superpower. Where Soviet ideology and socio-economic model have had only superficial influence in the Third World, the Soviets have found *entrée* and influence through their military. The earliest Soviet military client was the Republican side in the Spanish Civil War, followed by the Kuomintang Government of Chiang Kai-shek from 1938 to 1940. Since that time, the Soviets have armed the Arab World in its struggles with Israel, made Cuba a well-armed and trained force in the Carribean also capable of expeditionary adventures in Africa, and gathered a variety of other clients in Africa, Asia and the Middle East. The attraction has been the availability of Soviet arms, military advisers and political support.

The most successful and visible aspect of Soviet development has been the accumulation of military power along with the industrial and technological bases to support it. Where the civilian economy is still rife with shortages, delays, and low productivity and where civilian agriculture is such that the army tries to grow much of its own food, the military is the success story of the USSR. Whatever position the Soviets have in the world largely stems from accomplishments in the military sphere. The Soviets have fielded large modern forces and built an extensive defense industrial base which arms these forces with very acceptable weapons and material. Soviet technology has enabled the Soviet to keep abreast of, and in several instances ahead of, the US in the highly visible space race with its important military thrust for each side. The military is in fact the only area in which the Soviets successfully compete with the West and much of the USSR's accomplishment as a state is measured specifically in terms of the military competition with the United States. The Soviet military would indeed be aptly characterized by John Keegan's general observation that a military is 'a mirror of its own society and its values . . . an agent of national pride . . . a bulwark against national fears, or perhaps even the last symbol of the nation itself.'

Military Power and Soviet Security

Survival is the basic concern of any political regime but was especially so for the small group of Bolsheviks who seized power in Russia in October 1917. The country was still at war and the victorious army of Kaiser Wilhelm II was camped in Western Russia. Lenin solved that problem through diplomacy but the Bolsheviks

fought a long and bitter war with their White adversaries and then spent several more years in military conquest of the hinterlands of the former Russian state. The early Bolsheviks were also concerned about their ability to build the new communist state and lead their revolutionary movement abroad but fears of domestic counterrevolution and foreign attack quickly returned them to a more traditional conception of security under Stalin. To curb domestic opposition, Stalin created the world's first totalitarian state and used mass terror as an effective instrument of internal security. He also began the expansion of the armed forces and, equally important, began to build the defense industrial base necessary for modern military power.

Stalin early recognized the danger posed by Nazi Germany and attempted to make alliances against the future contingency of war. Rebuffed by France and Britain, he cynically tried to buy more time to prepare through the Pact of Steel with Hitler. When the long expected conflict came, the Soviets won over the long haul by

Below: V. I. Lenin, the first leader of the new Soviet state, was faced with major problems of internal and external security. Some were solved with diplomacy, but most were handled by the Red Army which was created and led by Trotsky.

Above: Internal security was a constant problem for the new Soviet state. The Red Army had as its major job policing a restive population.

Left: A unit of the Imperial Russian Army defects to the revolution in 1917.

ДА ЗДРАВСТВУЕТ СВОБОДНАЯ РОССІЯ

out-producing and out-gunning Hitler's Germans in a war of brute force. In a lesson not lost to this day, the Soviets survived their greatest challenge through raw military power bluntly applied.

Following the war, Stalin addressed himself to improving the condition of Soviet security by consolidating its military base through revamping the military, especially the army. He also expanded the Soviet security perimeter by establishing Soviet control over East Europe through the physical presence of Soviet troops in most cases. Though the pace and methods of creating these 'satellites' varied from case to case, Stalin was following a concept of territorial buffers which he had apparently developed during World War II. He had certainly made no secret of his designs on East Europe during the

Left: Building on the foundation laid by Stalin, the modern Soviet Army is well equipped. Here T-64 tanks are seen on realistic maneuvers.

later wartime conferences with Churchill and Roosevelt. This regional approach to security accomplished two goals in that the large scale presence of Soviet forces ensured the subservience of the satellite states and also gave the USSR a forward line of defense well to the west

of Soviet territory. Any future war was to take place in Europe well away from the Soviet homeland. The satellites, for their part, were not only to be subservient to Soviet needs and goals but indeed were expected to become mini-versions of the Soviet model faithful to the USSR. Thus they were to serve not only as a military buffer zone but also as a buffer against ideological and psychological challenge from the West.

After Stalin's death in 1953, his successors moved well beyond this extended concept of military and ideological security to a global concept forced upon them by the development of whole new dimensions of military power. Even though they inherited a strong position in East Europe and could look out on a weak West Germany and China, they also were confronted with the formation of NATO in 1949 and large American forces permanently deployed in Europe. Most importantly, however, the Americans had a small but growing nuclear arsenal and the means to deliver it on Soviet targets. The Soviets had no counter to this threat. Under Nikita Khrushchev, the Soviets came to see that their military power needed a global reach and especially a reach to the prime enemy in North America. Soviet security came increasingly to be defined as military competition with the United States. As the strategic nuclear

Left: A Soviet Kara class cruiser seen in 1982. In addition to their comprehensive missile and gun armament the Karas carry a Hormone-A anti-submarine helicopter.

Soviet troops on maneuvers, supported by Mil-8 Hip helicopters. The Mi-8 is the standard Soviet assault transport helicopter and most versions in service are armed with rockets or machine guns. They can carry 28 troops.

arsenals of each side developed, they became the main measuring sticks of the military competition because they were both crudely quantifiable and were seen as the ultimate measure of military power.

While the Soviets worked hard to overcome their deficit in this crucial area of military power, they also looked beyond their security perimeter to a Third World teeming with newly-independent countries and national liberation movements. The Soviets could offer their model of economic and political development and also step over the 'capitalist encirclement' to compete on a broader stage. Thus they embarked on a series of relationships with such figures as Nasser of Egypt, Sukarno of Indonesia, Nehru of India and, most importantly, Castro of Cuba. The gains were hard won and usually transitory and required a constant effort to consolidate. But the Soviets did make their presence known beyond the confines of their historic perimeter and did so at a time when the US was at the peak of its global influence and power.

While urgently pursuing the development of nuclear weapons, Stalin had not permitted his military theorists to consider their implications for warfare and thus left to his successors a military equipped and oriented only toward conventional war. The passing of Stalin, however, opened a floodgate of changes in both milit-

Pictured with Churchill and Roosevelt at the Teheran conference in 1943, Stalin made no secret of his postwar intentions to his erstwhile allies.

ary doctrine and strategy. Breakthroughs were being achieved in research, development, production and deployment of new nuclear weapon systems. By 1957, a general conclusion had been reached that the introduction of nuclear weapons and ballistic missiles had brought about radical changes in all aspects of warfare, forcing major revisions in basic concepts. Ultimately, the party leadership concluded that in any future war between the opposing socialist and capitalist social systems, the nuclear weapon and the ballistic missile would be the decisive factor. 'One of the important positions of this doctrine' wrote the Soviet theorist A. A. Strokov, 'is that a world war . . . will inevitably take the form of a nuclear rocket war, that is the kind of war in which the main means of striking will be the nuclear weapon and the basic means of delivering it to the target will be the rocket.' The Soviet expectation was that such a conflict would be short and immensely destructive. But Soviet theorists were careful to temper this conclusion with a belief that it was necessary to prepare for protracted conflict. Thus a new doctrine based on the preeminence of nuclear

weapons was developed.

As William and Harriet Scott have noted, the Soviet leadership traditionally uses slogans as an educational tool. The 'revolution in military affairs' was the slogan chosen to keynote the reorientation of the Soviet officer corps to the new doctrine of nuclear war. Throughout the 1960s and 1970s, almost everything written on military doctrine made some reference to this 'revolution.'

But what of the impact of the revolution on strategy and operations – how would such a 'nuclear missile war' actually be fought? The early 1960s were a time of turbulence as an extreme view usually associated with the policy of Nikita Khrushchev contested the more conventional approach of the military establishment. The Khrushchev perspective was epitomized by the formation of the Strategic Rocket Forces in 1960 as the premier military service to serve as the focus of Soviet long range missiles and nuclear weapons. The next world war was to take to the form of mass exchanges of strategic nuclear missiles. Conventional forces would still be required to mop up and occupy enemy territory but the decisive factor would be nuclear firepower, so the conventional forces could be – and were – reduced.

Khrushchev's wholehearted embrace of this extreme view of nuclear warfighting also fitted in well with his desire to reduce the resources devoted to the defense establishment. But the military theorists who dominated the establishment were never completely comfortable with this view. Khrushchev's war would be a short one, requiring little more than occupation operations from the army. But in the view of many of the Soviet marshals, nuclear weapons did not make the army superfluous but rather required large forces to absorb the horrendous casualties all agreed would be a main feature of nuclear war and to sustain operations in a nuclear environment.

His extreme view of war also led Khrushchev to abandon or alter the fundamental tenets of Leninist dogma about the inevitability of war with the capitalist camp and of communist victory, and also of the utility of war as an instrument of policy. Continued adherence to the doctrine of the inevitability of war would make the Soviets appear as advocates to a world nervous about 'the bomb'. The Soviets had also to offer some vision of the future to their own people other than inevitable armageddon. Khrushchev thus espoused the view that neither war nor

Seen here with President Eisenhower at Camp David, Nikita Krushchev challenged the United States in a bold and provocative manner by placing Soviet missiles in Cuba.

A ZSU-23-4 23mm self-propelled anti-aircraft gun is seen with its target-tracking radar mounted on the rear of the turret.

communist victory was inevitable and that 'peaceful coexistence' could be maintained indefinitely. Peaceful coexistence was broadly defined as vigorous competition with the capitalist camp in all areas short of armed conflict.

But Khrushchev paid dearly for this doctrinal revisionism and peaceful coexistence as these became a major factor in the Sino-Soviet split. The Chinese excoriated Khrushchev for these deviations, with the aging Mao still insisting on

the probability and even desirability of nuclear holocaust. Khrushchev's memoirs suggest that China was considered at least an adversary if not an outright enemy by 1959, thus adding a major item to the already long list of Soviet security concerns. Mao's China became a competing center of communist orthodoxy as the Chinese directly challenged the relevance of the Soviet model of development for the Third World. The Chinese also demanded redress for

Above: The Soviet
hegemony over Eastern
Europe has never been
easy. Here young Germans
challenge Soviet T-34
tanks in Berlin during
June 1953 in one of the
earliest episodes of
satellite unrest.

Right: Mikhail Gorbachev
and former US President
Ronald Reagan discuss
arms control at Geneva in
1985.

the unequal treaties forced on Imperial China
by a hungry Russian empire and laid claims to
Soviet territory as a result. The Soviets were
made painfully aware that there was a hostile
and potentially powerful state abutting their
Far Eastern borders which were vulnerable because of tenuous communications and a sparse
population of largely non-Russian inhabitants.
Much of the impetus for the large buildup of the
Soviet army in particular during the 1960s can
be laid directly to the Soviet conception of China
as a major security concern and the vituperative
and occasionally violent nature of their political-military confrontation.

While Khrushchev denigrated 'rifles and
bayonets' and asserted that defense was based
on 'the quantity and quality of our nuclear missile arsenal', his successors have taken a more
balanced view of military needs and policy and
developed Soviet military power across the
board, aided by a change in the position of the
military itself. After the extremes of the
Khrushchev period, the military came to the
view that war and victory were both possible

and that the best possible deterrent was a
strong, balanced force posture. It was increasingly recognized that a nuclear conflict
might well prove protracted, requiring large
combined-arms ground formations equipped
with their own tactical nuclear missiles. The
conflict might also begin with conventional
weapons only because of the balance of strategic
nuclear forces and NATO's doctrine of 'flexible
response' formally adopted in 1967. But the revolution in military affairs remains at the core
of Soviet strategy and doctrine and nuclear missile systems continue to represent the decisive
factor in any future conflict of the superpowers.
The Brezhnev regime continued and indeed considerably expanded Khrushchev's 'nuclear missile arsenal' but also paralleled these programs
with a huge and continuing investment in the
general purpose forces.

Even at the time of Khrushchev's fall in 1964,
the Soviets had made major gains in military
power but as that power continued to accumu-
late under Brezhnev, the Soviets remained
obsessed by their self-image of inequality with

the United States. American power and influence reached around the globe in political, military, economic and commercial aspects. While Soviet influence was growing, it was by comparison very modest and even tenuous and relied on the export of arms and training. And even as late as 1982, the Soviets could be haunted and embarassed by the specter of inequality when in Lebanon the Soviet equipment matched against the American equipment used by the Israelis was shown to be inferior. Israeli-flown US warplanes shot down 83 Syrian-flown Soviet warplanes without loss.

This may help to explain the apparent willingness of the Soviets to talk more openly with the West about arms control, characterized by the Summit meetings at Geneva (November 1985), Reykjavik (October 1986) and Washington (December 1987), the latter of which produced an agreement over intermediate-range nuclear forces in Europe. Mikhail Gorbachev, the Soviet leader since March 1985, has realized that, if the Soviet Union is to survive economically into the twenty-first century, a certain amount of *perestroika* (restructuring) has to take place, and this has led, in part, to a deliberate policy of *glasnost* (openness) both internally and in relations with the West. The vast investment in nuclear weapons was unlikely to diminish if confrontation continued – indeed, with President Reagan's Strategic Defense Initiative (SDI, or 'Star Wars') program of space-based anti-ballistic weapons on the cards, the Soviets would clearly have to match the capability to stay in the game – so negotiation and arms control was an obvious response to the rising costs of the arms race.

Soviet security concerns have become far more complex than the regional conception of Stalin's time or even the global conception of Khrushchev. The Soviets now measure their security not just in military terms but also in terms of political position, rights due, and even image. The core, however, is still the very complex military relationship with the United States which has developed over the last several decades. The Soviets have also arrived at the classic dilemma of the nuclear age superpower. Like the United States, their vast investment in a strategic nuclear arsenal has endowed them with awesome power, yet that power is not usable except in terms of the ultimate catastrophe. But the Soviets have another dilemma in that their vast military buildup over the years has provoked responses from their potential adversaries that continue to change Soviet perceptions of their requirements for military power.

The Warsaw Pact

The USSR has relied less than other countries on alliances, diplomacy and international institutions for security and much more on a strong military posture. Yet it does belong to an alliance which adds a significant dimension to its military potential. The Warsaw Pact is a multi-lateral military alliance formed on 14 May 1955. It was inspired by the creation of NATO and the need for a more unified command structure in the forward security buffer of East Europe. The original membership included Albania, which withdrew in 1968, and now comprises Bulgaria, Romania, Hungary, Czechoslovakia, East Germany and Poland in addition to the USSR. The Warsaw Pact is committed to the defense only of the European territories of its members.

The Warsaw Pact members are almost totally subordinate to Soviet control and interests, a subordination maintained by Soviet forces per-

Top: Soviet forces practice an amphibious landing with a PT-76 light tank supported by BTR armored personnel carriers.

Above: The Soviets strive for realism in training.

manently stationed in Poland, East Germany, Czechoslovakia and Hungary. The Soviet troops in Czechoslovakia and Hungary are in fact the continuing legacy of past insubordination. The highest organ of the Warsaw Pact is the Political Consultative Committee. There is also a Combined Military Command. All key Warsaw Pact positions are held by Soviets, including commander-in-chief and chief of staff. Non-Soviet forces are armed primarily with Soviet weapons and are dependent on Soviet logistic support in both peace and war. In wartime, the Soviet High Command would assume operational control of the forces of the other members. The Warsaw Pact air defense system is now commanded from Moscow even in peacetime.

The non-Soviet members have between them some 53 divisions plus other units to augment the Soviet effort. This would be a significant contribution if taken at face value. But the key question of how willing the non-Soviet forces would be to join the Soviets in a major war is one often discussed by Western analysts and surely by the Soviets as well. The history of Polish and

Romanian insubordination is well known while the Soviet interventions in Hungary in 1956 and Czechoslovakia in 1968 are continuing and embarassing testimony to the coercive nature of Soviet relations with the East European satellites. How the East Europeans would respond in wartime cannot be known in advance but the prognosis for wholehearted support of Soviet goals can hardly be seen as encouraging. On paper, the Warsaw Pact appears to be an important part of Soviet military power but the reality may be something else.

The Garrison Economy

There are within the USSR two economic sectors, defense and the rest. In contrast to the general sluggishness and shortage-plagued inefficiency of most of Soviet industry, the defense sector appears to be well-managed and productive, no doubt in part because of the absolute priority it has traditionally enjoyed in terms of resources and managerial talent. Over the last 25 years, the USSR has devoted an average of 12 or 14 percent of its Gross National Product to defense, and increased military expenditures in real terms.

The growth rate of the Soviet economy has declined sharply over the last decade, however, to force some hard decisions. In all of those decisions, military spending has emerged relatively unscathed, with most of the burden being born by civilian consumption and investment. In 1975, investment growth was cut by one third in a significant departure from the longstanding ideological devotion to the increasing allocation from national income to investment in order to assure continuing growth. Myron Rush has noted that the decision to sacrifice growth through the diversion of investment funds to defense came after the onset of detente. Rush argues that continued increases in defense spending, despite the worsening economic situation, suggest that defense is rather insensitive to changes in economic circumstances. Since Mikhail Gorbachev came to power in March 1985, however, this has been recognized officially and defense spending has come under scrutiny. The Soviets now face an inevitable diminution of defense resources. If the latter is accepted, the international scene has to be made more friendly, with less overt confrontation.

According to the US Department of Defense, the Soviet military industrial base is the world's largest in terms of number of facilities and physical size. Its physical plant has grown steadily over the last two decades through large amounts of financial and human resource investment. The industry devoted to military production includes 135 major final assembly plants producing weapons as end products, supported by over 3500 factories and related facilities. Qualitative improvements in production technology – the defense industrial sector has absolute priority on new technologies – has

Left: General Dmitry Yazov, the Soviet Union's former Minister of Defense.

Below: The Soviets were the first army to introduce an infantry combat vehicle in the BMP. The BMP has a Sagger anti-tank guided missile mounted next to its 73mm gun, a crew of 3 to 4, and can carry a squad of 8 soldiers into battle.

while capable of developing advanced systems, show signs of being unable to match the production of the more basic hardware industries, perhaps another incentive to simplicity. Western analysts have concluded that one of the great failings of Soviet industry is its inability to produce sufficient numbers of highly sophisticated goods in fields like electronics.

Whatever its failings, however, the garrison economy has been a major factor in the development of Soviet military power. It has produced the huge quantities of weapons and material required to arm and equip the forces, no mean feat in itself. Over time, it has also improved the quality of the product to the point that most Soviet equipment is as good as, and in some cases better than, its Western counterparts. The economic price that the Soviets have had to pay for these accomplishments, however, has been high, far higher than would have been required by a better organized and more efficient economy. Over the long term, the price may well turn out to have been too high because of its negative effect on the rest of the economy.

Above: Soviet troops roll past a Czech holding a bloodstained Czech flag during the Soviet intervention of 1968.

Right: A column of Soviet T-55 tanks on a side street in Prague during the Soviet intervention of 1968.

paralleled physical growth. The USSR alone produces more weapons systems in greater quantities than any other nation.

Despite their privileged position and relative efficiency, the defense industries suffer from the rigidities of a command economy and its technological shortcomings. The rigidly planned economy is ill-equipped to deal with sudden shifts in priorities while the production quota-oriented industrial sector resists the disruption implied by the introduction of new systems. Yet entirely separate design bureaus continue to work to produce new models. But the history of Soviet weapons development is replete with accounts of promising systems whose production versions failed miserably because subcomponent producers could not consistently maintain specifications. Soviet weapon systems tend to be rugged and reliable, indeed simple, and their production runs are typically long in time and huge in quantity. But this may be as much a product of the imperatives of the military economy as of the demands of the Soviet military. High technology industries such as electronics,

The Command of Military Power

The main function of the Soviet military is to operate in support of the decisions and objectives of the Communist Party. The Party controls the military through the Politburo which determines military policy and gives direction to the forces. The Politburo in turn uses the Defense Council to oversee military affairs and ensure that the forces, industry and Party are prepared for any defense contingency. This council was chaired by the late President Brezhnev and has been chaired in turn by his three successors, Yuri Andropov, Konstantin Chernenko and Mikhail Gorbachev. The Minister of Defense, currently Dmitry Yazov, is also a Defense Council member and presumably the liaison between his ministry and the other members of the Defense Council.

In wartime, the Soviets apparently plan to revert to the 'Stavka' or General Headquarters of World War II. In his standard work *Military Strategy,* the Soviet Marshal Sokolovsky wrote that 'The direct leadership of the Armed Forces in a war will obviously be accomplished, as be-fore, by the Stavka of the Supreme High Command. The Stavka will be a collegial agency of leadership under the chairmanship of the supreme commander-in-chief.' Brezhnev was supreme commander-in-chief. The Stavka would presumably include key political figures and top Ministry of Defense officials.

This superstructure of command exercises control through the General Staff which M.V. Frunze, its first chief in 1925, described as the 'brain of the army' and Sokolovsky later termed the 'main agency of the Stavka'. Senior to all services and branches, the General Staff is the main locus of activity within the Ministry of Defense. Similar to the strong German General Staff system, the Soviet General Staff is not only prestigious but exercises great authority and influence over all military matters, including the military budget, and directs all foreign military sales, assistance to client states, insurgent movements and 'wars of national liberation'. The General Staff formulates overall plans for the development and employment of the armed forces and has a direct role in their

A Soviet T-55 tank clears a barricade of burning buses set up by Czech resisters in 1968.

Main picture: A Soviet Tu-95 Bear reconnaissance plane overflies the USS *Kitty Hawk* escorted by two US F-4 Phantom interceptors.

Above: The late President Leonid Brezhnev, at lower right, and other members of the Politburo vote during a session of the Supreme Soviet in 1981. Brezhnev was replaced in 1982 by Yuri Andropov, former KGB chief, seen here in the middle of the back row. Andropov died in early 1984.

operations and control. Of the ten directorates of the General Staff, the most important is the Main Operations Directorate which is the center of war planning and operations, including training, plans, readiness, and control of operations. Next comes the Main Intelligence Directorate (GRU) which is the central military intelligence agency. On the basis of worldwide collection and analysis, the GRU prepares intelligence for the General Staff on the military capabilities and intentions of other countries but especially potential adversaries. The other directorates are Communications, Armaments, Military Assistance, Topography, Cryptography, Military Science, Organization and Mobilization, and the Warsaw Pact.

The General Staff is also the vehicle through which the Minister of Defense commands the

Above: After 18 years of power, Leonid Brezhnev died on 10 November 1982 to open a new era in Soviet politics.

Above right: Admiral Vladimir Chernavin, the Commander-in Chief of the Soviet Navy, gained his position after the retirement of Gorshkov in 1985.

Main picture: A Soviet Foxtrot class submarine cruises in the Mediterranean. The Foxtrot is a diesel-electric powered attack submarine with a surface displacement of some 2000 tons.

forces. Western forces are typically organized into land, air and naval components but the Soviets have five distinct services: the Strategic Rocket Forces, Army, Air Forces, National Air Defense Forces, and Navy. Each service has its own commander-in-chief who is responsible for training, organization, administration and logistics through his staff and directorates similar to those of the General Staff. The exercise of operational command by the services, however, is limited by the amount of direct command authority residing in the General Staff. The Strategic Rocket Forces and the Army are the two premier services and have the primary offensive missions in the Soviet forces. In charge of all land-based ballistic missiles with ranges of 1000 km or more, the Strategic Rocket Forces was officially established in 1960 to displace the Army as the number one service. Historically the most important, the Army is the largest service by far and in peacetime is deployed throughout the sixteen Military Districts of the USSR and four 'Groups of Forces' in East Europe. In wartime, the Military districts and Groups of Forces would become 'fronts', the highest operational unit, especially those Military Districts located near main areas of conflict. The Air Forces are composed of Long Range Aviation, Frontal (tactical) Aviation, and Military Transport Aviation. The National Air Defense forces are the antiaircraft guns, surface-to-air missiles, radars and interceptor aircraft which protect the homeland against air attack. Still a distinctly junior service, the Navy has four fleets – Northern, Pacific, Black Sea, and Baltic Sea – as well as a strong land-based air arm and 17,000 naval infantry in five independent regiments.

Military Power and the Future

Under Brezhnev, the Soviets muted the themes of economic and ideological competition with the West and sought detente while building all dimensions of their military power to a degree both puzzling and perturbing to the West. Brezhnev's death on 10 November 1982 left to his recent successors a country with not only serious economic problems and social malaise

---

COMPOSITION OF THE GROUP OF SOVIET FORCES, GERMANY

Headquarters – Zossen-Wunstorf
(Also HQ of 16th Air Army, 975 tactical aircraft)

Second Guards Tank Army – HQ Furstenberg
Component Units
9th Guards Tank Division (Neustrelitz)
32nd Guards Motor Rifle Division (Perleberg)
94th Guards Motor Rifle Division (Schwerin)

Third Shock Army – HQ Magdeburg
Component Units
25th Tank Division (Templin)
12th Guards Tank Division (Neuruppin)
10th Guards Tank Division (Potsdam)
47th Guards Tank Division (Altmark)
207th Motor Rifle Division (Stendal)

Eighth Guards Army – HQ Weimar
Component Units
20th Guards Tank Division (Jena)
20th Guards Motor Rifle Division (Grimma)
39th Guards Motor Rifle Division (Ohrdruf, Thuringia)
57th Guards Motor Rifle Division (Naumburg, Saale)

Twentieth Guards Army – HQ Eberswald
Component Units
6th Guards Motor Rifle Division (Bernau)
14th Guards Motor Rifle Division (Juterborg)
19th Motor Rifle Division (Potsdam)

First Guards Tank Army – HQ Dresden
Component Units
6th Guards Tank Division (Wittenberg/Lutherstadt)
7th Guards Tank Division (Dessau/Rosslau)
11th Guards Tank Division (Dresden)
27th Guards Motor Rifle Division (Halle)
9th Tank Division (Riesa)

Additional Units Include:
34th Guards Artillery Division (Potsdam)
Two Assault Engineer Regiments (Zossen, Berlin)
Two 36-ship Hind helicopter Regiments (Parchim, Stendal)
One Airborne Brigade (Neuruppin)

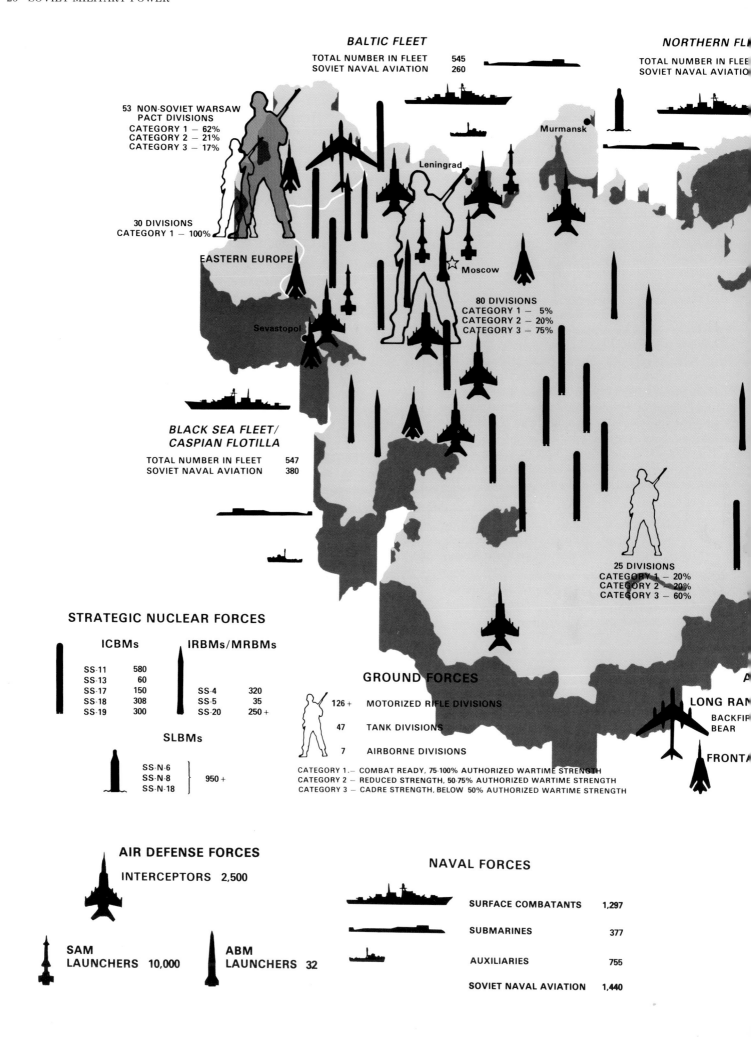

BALTIC FLEET

TOTAL NUMBER IN FLEET   545
SOVIET NAVAL AVIATION   260

NORTHERN FL...

TOTAL NUMBER IN FLEE...
SOVIET NAVAL AVIATIO...

Murmansk

Leningrad

Moscow

53 NON-SOVIET WARSAW
PACT DIVISIONS
CATEGORY 1 — 62%
CATEGORY 2 — 21%
CATEGORY 3 — 17%

30 DIVISIONS
CATEGORY 1 — 100%

EASTERN EUROPE

80 DIVISIONS
CATEGORY 1 — 5%
CATEGORY 2 — 20%
CATEGORY 3 — 75%

Sevastopol

**BLACK SEA FLEET/
CASPIAN FLOTILLA**

TOTAL NUMBER IN FLEET   547
SOVIET NAVAL AVIATION   380

25 DIVISIONS
CATEGORY 1 — 20%
CATEGORY 2 — 20%
CATEGORY 3 — 60%

STRATEGIC NUCLEAR FORCES

ICBMs		IRBMs/MRBMs	
SS-11	580		
SS-13	60		
SS-17	150	SS-4	320
SS-18	308	SS-5	35
SS-19	300	SS-20	250 +

SLBMs

SS-N-6	
SS-N-8	950 +
SS-N-18	

GROUND FORCES

126 +	MOTORIZED RIFLE DIVISIONS
47	TANK DIVISIONS
7	AIRBORNE DIVISIONS

CATEGORY 1 — COMBAT READY, 75-100% AUTHORIZED WARTIME STRENGTH
CATEGORY 2 — REDUCED STRENGTH, 50-75% AUTHORIZED WARTIME STRENGTH
CATEGORY 3 — CADRE STRENGTH, BELOW 50% AUTHORIZED WARTIME STRENGTH

LONG RAN...

BACKFI...
BEAR

FRONTA...

AIR DEFENSE FORCES

INTERCEPTORS   2,500

SAM
LAUNCHERS   10,000

ABM
LAUNCHERS   32

NAVAL FORCES

SURFACE COMBATANTS	1,297
SUBMARINES	377
AUXILIARIES	755
SOVIET NAVAL AVIATION	1,440

The maps show the deployment of Soviet forces and the main military research centers.

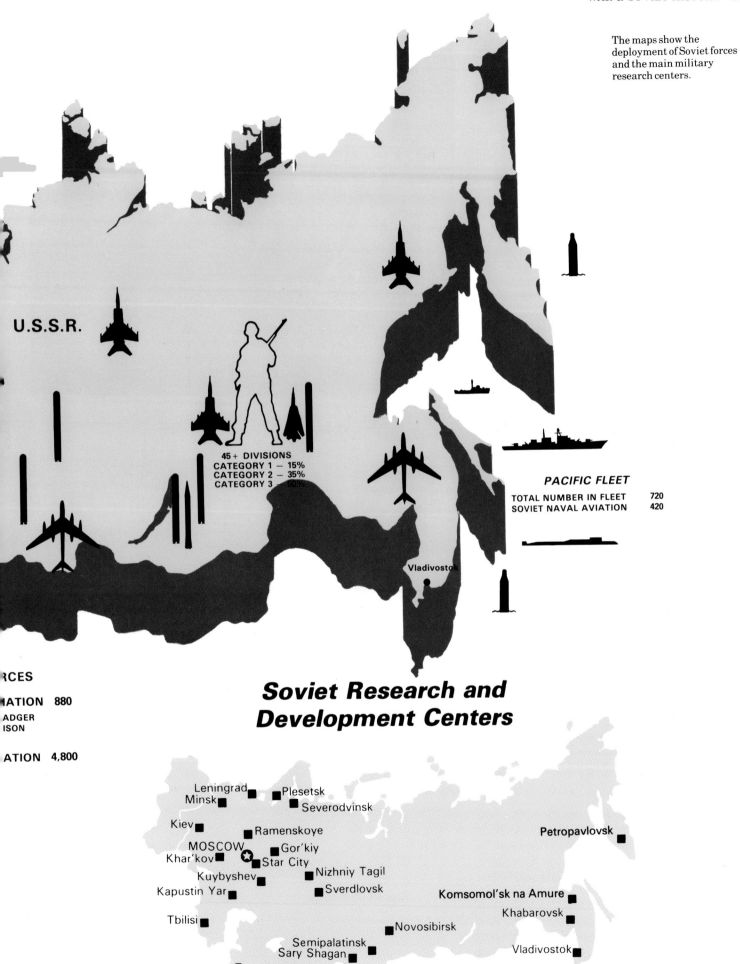

U.S.S.R.

45 + DIVISIONS
CATEGORY 1 — 15%
CATEGORY 2 — 35%
CATEGORY 3 — 50%

PACIFIC FLEET

TOTAL NUMBER IN FLEET   720
SOVIET NAVAL AVIATION   420

Vladivostok

RCES

IATION 880

ADGER
ISON

ATION 4,800

Soviet Research and Development Centers

Leningrad
Minsk
Plesetsk
Severodvinsk
Kiev
Ramenskoye
Petropavlovsk
MOSCOW
Gor'kiy
Khar'kov
Star City
Kuybyshev
Nizhniy Tagil
Kapustin Yar
Sverdlovsk
Komsomol'sk na Amure
Tbilisi
Khabarovsk
Novosibirsk
Semipalatinsk
Sary Shagan
Vladivostok
Tyuratam

but some new and some renewed security concerns. There is the southern border where the ferment in Iran and record of resistance in Afghanistan threaten both the internal and external security concerns of the USSR. There is continued confrontation, despite the era of 'New Detente,' with the West, and the reality of American force strength worldwide. Most importantly, there is the recognition that the Soviet Union, if it is to survive economically, must channel resources away from defense spending into investment and massive industrial reorganization.

All of this has led Mikhail Gorbachev to pursue some surprising policies, both at home and abroad. In domestic terms, he has carved out a power base in the Politburo which, by 'purging' long-term Brezhnev supporters like Minister of Defense Dmitry Ustinov, has clearly affected the influence of the armed forces, while the policy of *glasnost* has awakened demands among the Soviet people for consumer goods that can only be provided by cutting down defense spending. Abroad, Gorbachev has im-

proved relations with the United States through the various Summit meetings and the INF Agreement (December 1987) and has even mended fences with China, for long a source of border tension in the East. In addition, an agreement has been made to pull Soviet troops out of Afghanistan by February 1989, and the number of Soviet 'advisers' worldwide has been cut. The overall result is a noticeable thaw in East-West relations which may reflect Gorbachev's desire to lessen the threat to his country as a preliminary to force spending cuts. However, this has yet to be translated into deep reductions in the size or structure of Soviet armed forces, which remain formidable instruments of political power. Until such reductions are seen to happen, the West has to remain on its guard. Gorbachev's statement to the United Nations in December 1988 outlining large troop and equipment cuts in Western Europe was widely seen as a positive move to reduce international tension.

Above: The Victor class nuclear-powered submarines are the mainstay of the Soviet attack submarine fleet.

Top: Former Soviet Minister of Defense Dmitry Ustinov was one of the architects of the Soviet military build-up over the last 20 years.

Top right: The MiG-21 fighter, seen here in the later Fishbed L model, is the most widely deployed fighter aircraft in the world.

Right: The first *Sovremennyy* class guided missile destroyer began its trials in 1980.

THE NUCLEAR

SUPERPOWER

An important turning point of Soviet history occurred not in the halls of the Kremlin nor even in the USSR but at Glassboro State College in New Jersey in 1967. In that unlikely locale, President Lyndon Johnson broached to a Soviet representative a proposal for negotiations on managing the strategic nuclear arsenals of the two countries to reduce the risk of nuclear war and head off a possible new round in the nuclear arms competition. Formal negotiations did not get underway for about two years, however, as the Soviet invasion of Czechoslovakia intervened in 1968. Known under the acronym of SALT for Strategic Arms Limitation Talks, the negotiations produced four formal treaties and other agreements over the next decade. The USSR, and Imperial Russia before it, had traditionally been a continental land power able to dominate or at least influence its neighbors but never a global arbiter of events as was, for example, Britain in the nineteenth century or the United States since World War II. Johnson's overture on that fateful day marked implicit US acknowledgement that it would have henceforth to share the global arena with the Soviets. In the eyes of the watching world, a second superpower had been born.

The Soviet elevation to superpower status stemmed from the conscious development of a whole new dimension of Soviet military power. That dimension was the growth of a large force of intercontinental ballistic missiles (ICBM) which for the first time brought the entire US under credible threat of large scale attack. In a future war, no longer would the US be able to contribute men and material while its population, industry and government remained well removed from any physical threat as they had in World Wars I and II. Fortress America was no longer impregnable and the strategic nuclear monopoly on which postwar US defense policy had centered no longer existed.

The new dimension of Soviet military power grew out of what the Soviets term the 'revolution in military affairs' which was simply the marriage of the nuclear warhead with the means to deliver it over long, even intercontinental, distances. As the Soviet military theoretician I. Zavilov wrote in *Red Star* in 1970, 'The creation of nuclear warheads and the combination of them with missile carriers . . . brought about a complete revolution in the art of warfare . . . and demanded a reappraisal of the existing principles of the art of war.' Zavilov went on to note four primary ways in which warfare would be affected by the 'revolution'. First, the spatial dimension of war would be greatly expanded since no combatant would be spared attack. Second, the time dimension would be accelerated since wars would no longer take years but might be decided in days or even hours by nuclear salvoes. Third, the surprise factor would be increased since the enemy could be totally destroyed by a sudden nuclear strike. Finally, the usual complexity and chaos of war

would be multiplied many times by the awesome power of nuclear weapons.

The meaning and impact of nuclear weapons not only on warfare but on international relations in general has indeed been one of the great imponderables since the US dropped two small nuclear bombs on Japan in August 1945. Although nuclear weapons have fortunately never been employed again, the simple fact of their existence has been a major factor in the relationship of the US and USSR and now has come to affect the political-military confrontations between such local rivals as India and Pakistan, Israel and the Arab world, and South Africa and its African antagonists.

The nuclear arms competition with the US which eventually carried the USSR to nuclear parity and attendant superpower status began in the wake of the Hiroshima and Nagasaki

Above: An SS-8 ICBM on parade in Red Square.

Top: An AS-1 Kennel anti-shipping missile. Two of these now-obsolete missiles can be carried by the Tu-16 Badger medium bomber.

Right: The monster SS-9 ICBM greatly disturbed the US because of its massive warhead.

Previous page: An SS-4 medium range ballistic missile lifts off a soft pad. The SS-4 has a range of perhaps 1200 miles and a nuclear warhead in the megaton class.

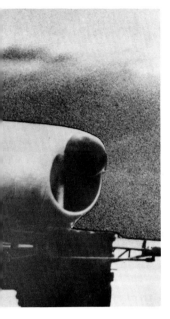

bombings. Shaken by the potential military dominance then in US hands, Stalin within days called together his chief weapons designers and reportedly instructed: 'A single demand of you, comrades: provide us with atomic weapons in the shortest possible time . . . The equilibrium has been destroyed. Provide the bomb – it will remove a great danger from us'. In a truly remarkable achievement, Stalin's scientists exploded a nuclear device within four short years.

Nuclear weapons have their roots in late nineteenth century physics, particularly that of the French scientist Henri Becquerel who identified the nature of radiation and discovered electrons as sub-atomic particles. Pierre and Marie Curie isolated the natural elements radium and polonium at approximately the same time. By the 1920s, work on nuclear physics was expanding and included the early research of those most associated with the first atomic bomb – Enrico Fermi, Edward Teller and J. Robert Oppenheimer. Soviets were involved in European research in the 1920s as, for example, V. I. Vernadsky worked at the Curie Radium Institute in Paris and Peter Kapitsa in Lord Rutherford's Cambridge laboratory.

Nuclear research in the USSR got underway in the 1930s with enough success that the Leningrad Radium Institute built the first cyclotron in Europe in 1937. The Soviets launched a modest development program for nuclear weapons in 1942 and kept abreast of the Anglo-American work in the Manhattan project through spies such as Klaus Fuchs and the Rosenbergs. When the crash development program was ordered in August 1945, the fruits of this espionage were very valuable. The first Soviet reactor, built in 1947, was almost a replica of the US reactor producing weapons grade material at Hanford, Washington. The early programs of the US and USSR had more in common than just the universal laws of physics.

Nuclear weapons result from the discovery of the fact that splitting the nucleus of an atom with neutrons releases tremendous energy in a process called fission. Only the heaviest natural elements such as uranium, or the man-made plutonium, will split readily with a relatively small energy input. Each split nucleus of these elements releases about twenty million times as much energy as each atom involved in the chemical reaction of a TNT explosion. Once atoms begin to split in the nuclear fission process, they produce more neutrons which in turn split more nuclei and begin a chain reaction. A balanced and controlled chain is the basis for the steady production of nuclear reactors, while a sudden unbalanced reaction produces a nuclear explosion. The explosive power or 'yield' of fission weapons is expressed in terms of the kiloton, equal to 1000 tons of TNT.

The early US and Soviet weapons were small yield fission bombs. The Hiroshima bomb, for example was 12.5 kilotons. But within a few

years, weapons designers of both sides had developed the hydrogen bomb based on a process called fusion. Whereas fission splits the nuclei of heavy elements, fusion combines the nuclei of light elements (typically hydrogen to lithium) into heavier nuclei. The fusion bomb uses the heat produced by a fission trigger to start the fusion process, which is termed thermonuclear because the reaction is sustained by heat rather than neutrons. Fusion weapons are far more powerful than fission weapons, hence their yields are usually measured in terms of the megaton, equivalent to one million tons of TNT. Because fusion weapons do not depend on critical mass as do their fission counterparts, they can be packaged in any size without the problem of premature detonation. The largest nuclear device ever detonated was a monster 50 megaton bomb tested by the Soviets in 1961. Weapons of that magnitude, however, are simply not efficient in military terms. It is preferable to use more smaller weapons than a few large weapons. The trend of the 1970s has been toward smaller weapons to be delivered in much larger numbers.

The other partner in the 'revolutionary' marriage has been the delivery system to place the nuclear weapon on, or at least somewhere in the vicinity of, its intended target. The US and USSR both early relied on bombers but these were supplanted, particularly for the Soviets, by the development of long range ballistic missiles in the 1950s and 1960s. The two key factors were design advances reducing the size and weight of the warhead and the development of increasingly accurate guidance systems. Since the 'missile gap' days of the 1960 presidential campaign, the USSR has committed itself to a long term effort to achieve equality if not supremacy in ICBM arsenals with the US. Intertwined with the ICBM competition has been the highly visible competition in space in which the Soviets have competed from the beginning on at least an equal footing.

The Soviets attached so much importance to the role and development of their long range missile force that they created an entirely new service in 1960 to provide an independent home for these weapons. The Strategic Rocket Forces (SRF) from its inception displaced the army as the premier service arm. Regardless of actual rank, its commander takes precedence over the other service commanders. Nuclear strike is the sole mission of the SRF which is responsible for all land-based ballistic missiles with ranges of 1000 kilometers or more. This includes not only the largest and most formidable ICBM force in the world but a large and potent force of medium and intermediate range missiles covering potential adversaries from Europe through the Middle East to the Far East. While the US has chosen to spread its nuclear warheads fairly evenly among the ICBM, bomber, and submarine-launched ballistic missile (SLBM) legs of its 'strategic triad' the Soviets have invested

Main picture: The Soviet Soyuz spacecraft seen from the US Apollo spacecraft during the joint Apollo-Soyuz mission in July 1975.

Inset, top: After a record-setting 175 days in orbit, two Soviet cosmonauts are seen after their return to earth. Many cosmonauts are serving military officers and manned space flights often have military purposes.

Inset, lower: Two Soyuz spacecraft dock during a 1969 flight. The Soviets have considerable experience with manned space stations. At least two of the Salyut space stations have been used exclusively for military purposes, according to reports in the Western press.

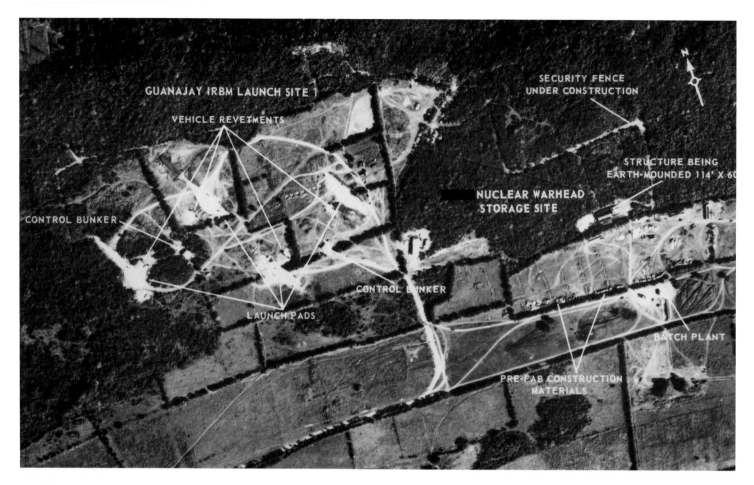

GUANAJAY IRBM LAUNCH SITE 1

VEHICLE REVETMENTS

SECURITY FENCE
UNDER CONSTRUCTION

STRUCTURE BEING
EARTH-MOUNDED 114' X 60

CONTROL BUNKER

NUCLEAR WARHEAD
STORAGE SITE

CONTROL BUNKER

LAUNCH PADS

BATCH PLANT

PRE-FAB CONSTRUCTION
MATERIALS

US aerial reconnaissance photo of a Soviet SS-5 intermediate range ballistic missile site in Cuba during the Cuban missile crisis of 1962. Such missiles could have targeted much of the US from Cuba with their 2000 mile range and one megaton warheads.

most of their strategic nuclear power in the land-based missiles of the SRF.

The Soviets have indeed had a longstanding interest in rockets and had a body of experienced rocket scientists available in 1945 when the need and the opportunity arose. These scientists largely stemmed from the work of the 'father of Soviet rocketry', Konstantin Tsiolkowski, who did much early conceptual work and trained enough pupils and colleagues to populate three rocket research centers. Surprisingly, almost the only Soviet use of rockets in World War II was the famous Katyusha 'Stalin organ', simple unguided rockets ripple-fired from multiple, truck-mounted launchers to sometimes devastating effect on the battlefield.

The postwar missile program profited immeasurably from the Soviet seizure of many of the German rocket scientists and much equipment. Two complete German rocket factories fell into Soviet hands and were packed up and moved to the USSR. More importantly, the plans and test data for the A-9, a two stage missile with New York as its intended target, and other longer range weapons also came into Soviet hands intact with their associated personnel. But it was the V-2, precursor of the ICBM, which launched the early Soviet missile program because of its proven powerplant and aerodynamic design. Improvements on the V-2 design by Soviet and German scientists enabled the Soviets to begin fielding the medium range SS-3 and SS-4 (SS stands for surface to surface) ballistic missiles and short range tactical mis-

siles such as the SS-1 and SS-2 in the early and mid-1950s. In the early 1960s, the Soviets added the intermediate range SS-5.

When the SRF thus came into existence, it was armed with the 1100 nautical mile SS-4 and 2200 nautical mile SS-5. By the mid-1960s, about 600 SS-4s and 100 SS-5s were deployed. The missions of these weapons were industrial and military targets in Europe and US bases in the Middle East and Far East, particularly air bases, nuclear storage sites and Thor and Jupiter missile sites. Neither weapon was very accurate and both were deployed in sites vulnerable to attack. Still, they provided the primary counter to the ring of US bases around the Soviet periphery and menaced NATO Europe with a credible nuclear threat.

More important to the Soviets, however, was a missile to threaten the US. In 1957, they launched the world's first ICBM in the SS-6, a monster of a missile with 32 engines. The SS-6 was a failure as a weapon, however, because it was fuelled with non-storable liquid requiring hours to load before launch and its radio guidance could be disrupted by jamming. Like the SS-4 and SS-5, the SS-6 also used vulnerable, aboveground launch pads. As a result, only a token deployment was made, possibly as few as four launchers. Because of its large payload capability, however, the SS-6 has been a workhorse space booster over the years and highlighted the Soviet space challenge to the US when it lifted the world's first satellite into orbit on 4 October 1957 in the full glare of international publicity.

5 NOVEMBER 1962
MARIEL PORT

6 MISSILE TRANSPORTERS

ERECTOR

3 MISSILE TRANSPORTERS

IRBM
PROPELLANT TRAILERS

OXIDIZER TRAILERS

The SS-6 again impressed a watching world when it sent Yuri Gagarin aboard the Vostok I spacecraft into history as the first man in space. While the Soviets were spectacularly preempting the US in space, however, the US did succeed in deploying an operational force of Atlas ICBMs beginning in 1959, though these missiles had many of the same operational drawbacks as the SS-6 and were phased out in 1965 four years ahead of schedule as a result.

The Soviets began to deploy a second generation of ICBMs in the SS-7 and SS-8 in 1961. Around 197 SS-7s were deployed but only 23 SS-8s, apparently because the Soviets saw this missile as inferior. The SS-7s and SS-8s, the second generation of Soviet ICBMs, remained in service until 1977 when deactivated under the terms of the SALT I Interim Agreement. Initial deployment was above ground but subsequently about 75 percent of the force was placed in impressively hardened silos. The silo was intended to minimize the vulnerability inherent in 'soft' sites and was a round, underground, reinforced concrete and steel structure designed to withstand overpressures of several thousand pounds

per square inch and to reduce thermal and radiation effects. Neither missile was very accurate, however, and still used volatile chemical fuels. Lack of accuracy was partially compensated for by a three megaton warhead.

Silos would have been the perfect instrument for safeguarding the delicate ICBMs against enemy nuclear attack had it not been for the near simultaneous appearance of the photoreconnaissance satellite. Prior to the advent of strategic photoreconnaissance neither side could seriously consider attacking the opponent's embryonic ICBM force and other point targets because locations were known only in the most general terms. The only mission these early missiles were really capable of was to attack large, soft area targets such as cities, industrial complexes, and large military installations. The cameras of the satellites were able to map the coordinates of each and every silo and other target and so made possible a more defined counter-military mission. Lacking, however, were guidance systems with enough accuracy to carry out such a mission. Thus the Soviet and US ICBM forces remained

Aerial photo of the Cuban port of Mariel showing Soviet ships and missile-related equipment in November 1962.

Above: A tactical FROG
(Free Rocket Over Ground)
ballistic missile on its
transporter-erector-
launcher. The FROG is an
unguided rocket not known
for its accuracy.

Right: A Soviet lieutenant
and soldier prepare missile-
related equipment in the
field.

secure in their silos and ICBM employment remained restricted to 'countervalue' (civilian
and industrial) rather than countermilitary
targets.

It was also at this time that the USSR and the
US first stumbled to the brink of nuclear war.
The failure of the early Soviet ICBM program
apparently led Nikita Khrushchev to emplace
SS-4s and SS-5s in Cuba where they could
threaten part of the US. In this way, the Soviets
may have hoped to take a shortcut while await-
ing a successful ICBM program by planting a
covey of missiles on the doorstep of the US as the
US had missiles and bomber bases ringing the
USSR. In a gripping drama in 1962, President
Kennedy subtly rattled US ICBMs at Khrushchev on the strategic level while imposing a

Left: A FROG rocket is launched.

Below: A FROG rocket in the launch position. The FROG has a maximum range of 45-50 miles and a warhead of 25-40 kilotons.

Above: Soldiers do geodetic preparation of a FROG field launch site. Precise surveying of a missile's launch position is essential to accuracy.

naval 'quarantine' around Cuba in a local demonstration of force. At the time of the crisis, the US with 294 ICBMs and 144 SLBMs had a substantial preponderance of strategic nuclear capability over the 75 Soviet ICBMs and handful of SLBMs. Humiliated before the world, the Soviets withdrew their missiles from Cuba and, it is widely believed, vowed never again to suffer such a defeat.

The leaderships of each country, however, were sobered by the potential for accidental war. As Khrushchev himself wrote in his memoirs, 'Of course I was scared. It would have been insane not to have been scared'. In the aftermath of the crisis, both powers did accept their common interest in drawing some limits around nuclear weapons, an acceptance which has led to a number of modest agreements and treaties over the years.

After the Cuban missile crisis, the ICBM forces of each country began a period of rapid expansion and major technological improvement. The US began to deploy its current ICBM force – the third generation Minuteman family in 1963 and halted deployment in 1968 when force size had reached 1000 silos. In addition, 54 of the older, second generation Titan II ICBM launchers were retained. In 1966, the USSR began to deploy its third generation – the SS-9, SS-11, and SS-13 – and reached a force size of

over 1600 launchers when deployment was frozen in 1972 by the Interim Agreement of SALT I. The Soviets might very well have gone on to deploy considerably more ICBM launchers had it not been for the opportunity to curtail the US threat presented by SALT. Except for the retirement of the 220 SS-7s and SS-8s, force size has remained static on each side to date. Instead, both sides have refined their missiles in terms of technological performance to the point where a number of complex countermilitary employment options have theoretically become possible.

While the US developed a force of small, reliable, relatively accurate ICBMs in the Minuteman I, II, and III, the USSR took a different route and ended up with a more diverse but highly effective force. The mainstay of the Soviet ICBM force until the late 1970s was the SS-11, a liquid fuelled missile a little larger than the Minuteman. The Soviets put over 1000 SS-11s into the field between 1966 and 1972 in an impressive effort which balanced the Minuteman program. The SS-11 has three versions or 'mods'. The mods 1 and 2 are single warheads of about one megaton yield while the mod 3 carries three small warheads which are not independently targetable but fall into a fixed pattern.

Particularly disturbing to the US was that in

addition to the large SS-11 force, the Soviets also deployed 288 SS-9 heavy ICBMs. These giant missiles in several single warhead versions had yields of a staggering 25 megatons and in a three warhead mod of 3.5 megatons. Because of its huge warhead, the SS-9 was interpreted in the US as a Soviet attempt to develop a 'hard target' capability. It was assumed that the mission of the SS-9 was to attack hardened command and control centers and missile silos, thus the US went to great lengths to negotiate a limit of 308 launchers for the Soviets on heavy missiles of this sort in SALT I.

The Soviet deployment of third generation ICBMs was probably driven by two main factors as suggested by Robert Berman and John Baker. First was the need to get a credible ICBM force in the field and particularly a force which matched the US in number of launchers. For political reasons, the Soviets could not be seen as numerically inferior which helps to explain the size of the SS-11 force. Second was the military need to provide some counter to the threat of the Minuteman force. The SS-9 with its large yield warheads may well have been targeted against the 100 Minuteman launch control centers whose destruction would have largely neutralized the Minuteman force. But the SS-9 was an expensive weapon which would have required over a decade to become numerous

Above: Aerial view of a Soviet ship whose crew voluntarily opened the crates on its deck for US inspection shortly after the Cuban missile crisis. The crates contain Il-28 Beagle tactical bombers.

Left: Suspicious crates on the deck of the Soviet ship *Kasimov* bound for Cuba in December 1962. Close inspection (above) revealed that the Soviets were keeping their agreement that missiles would not be sent to Cuba. Krushchev's failure in the Cuban crisis is believed to have played a large part in bringing about his personal fall from power.

Above: Paratroops in training simulate an attack on a missile site in the enemy rear.

Right: A rare picture of a Soviet ICBM in its silo.

enough to offset the Minuteman silos. Thus Berman and Baker suggest that as an interim response, the Soviets used the SS-9 to meet part of the Minuteman threat and mass-produced the smaller, cheaper SS-11 to match the US politically and militarily. With its modest yield and accuracy, the SS-11 did not have the capability to threaten Minuteman silos but was probably intended to attack urban and industrial centers. Berman and Baker also suggest that over 300 of these weapons may have been assigned to cover targets in Europe, the Far East, and the Middle East to take advantage of the weapon's flexibility in range and provide a dimension of capability beyond the SS-4s and SS-5s. No new shorter range missiles were deployed in this period to modernize the SS-4 and SS-5 force, apparently because the SS-X-14, a mobile IRBM, turned out to be a failure. Shorter range missions thus continued to fall on the SS-4 and SS-5, assisted by the SS-11.

The rapid growth of this formidable force of ICBMs persuaded then US Secretary of Defense Robert McNamara that the ICBM race should

Soviet training takes full account of the contingency of the nuclear battlefield. Here Soviet troops in full nuclear-bacteriological-chemical protective clothing practice battlefield tasks which are many times harder to perform in that gear.

be at least slowed if not halted. It was this recognition that led the US to make the initial overtures to the USSR on strategic arms limitations in 1967. The initiation of these talks in 1969 was an implicit US recognition of the USSR as a strategic equal and an admission that the USSR had effected one of the great shifts in the international balance of power in history.

Apart from the political symbolism, however, the Soviets probably were disposed toward negotiations for several compelling reasons. As the US was concerned with the scope and pace of the Soviet ICBM program, the USSR was concerned with the US antiballistic missile (ABM)

program and undoubtedly wanted to avoid an expensive 'ABM' race which the US would probably have won. The Soviets probably also wanted to improve general relations with the US at a time when relations with Mao's China were reaching vitriolic, and occasionally violent, lows. But most importantly, the Soviets surely were and are concerned about the dangers of nuclear war. As the Soviet Marshal Sokolovsky wrote in his widely read work *Military Strategy:* 'The losses in a world nuclear war would not only be suffered by the USA and their NATO allies but also by the socialist countries'. At the time, SALT seemed to offer to both sides a

A Yankee class ballistic missile submarine on patrol. Sixteen missile launch tubes for SS-N-6 ballistic missiles are located behind the sail.

An SS-N-6 submarine launched ballistic missile on parade in Red Square. The SS-N-6 with a range of 1300 to 1600 miles requires that the Yankee class submarines patrol close to US shores.

way to curb the further growth of already extensive arsenals and to establish a few simple mechanisms to manage future crises. Unfortunately, it was not to be so simple.

Characterized as 'complex, technical and bedeviled with jargon', the goal of SALT I was an equitable and verifiable agreement to limit force levels without military disadvantage to either side. The negotiations required several years, not least because of the difficulty of comparing two arsenals so different in their characteristics. In the end, only an interim agreement was reached rather than a treaty because the parties recognized that more time was needed to

resolve the issues. The SALT I agreement and the subsequent Vladivostok Accord of 1974 essentially codified the sizes that both strategic arsenals had already reached but did not prevent the introduction of new ICBMs or the refinement of existing weapons. Even as the ink was drying on the Interim Agreement in Moscow on 26 May 1972, the USSR was already flight testing a fourth generation of ICBMs and the US had its MX ICBM in the design stage.

As the 1970s unfolded, the Soviet ICBM force was transformed from a large force of distinctly inferior but serviceable weapons to a slightly smaller force of weapons as good as, if not better

Soviet ICBM Deployment

MIRVed ICBMs

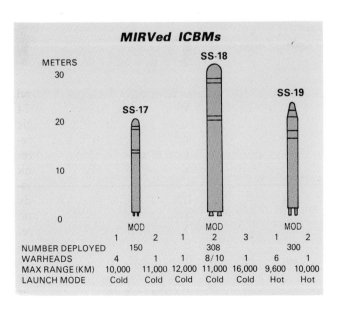

	SS-17			SS-18		SS-19	
METERS							
MOD	1	2	1	2	3	1	2
NUMBER DEPLOYED	150			308		300	
WARHEADS	4	1	1	8/10	1	6	1
MAX RANGE (KM)	10,000	11,000	12,000	11,000	16,000	9,600	10,000
LAUNCH MODE	Cold	Cold	Cold	Cold	Cold	Hot	Hot

than in some cases, their US counterparts. As the US made a few improvements to Minuteman III, deferred others for lack of funds, and regularly postponed the MX ICBM (eventually deployed as the Peacekeeper in modified Minuteman silos), the USSR overhauled virtually its entire ICBM force. Four new ICBMs were tested and three extensively deployed. Between 1975 and 1980, the Soviets replaced the entire SS-9 force with the SS-18 and about half of the SS-11 force with the SS-17 and SS-19. Deployed in harder silos, the new weapons had versions carrying 'multiple independently targeted reentry vehicles' or MIRV for short.

The MIRV was a revolutionary advance in missile technology introduced by the US on Minuteman III which uses one missile to deliver three warheads on three separate targets. A MIRVed force thus need only use a fraction of its missiles to deliver a large number of its warheads and still retain a reserve of weapons. The innovation was controversial at the time because it appeared to take the US far beyond the requirements of mutual deterrence but it was argued that MIRVing the force was necessary to penetrate the ABM system the Soviets were then deploying. Probably equally important was the fact that the technology was available to give the US a cheap (albeit temporary) military advantage over the USSR.

The SS-18 is roughly the same size as the SS-9 and has a single warhead version with the same large yield and a MIRVed version carrying eight to ten smaller warheads. Even within the

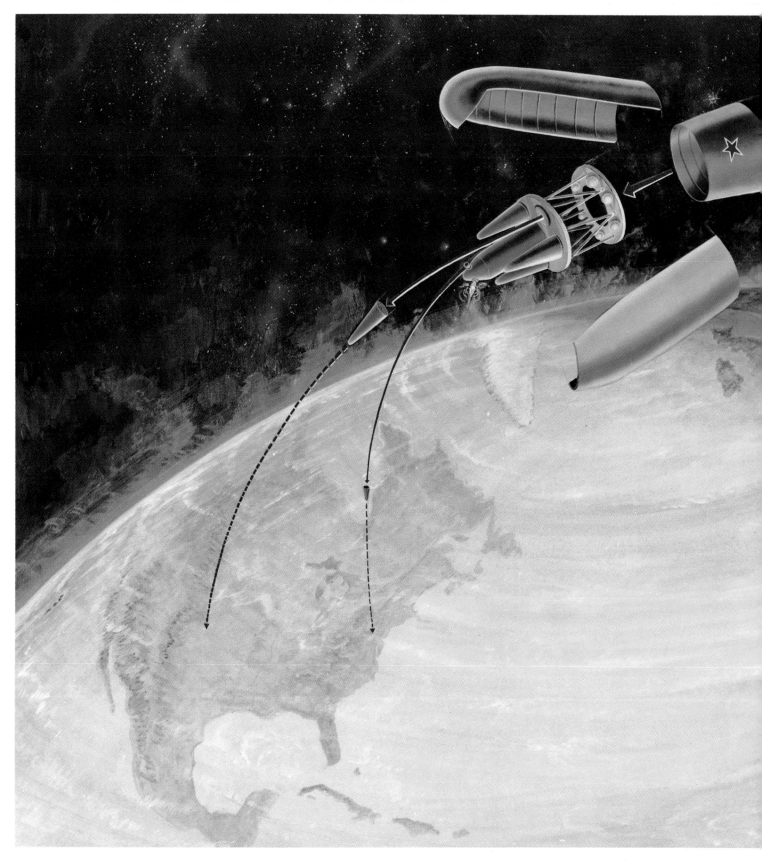

An artist's conception of the flight track of a MIRVed ICBM, shown with the nose cone of the missile opening and the warheads beginning to deploy to their individual targets.

SALT I permitted limit of 308 launchers, the MIRVed version of the SS-18 is fully capable of attacking the silos of the US Minuteman force without assistance from the remainder of the ICBM force. The SS-17 and SS-19 also have MIRVed versions with four and six warheads respectively. The USSR now has a formidable arsenal of modern, accurate ICBM warheads which, in addition to the SS-18s, includes 300 SS-19s and 150 SS-17s as well as the remainder of the third generation force. The extreme accuracy of the SS-18 and SS-19 in particular are the basis for fears of a 'window of vulnerability' for the Minuteman force in the early to mid-1980s in some segments of the US defense community and the push to deploy the MX in a more survivable mode than fixed silos.

The MIRVed version of the SS-18 is probably

the main Soviet counter to the Minuteman force but the SS-19 is also well suited to this mission. Each system, however, probably must use two warheads for a high probability of destruction against a Minuteman silo. The SS-17 is probably intended more for the soft area targets originally assigned to the SS-7 and subsequently the SS-11.

Concurrent with the fourth generation ICBMs, the Soviets began to introduce a new regional missile in the SS-20 IRBM. The SS-20 is mobile to improve its survivability and carries three MIRVs. In recent years, it has replaced much of the old SS-4 and SS-5 force to mount a more potent threat against the Far East but particularly against Europe. The SS-20 has improved Soviet regional capabilities so much that it is the centerpiece of the US-USSR negotiations on intermediate range nuclear forces which began in Geneva in 1981. Indeed, the increased nuclear threat to NATO from the SS-20 was a main factor in the December 1979 decision of that alliance to deploy beginning in 1983 a more potent intermediate range nuclear capability of its own in the Pershing II medium range ballistic missile and the ground-launched cruise missile.

Remarkably, the amazing increase in Soviet ICBM capabilities occurred under the provi-sions of the SALT I Interim Agreement which limited little more than force size. Over the succeeding seven years, the negotiators wres-tled with the complex problems of regulating the modernization and certain operational aspects of two very different strategic nuclear forces. In addition to ICBMs and SLBMs, SALT II dealt with bomber modernization and the complicated issues of cruise missiles and mobile ICBMs. A treaty was finally signed in 1979 by Presidents Carter and Brezhnev but was so con-troversial in the US that the Carter administra-tion ultimately chose not to submit it for Senate approval. Controversy centered on whether the treaty was verifiable and overly favorable to the USSR at the expense of US interests. Disavow-ing the SALT II treaty, the Reagan administra-tion in 1982 launched the Strategic Arms Re-duction Talks. In the meantime, the US went ahead with its plans to deploy the MX ICBM Peacekeeper, while the Soviets continued test-ing two new ICBMs – the SS-24 and SS-25. In March 1983, President Reagan announced Star Wars. START failed to materialize.

The emergence of the USSR as a superpower has thus been marked by the initiation of SALT while the subsequent development of the Soviet strategic forces, but especially the ICBM force, has been intertwined with the SALT negotia-

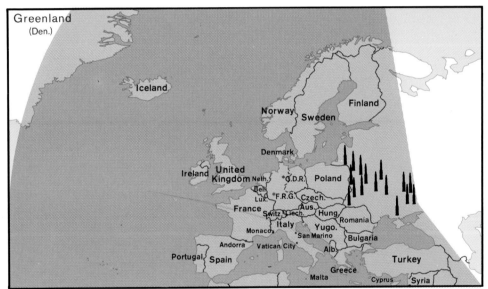

Above & right: The Soviet deployment of SS-20 missiles and the targets they can reach, with a comparison between the SS-20 and the Western Pershing 1A missile. The Pershing II, with a longer range than the Pershing 1A, was about to be deployed to NATO sites in West Germany when Ronald Reagan and Mikhail Gorbachev signed the INF Treaty in December 1987. Since then, both sides have agreed to dismantle their ground-based intermediate-range missiles.

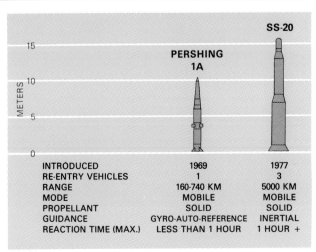

	PERSHING 1A	SS-20
INTRODUCED	1969	1977
RE-ENTRY VEHICLES	1	3
RANGE	160-740 KM	5000 KM
MODE	MOBILE	MOBILE
PROPELLANT	SOLID	SOLID
GUIDANCE	GYRO-AUTO-REFERENCE	INERTIAL
REACTION TIME (MAX.)	LESS THAN 1 HOUR	1 HOUR +

Right: An SS-12 Scaleboard medium-range theater nuclear ballistic missile. The Scaleboard has a range greater than 400 miles.

Above: A snowy SS-13 ICBM on its trailer. Only 60 of these missiles have been deployed as the Soviets apparently prefer the more capable and widely deployed SS-11.

Right: A Galosh anti-ballistic missile. Originally deployed in the 1960s, the Galosh missiles have recently been uprated and incorporated into a more sophisticated defense system around Moscow.

tions. Discussions of ICBMs tend to stress these as objects in arms control negotiations but ICBMs are also potential weapons of awesome power – potential because they have never yet been used in war and there have always been questions as to how they would or should be used. Both sides have had doctrines for ICBM employment but it is only in recent years that western students have made a serious effort to understand Soviet thinking about strategic nuclear war and begun to accept that it is very different from that of the US.

US strategic theory has tended to focus on 'deterrence' in one form or another. American strategic thinkers with a few notable exceptions have declined to 'think the unthinkable' in Herman Kahn's old but apt phrase and generally considered that ICBMs were fulfilling their true function if they were never used. To ensure that the Soviets were deterred, the US first threatened 'massive retaliation' in the 1950s in a crude use of the US strategic nuclear monopoly. Once the Soviets had gained some capability to strike the US and thus rendered massive retaliation questionable as a strategy, the US moved to 'mutual assured destruction' under Robert MacNamara, threatening to attack Soviet cities and economy under the assumption that such a price would be too high for the Soviets to contemplate war. Under the Nixon administration, the US began to incorporate more limited nuclear responses in its strategy to give the president more flexibility in responding to given situations but the emphasis remained generally on deterrence through the threat of a broad retaliatory attack.

The Soviets by contrast have been skeptical of US concepts of deterrence and especially of notions of controlling nuclear use in a major war. 'There are as yet no rules of behavior in a nuclear war' wrote one leading Soviet commentator on strategic affairs in 1980. As Berman and Baker aptly note, the idea of limiting nuclear warfare to theaters surrounding the USSR has understandably little appeal to the Soviets since the USSR would suffer substantial destruction while the US remained relatively unscathed. Once war has begun, the Sovets stress using the full range of forces available to defeat the enemy. Soviet doctrine has always emphasized the probability, if not the inevitability, of mass strategic nuclear exchanges centering on ICBM forces.

Soviet military strategy appears to have a dual thrust. One is to defeat NATO forces and overrun Western Europe while the second, equally important, is to neutralize the power of the US to attack the USSR and support the war in Europe. China would probably be an important but secondary enemy since it is not presently capable of mounting a major nuclear threat to the USSR while its conventional forces pose only a local threat to the Soviet Far East. The burden of neutralizing the US would fall on the Soviet ICBM force, supplemented by SLBMs.

Long-Range Theater Nuclear Weapons

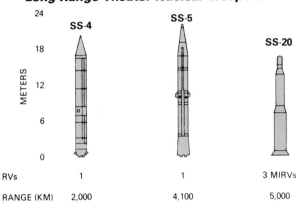

	SS-4	SS-5	SS-20
RVs	1	1	3 MIRVs
RANGE (KM)	2,000	4,100	5,000

Above left & left: Characteristics and deployment areas of Soviet medium range missiles. The SS-5 no longer figures in Soviet forces, having been replaced by the SS-20. These missiles are currently being dismantled.

Soviet strategy for the use of strategic forces was broadly outlined by Marshal Krylov, commander of the SRF, in 1967. 'In a future war with the use of nuclear-missile weapons' he wrote, 'the strikes will be inflicted simultaneously both against the armed forces and against administrative-political and military-industrial centers of the country, the destruction of which will disorganize state and military control, undermine the military-economic potential, deprive the enemy of the opportunity to conduct extended combat operations, and lead to his destruction'. The Soviet forces would attack as their most important targets US missile fields, missile submarines, and long range bombers in which reside the US strategic nuclear threat to the USSR. General military forces would also be targets. Because the Soviets see

guine about their ability to execute such a doctrine both for technical and operational reasons. ICBMs are untried weapons which would have to be launched on 5000-6000 mile journeys, partly through inner space. They are made up of thousands of subsystems, any one of which can cause the missile to fail in its mission. ICBM accuracy, the crucial factor in planning a sophisticated attack against hardened military targets, is so relative that it is expressed in probabilities that 50% of the warheads would fall within the specified radius of a circle around the target and the remainder outside. Both sides test their ICBMs under carefully controlled conditions and can only model mathematically the gravinometric fields over the north pole over which wartime ICBM tracks would be. For these and many other reasons, the technical

Right: A FROG rocket in the ready-to-launch status. The FROG is widely deployed with the Soviet ground forces.

Opposite: Scud short range ballistic missiles, historically the main nuclear fire power of the Soviet ground forces, pictured here in the ready-to-launch position on the cover of a Soviet magazine.

such a war as a struggle between two political systems, they would also include the US political structure and the economy that supports the war effort. Military command and control as well as civilian continuity of government would be included while destruction of industrial resources would prevent the US from supporting the war in Europe and elsewhere and sustaining a longer war.

Many observers feel that the Soviets appear to have a more coherent doctrine for their strategic nuclear forces than does the US which, for domestic political reasons, has generally been reluctant to look beyond the unthinkable failure of deterrence. A move more in the direction of contingency nuclear warfighting, begun by the Carter administration and expanded by the Reagan administration, has touched a strong chord of negative response from varied sectors of the American body politic.

Though the Soviets may take some comfort from what they consider a more realistic approach to nuclear war than their potential adversaries, they surely cannot be overly san-

uncertainties associated with a mass launch of ICBMs would be enormous. Technical uncertainites aside, the operational problems of trying to mount effective operations with strategic nuclear forces in wartime would be staggering and are an important theme in the recurring debates in the US defense community over the future of strategic forces.

Another factor that could assume increasing importance in coming years is the possibility of effective defenses against ICBM and SLBM attack. To date neither side has been able to mount such defenses because of technical problems and high cost. Indeed, the difficulties have been so great that both sides have mutually foresworn more than token deployment of defenses and have instead relied on deterrence. In fact, the development of ABM programs began almost concurrently with the early ICBM programs. By the late 1960s, the US had developed the Safeguard system based on the Sprint and Spartan interceptor missiles and the USSR first the Griffon and then the Galosh system. All systems rely on radar to locate and track the

Техника и Вооружение

10/81

ISSN 0201—7490

Right: SS-11 ICBMs on parade in Red Square. Along with the SS-9, the SS-11 was the main factor in the Soviet achievement of superpower status.

incoming warheads and to direct the ABM to the intercept point. Neither the American nor the Soviet efforts would have been very effective even against the older ICBMs.

As part of the early SALT process, the US and the USSR signed a treaty in 1972 which limited each side to 200 interceptor launchers, subsequently reduced to 100. The Soviets deployed only 64 Galosh interceptors around Moscow while in 1976 the US unilaterally deactivated the few interceptors it had deployed. The ABM treaty does allow research and development, however, and advancing technology is clearly outrunning the treaty and its simple premises. Both sides are believed to have the capability to produce laser ballistic missile defenses, for example, which could be ground or space-based, at some point in the 1990s. There has been a strong renewal of interest in ABM defenses in the US whose prospects for laser defenses and more conventional approaches of the earlier ABM type are seen as considerably better than those of the USSR. Indeed, President Reagan's announcement in March 1983 that the US would strive to produce an anti-nuclear 'umbrella' of space-based laser and charged particle beam weapons by the beginning of the twenty-first century, caused grave concern in the Soviet Union. If it was to be matched, the expense would probably cripple the Soviet economy – hence Mikhail Gorbachev's constant striving to include 'Star Wars' in arms control negotiations.

Secure in their superpower status for over a decade now and enjoying at least strategic nuclear parity with the US by any measure, the Soviets can take satisfaction and comfort in this dimension of their military power.

Yet at longer range, the Soviets have reasons for strong concern. A dramatic US breakthrough in the ABM sphere, a very real possibility, could render the monster SS-18s and sleek SS-19s impotent and rob the USSR of its hardwon strategic power. The US could opt to abandon land-based missiles entirely and put its warheads to sea aboard elusive SLBM submarines, a course which has many American advocates, to solve the vulnerability problem of US ICBMs created by the super accuracy of the new Soviet missiles. And the US already has an SLBM with hard target capability on the drawing boards in the D-5 missile. The US strategic nuclear force is already expanding with new, hard to locate, and potentially numerous weapons such as the cruise missile, scheduled for deployment on land and at sea and already operational with the US B-52 force since December 1982. The coming years could indeed show a strong erosion of the Soviet gains of the 1970s but the Soviets have their own counters under development, including a mobile ICBM. The superpower game has been long and expensive for the Soviets but they have demonstrated that they can stay the course and are willing to pay the price.

LAND POWER

Above: One of the foremost Russian and Soviet military heroes is General M. I. Kutuzov who defeated Napoleon in a campaign of strategic retreat and ultimately brought about Napoleon's downfall, 1812-1814.

Above right: Troops at the front read an illegal Bolshevik newspaper in 1914.

Previous page: Infantry on maneuvers. They are armed with Kalashnikov assault rifles and AGM-37 grenade launchers. BMP infantry combat vehicles move up in support.

Right: Russian troops on the Eastern Front suffered immense casualties during World War I and, particularly in the first two years of war, from a lack of weapons and ammunition.

The Soviet Army was officially established in September 1946 as the successor to the hard-worked Workers-Peasants Red Army that had seen the USSR through its formative years and its great test of survival in World War II. At the end of the war, the Red Army had some 6.2 million men in over 500 divisions under arms and had fought a gruelling and bloody campaign from Moscow to Berlin and beyond. It is the western image of this army – herding its infantry through minefields to give the enemy less time to dig in, lining thousands of guns hub to hub in immense barrages, and absorbing by its own (probably under-) estimate four and half million casualties in the first year of the war – that conveys the elemental reality of Soviet military power. Massive, brutish, lavish in its use of firepower and cannon fodder, the Red Army also reflected the reality of the USSR under the rough hand of Stalin.

Under the more restrained touches of Stalin's successors, the Soviet Army has developed into the most formidable modern army in the world, still massive but also sophisticated in doctrine and up to date in equipment. Even though the army is no longer the premier service, it is still used among Soviets as a synonym for all the military forces and still retains a disproportion-

ate influence in the high command and on military policy and organization. Indeed, army officers still predominate in the General Staff and the upper echelons of the Ministry of Defense. This is all the more surprising given the postwar vicissitudes of Soviet military policy and thought, the Soviet fascination with long range nuclear weapons, and the emergence of powerful sister services with attendant internecine bureaucratic strife. On balance, the army has shown itself to be both durable and adaptable and, despite its period of eclipse, to be emerging into new importance as an instrument of Soviet policy in the present age of nuclear standoff.

The main role of the army is to fight and win any conflict with NATO and to secure Soviet interests in the Far East against China, Japan and the US or any combination thereof. To win a war with NATO would require, in Soviet eyes, the military disarmament and political disintegration of that alliance, no easy task under any circumstances. The importance the Soviets attach to this role can be inferred from the fact that they provide 60% of the Warsaw Pact forces in Eastern Europe, a sharp contrast with the US role in NATO.

Beyond the longstanding military-political confrontation with NATO, the army serves a broader defense purpose by guaranteeing the security of the historically long and vulnerable borders of the state. It enforces the traditional Russian hegemony over Eastern Europe by physical presence and occasionally active military intervention. Indeed, the high visibility of the large ground forces in Europe renders a variety of political benefits. They maximize the Soviet strategic position and remind Europeans that the USSR is the only superpower indigenous to that continent. But Soviet land power is limited to the Eurasian landmass because it lacks strategic mobility and thus cannot be projected much beyond the Soviet periphery.

The Army and Russian History

The army was always Russia's primary instrument of national defense and national aggrandizement. Until the early eighteenth century, Russia was weak vis-à-vis her western neighbors because her army was little more than feudal levies raised by vassal lords owing military service to the Tsar in return for land and serfs bound to that land. As elsewhere, this type of military organization tended to foster local warlordism and low military effectiveness because of lack of training of both leaders and led

A Russian heavy gun position near the Austrian fortress of Przemysl during World War I.

Above: Russian soldiers prepared for German gas attacks during World War I. Gas was used for the first time in the war on the Eastern Front.

Right: From left Budenny, Frunze and Voroshilov discuss tactics during fighting in the Crimea in the course of the Revolution. Budenny and Voroshilov lived through Stalin's Great Purge and had fairly undistinguished careers in World War II.

Second right: Marshal Tukhachevsky argued for the introduction of strong tank forces in the early 1930s but he was killed during the Great Purge and his ideas were largely ignored in the years leading up to World War II.

and haphazard command arrangments. As Europe awakened to a new military age in the sixteenth and seventeenth centuries, the Russians fared poorly against their immediate enemies, the more modern Poles and Swedes. Beginning with Ivan IV, the first Tsar of Russia (1547-1584), the rulers resorted to the same strategy as the Western European monarchs to escape the strictures of feudal military organization. Ivan's units of *streltsy* or musketeers were the beginning of the regular Russian army and gave the Tsar the first forces under his direct control. Unlike the Europeans, however, the Russians were much slower to develop the military and fiscal bureaucracies which were so integral in the centralization of power in the monarch and thus also in the development of the modern state.

Only in the early eighteenth century did Peter the Great build a modern army able to compete with the Westerners, exemplified by his victory over Charles XII of Sweden at Poltava in 1709. By 1725, Peter had 200,000 regular troops (on 25-year terms of service) and 100,000 Cossacks and had built the military industry to support this military establishment which was very large by the standards of the time. He also founded the navy which had just one ship when he took the throne in 1682. Reminiscent of Stalin's motivation for launching the first Five Year Plan in 1928, Peter wanted to meet the West on a better than even footing. And he succeeded because by virtue of her new military power, Russia became a major European power in the eighteenth century.

The following century by contrast was a time of military decline. Though the regular army numbered half a million and was supported by well-developed military industries, it had been seized by formalism and concerned itself with such matters as parade ground drill, inspections and proper uniform. Russia survived the invasion on 21 June 1812 by 500,000 veteran French soldiers under Napoleon Bonaparte because the army was forced to fight only one major engagement – Borodino where each side lost 50,000 men – and instead ultimately triumphed through a strategy of strategic withdrawal. The campaign of 1812 with its theme of heroic struggle and sacrifice on the soil of the motherland was a major focus of Soviet internal propaganda in World War II to boost morale and a belief in ultimate victory.

But the rest of the nineteenth century was not a glorious military time for Russia. Numerous military interventions were conducted in Eastern Europe but some were debacles such as the Crimean War of 1853-1856. In response to this particular disaster, extensive reforms occurred in the military system under the direction of Dmitry Milyutin, Minister of War.

Reforms notwithstanding, the army fared poorly in the Russo-Japanese War of 1904-05 which was a direct harbinger of the land warfare of World War I and, for Russia, of army performance as well. At the beginning of World War I, the regular army fielded 1.5 million troops and had three million reserves ready for immediate mobilization and two million more within a few months. By late 1915, around ten million men were under arms. But this mass was vitiated by a military system which barely functioned and very incompetent leadership. Rifles and cartridges were in short supply and artillery was often restricted to firing one or two rounds a day. The troops often went unfed for days at a time because of the creaky logistics system. But worst of all was the leadership

which lost 300,000 men and 650 guns at Tannenberg alone and suffered losses of a million or more in the campaign seasons of 1914, 1915 and 1916. Only against the Austrians and Turks in the Caucasus did the army do well. The Tsar himself finally assumed direct command of the Eastern Front which was in stalemate by 1916 as the Germans focussed their resources to the west. But the Tsar was no better than his generals, although it should be remembered that no country had better than mediocre leadership in World War I.

Despite the defeats, horrendous losses and incompetence, the army somehow survived intact but the home front crumbled from war weariness. Peace was the most popular Bolshevik slogan and one of Lenin's earliest acts was to take Russia out of the war with the dictated terms of the Treaty of Brest-Litovsk in March 1918.

The Red Army 1917-1941

The vehicle through which the Bolsheviks seized power on 6 November 1917 was the Red Army, a motley collection of some sailors, a few Latvian rifle regiments and about 20,000 Red Guards – mainly factory workers. Because the regular army was war weary and infiltrated by Bolshevik agents, it was neutralized and allowed a handful of revolutionaries to seize a country of 150 million. Within five years, however, that handful had become an army of

Soviet armor in 1941 after the onset of the German attack.

Foreigners can never know
the suffering experienced
by the Soviet population in
World War II. The Soviet
leadership fears the
younger generation of
Soviets also does not know it.

five million as the Bolsheviks barely staved off the White counter-revolution and armed interventions by the Allied powers.

The architect of the new army was Leon Trotsky, First Commissar of War, who tried to point the Red Army in the direction of standing professional forces. Despite his role in the success of the army in the civil war, Trotsky's military policies led to his downfall in the Byzantine jockeying for power after the end of the civil war in 1923. Supported by most of the Tsarist officers who had joined the Bolsheviks, Trotsky argued for a small regular army as a defense against counter-revolution at home, particularly peasant dissatisfaction with the new regime and its policies. With M. V. Frunze as their spokeman, a group of Bolshevik generals including Voroshilov, Budenny, and Tukhachevsky vigorously espoused a new 'proletarian military doctrine' based on the tenet that the organization, training, tactics and strategy of an army stem from the class character of the state. Based on the experience of the civil war, this view rejected positional warfare in any form and stressed the offensive, maneuverability and repelling the foreign threat.

To weaken Trotsky politically, Stalin and his political cohorts espoused proletarian military doctrine and labelled Trotsky a supporter of 'reactionary military doctrine'. Using military policy and army efficiency as his avenues of attack, Stalin succeeded in deposing Trotsky as Commissar of War in 1925 and rewarded most of his supporters in the military by having them shot in 1937.

Frunze succeeded Trotsky as Commissar of War and developed a compromise solution to the problem of what kind of army was appropriate for the new communist state. A regular army of 560,000, which the Soviets termed the cadre army, and a territorial militia, mainly infantry, were created. The cadre army included the cavalry, air force, tanks, signals, and technical services along with infantry. The militia received only six weeks to three months of training per year because of the need for productive manpower in the economy. The Red Army thus emerged as a horde of essentially untrained infantry kept under control by a cadre of regular troops. Frunze also revamped the army staff and pointed the officer corps in the direction of professionalism. Frunze died in late 1925, quite possibly the first of Stalin's military victims, to be succeeded by Voroshilov. A political soldier, Voroshilov knew little about military matters and the cadre-territorial army was left relatively unchanged into the mid-1930s. The Red Army also enjoyed a fruitful collaboration with the German Army and about 120 Soviet officers received training in Germany. In 1933, however, the politics of the two governments became too incompatible for their military relationship to continue.

The cadre-militia compromise was very unsatisfactory to Stalin and his generals.

Although large, the Red Army lacked modern weapons, had only a few obsolete tanks and armored vehicles, and a small antiquated air force. If the USSR was to compete with its potential enemies in Europe, it needed a large standing army well equipped with up to date weaponry. The Soviets early realized the industrial foundation of a modern military establishment and instituted the first Five Year Plan to build up industry in 1928. By the end of the second Five Year Plan, the Soviets had advanced far toward their industrial goal and were producing large quantities of military equipment. The standing army also grew rapidly, reaching 940,000 by 1934 and five million by 1939. The Universal Military Service Act made service compulsory for all citizens in 1939.

On the eve of World War II, the Red Army had grown into a huge and relatively well equipped military machine but remained untested in battle. Although the Soviets sent military equipment to the Republicans in the Spanish Civil War from 1936, they carefully avoided a commitment of troops and sent at most 1000-2000 instructors and technicians. Spain, however, provided the opportunity to test new equipment in battle against German equipment. The army did engage in combat with Japanese forces in the Far East. The Changkufeng Incident in 1938 saw a sharp battle in which Red Army units performed well defending the Soviet supply line to the embattled regime of Chiang Kai-shek. In what the Soviets term the Khalkin-gol Incident of 1939, a substantial force of the Red Army under Georgi Zhukov, soon to become the leading Soviet general of World War II, fought a

Soviet troops and T-34 tanks on the attack near Minsk in World War II.

Manufacture of heavy anti-aircraft guns at a factory in the Urals during World War II.

small war lasting several months with Japanese forces over a small, dusty piece of territory on the Mongolian border with the then Japanese puppet state of Manchukuo and forced a Japanese withdrawal.

However well the skirmishes in the Far East went for the Red Army, its true measure was revealed in the Finnish War of 1939-1940. In late 1939, the Soviets invaded Finland in a dispute over adjustments to the border. Even though the Finns had a small, ill-equipped army, they still turned the Soviet offensive into an unmitigated disaster. Reorganized and reinforced in early 1940, the Soviets finally overwhelmed the out-manned, out-gunned Finns and dictated a peace treaty. Admitting to some 200,000 casualties, Stalin was made aware of the price of the military purge of 1937-1938 in competent, experienced officers and the army's serious problems with training, staff work and coordination of effort and planning. On the eve of World War II, he launched a major effort at reform and expansion and tried to bolster belatedly the sagging morale of the battered officer corps.

The Great Patriotic Fatherland War

World War II was the great test of the Red Army and a deeply traumatic experience for the communist regime. Still termed the Great Patriotic Fatherland War, it has become the heroic epic of Soviet history and steeled two generations of Soviet leadership in the grim struggle for survival. It also shaped the subsequent structure and doctrine of the army in important ways and remains a subject of intense operational study by the military in search of doctrinal truths and timeless operational axioms.

The onset of the war was the most momumental disaster in Soviet history. Stalin had unrealistically hoped that the Germans, French and British would exhaust themselves in the west and leave him the arbiter of continental Europe. At the least, he hoped for several years of grace to complete the reform and expansion of the army. But the speed of the German conquest of the west dashed both hopes. The real disaster, however, arose from Stalin's failure to heed either specific and authoritative intelligence warnings of German plans, including the scheduled invasion date and time, or the deployment of the Wehrmacht which made no attempt to mask its preparations. When the Wehrmacht, some three million strong, crashed into the USSR on 22 June 1941, Stalin's more than 200 divisions and 15,000 tanks were literally flatfooted. In the first two days, 2000 planes were lost, most on the ground. In the succeeding weeks, the Germans captured whole armies and corps in rapid envelopments and were 500 miles into the USSR. German Army Group Center alone took 287,000 prisoners and Army Group South won an immense victory and 665,000 prisoners at Kiev by mid-September.

But the German campaign faltered in the following months because of Hitler's indecision and refusal to yield an inch of conquered ground. Despite the loss of millions of men and thousands of planes, tanks and artillery pieces, the Soviets drew in fresh forces, especially from the Far East, and counter-attacked in defense of Moscow in December. With the enemy greatly overextended and hampered by the onset of winter, the offensive removed the threat to Moscow and pushed the Germans back in some sectors. Throughout 1942 and well into 1943, the Soviet and German war machines wrestled in the mud and snow of the Eastern Front while Soviet industry worked furiously to turn out vast numbers of the new T-34 medium and KV heavy tanks, planes, trucks and artillery. As the Red Army ground away at it, the Wehrmacht's turn came to lose huge numbers of men – 300,000 at Stalingrad alone. The turning point of the war came in the great tank battle at Kursk in the summer of 1943 where 3600 Soviet tanks defeated 2000 German tanks. From that event, the Germans, outmanned, outgunned and laboring under Hitler's standfast strategy, were irrevocably on the defensive. Although the war went on for two more years, they were a march of triumph for the Red Army as it had saved the Soviet regime and laid the groundwork for the postwar Soviet hegemony over East Europe.

The Soviet victory can be laid to several factors. The Soviets fought a one front war on which they were able to concentrate all of their resources. Soviet industry played a major role by mass producing the necessary military hardware, including over 100,000 tanks and self-propelled guns. Further blessed with substantial aid from the Allies and excellent commanders such as Zhukov, Shaposhnikov and Vasilevsky, the Soviets basically outproduced and overwhelmed the enemy in a local war won by brute force.

The Emergence of the Soviet Army

The Red Army at the end of World War II was an immense military machine camped in East Europe. Like all the postwar victors, it demobilized and began to revamp in accord with the seeming lessons of the war and the military requirements of the postwar period. These arose from the fact that the wartime alliance of the victors quickly collapsed into overt antagonism and left the USSR confronting a new array of potential enemies. And one of those enemies was in possession of the ultimate weapon – the atomic bomb. Thus the emergence of the new Soviet Army was shaped to no little extent by the contingencies of a new war – the Cold War.

The immediate postwar mission of the army, was, as Thomas Wolfe has written, 'to make the threat of Soviet land power against Europe the counterpoise to US nuclear power'. Thus the army remained massive and highly visible in East Europe to hold West Europe hostage to an

Soviet sailors raise the Soviet flag over Port Arthur in 1945 after the swift and successful Soviet campaign against the Japanese forces on the Asian mainland in the last month of the war. The belated Soviet involvement in the war against Japan also helped bring about the Communist presence in North Korea.

Right: An ASU-57 57mm self-propelled assault gun. Such guns were widely used by the Soviets during World War II but have only light armor protection. This model was introduced in the late 50s and continues to serve with airborne formations although now largely replaced by the more formidable ASU-85.

Above: A ZIL-131 cargo truck negotiates rough terrain on a test ground.

Left: An S-60 57mm anti-aircraft gun ready to fire.

A Soviet reconnaissance
patrol composed of a
motorcycle and a BRDM
armored scout car.

invasion, the best strategy Stalin could find given the US nuclear monopoly. The measure of the threat can be seen in the three to one advantage in divisions the Soviets held over France, Britain and the US. The menace of the Soviet Army in East Europe was the main impetus behind the creation of NATO in 1949.

Although publicly denigrating the atom bomb as just another weapon, Stalin ordered a crash program for a Soviet bomb which was detonated only four years after Hiroshima and Nagasaki. But even while Stalin's scientists worked furiously on his bomb, he strangely refused to allow his military thinkers to explore the implications of nuclear weapons for warfare. Instead, he continued to insist that the basis of power lay in his 'Five Principles of Victory': security of rear areas through political stability, good morale, adequate quantity and quality of forces, adequate amounts of equipment, and the skill and ability of officers. The last was particularly ironic because one of Stalin's first postwar acts was again to savage the

officer corps in a 'purge of the victors'. One result of the purge was to complicate further the already complex problem of reorganizing the army.

Two lessons the Soviets immediately drew from their World War II experience were the need for more firepower and more maneuverability through mobility. By 1948, the 500 wartime divisions had been reduced to 175, of which about 65 were reorganized as tank and mechanized divisions to serve as armored strike forces. Tank divisions were streamlined to 10,500 men and three tank regiments and mechanized divisions to 12,000-13,000 men with three mechanized and two tank regiments. The infantry division was turned into the rifle division with three rifle regiments and 11,000 men. The wartime artillery and antiaircraft divisions were retained.

The tank was seen as the main strike weapon. The T-34 medium and KV and Joseph Stalin heavy tanks with their distinctive low silhouettes had been used very effectively in the latter

Right: A bemedalled Marshal Zhukov seen just after the end of World War II. Zhukov later played a part in helping Khrushchev take power but was sidelined soon after.

Bottom: Along with the BMP infantry combat vehicle, the standard Soviet armored personnel carrier is the BTR-60PB. Unlike the BMP troops would dismount from the BTR to fight.

Below: A 152mm self-propelled howitzer. This weapon can fire to a range of 24-37 Km.

part of the war. Soviet tactics were to concentrate an enormous superiority of forces and equipment on a narrow front while other sectors remained on the defensive or made diversionary attacks. After immense artillery barrages, a wave of heavy tanks broke the defenses, followed by a second wave of medium tanks to exploit the breakthrough. Even better was two breakthroughs to envelop and destroy the defense in a pincer movement. Basically adapted from German tactics against the Soviets in 1941, these tactics were widely and successfully used in 1944-1945.

The problem was the limited mobility of the infantry, hence the thrust of the reorganization was to motorize the infantry and, for the first time, integrate tank and infantry units into streamlined strike forces. Toward this end, the Soviets created the Combined Arms Army consisting of two to three corps (a corps was two rifle and one mechanized divisions) and the Mechanized Army of two tank and two mechanized divisions.

A total of 23 divisions was deployed in East Europe in two field formations: The Group of Soviet Forces Germany and the Northern Group of Forces in Poland, with six additional divisions in Rumania, Hungary and Austria. Backing these were 30 more divisions in the Western USSR. Matched against this formidable array was a total of nine US, British and French divisions, giving rise to the banality that all the Soviets needed to conquer Europe was 'boots for marching.'

The army remained locked into Stalin's dogma until his death in 1953. Under Georgi Zhukov as Minister of Defense, the army then began to take on its modern configuration with stress on modernization of equipment, more mobility and the creation of effective 'shock' or offensive power. When Zhukov was abruptly deposed in 1957, his successor Malinovsky continued the program.

In order to integrate tank and infantry forces, the unwieldy mechanized division became the current compact tank division and the rifle division became the motor rifle division. The corps was abolished and the Combined Arms Army given instead two to three motor rifle divisions and one tank division. The Mechanized Army became the Tank Army with three to four tank divisions. With the passing of the corps, the division became and has remained the basic tactical unit. At the same time, the first tactical nuclear missiles appeared in the ground forces to replace the heavy artillery at army and division level and the antiaircraft gun was supplanted by surface-to-air missiles (SAM).

Thus the army took its first step into the nuclear age, along with being streamlined and somewhat modernized in hardware in line with a post-Stalin emphasis on the offensive as the centerpiece of strategy. Doctrine shifted away from mass and brute force in the mid-1950s to an emphasis on high speed offensive operations

Left: The T-55 tank was the standard Warsaw Pact battle tank until displaced by the T-62.

Below: A T-12 100mm anti-tank gun. Like their western counterparts, the Soviets are moving away from anti-tank guns in favor of guided missiles.

Above: Supported by a BMD infantry combat vehicle paratroops move into action during training. Along with the strategic rocket forces, the airborne forces are the elite of the Soviet military.

Right: The Sagger anti-tank guided missile is a simple but effective weapon against armor and was used effectively by the Egyptians in the 1973 Middle East War.

Opposite: A battery of twin-barrelled ZU-23 23mm anti-aircraft guns.

keyed to breaththroughs in selected sectors and operations in depth. The organizational and doctrinal changes further took place in the context of massive reductions in manpower. Total strength in the armed forces was reduced from about 5.8 million in 1955 to a little over three million in 1961. In this reduction, however, the Soviet forces in East Europe were virtually untouched. There was also a major reduction in logistics and artillery, both of which were seen as unnecessary impediments to mobility.

Even as these changes were being made, however, Soviet military policy was in upheaval from what the Soviets term the 'revolution in military affairs', more precisely the effect of nuclear weapons on warfare. From the Stalinist extreme of refusing to recognize nuclear weapons, the Soviets under Nikita Khrushchev swung to the opposite extreme of insisting that the unique characteristics of these weapons invalidated most previous military experience. Any future general war would inevitably and immediately be determined by the massive use of nuclear weapons. Such a war would be short, perhaps days long, and intensely violent because of the power of these weapons. Long range ballistic missiles and bombers carrying nuclear warheads thus were to play the central role in achieving Soviet military and political goals. The creation of credible strategic nuclear forces was the main focus of military policy under Khrushchev from 1955 to his ouster in 1964. The transition was accompanied by intense discussion and debate in the military and no little

T-55 tanks supported by infantry on maneuvers. In the foreground is a soldier with an RPG-7 40mm anti-tank grenade launcher.

amount of interservice strife over control of the new strategic missions and weapons.

The main victim in this revolution in policy was the army which ceased to be the central component of Soviet military power and was cast in a supporting role. This major break with Russian and Soviet tradition occurred because of questions about the role of the army in the new concept of war. Its brevity would make impossible the employment of large field forces which indeed would simply be annihilated by nuclear weapons. In the end, the army was conceived as contributing small, highly mobile armored forces to mop up and occupy the defeated states after the nuclear barrage. The battle over the role of the ground forces was bitterly fought for years. The depth of the slide in status and importance can be seen from the fact that in 1964, the army ceased to be an independent service with its own commander-in-chief but rather was administered directly by the Ministry of Defense.

But the eclipse of the army did not much outlast Khrushchev who was forced to depart the halls of power in October 1964. Almost immediately, there was a major overhaul of military policy and programs by the new Brezhnev-Kosygin leadership. The overhaul was spurred on by a perceived worsening of the international situation, highlighted by US military involvement in Southeast Asia, the continued decline in Sino-Soviet relations, and particularly the Chinese explosion of a nuclear device in 1964. The Soviet belief that US power was being committed to the suppression of national liberation movements, the Chinese challenge to the Soviet model of national development and leadership of the third world revolutionary movement, and the immediate matter of the Soviet political and military commitment to North Vietnam, caused the regime to raise its estimate that the USSR might be drawn into armed conflict. It also considered the question of improving Soviet military capabilities to support and even intervene in distant local conflicts. After years of debate, the milit-

Left: T-55 tanks are serviced in the field. The T-55 mounts a 100mm gun.

Left: The M1974 self-propelled 122mm gun.

Below: T-55 tanks on wintry maneuvers.

ary had also moved toward a less restrictive view of the nature of future conflict, particularly as it watched NATO progress from debate through military exercises to formal adoption of a more flexible and limited nuclear response policy between 1961 and 1967. Some recognition that nuclear weapons had limitations began to dawn, along with greater uncertainty about whether a war would be long, short or even inevitably nuclear. There was thus renewed interest in conventional operations by the ground forces. Since the mid-1960s, the army has thus undergone an important renaissance, symbolized by its restoration as an indepedent command in 1967, and regained much of its former dominance in shaping Soviet conceptions of future conflict.

The Modern Army

The Army has been sized and developed to deal with a much wider range of contingencies than envisioned in the Khrushchev period. These range from local interventions in the border areas, such as Czechoslovakia in 1968, Afghanistan in 1979 and conceivably Poland in the future, to World War III in which the army would have to deal with NATO in the West and possibly China, Japan and the US in the East. The Soviets now admit the possibility of important conventional operations in a general war. Army operations are now geared more than ever to the 'combined arms' concept which holds that the diversity of and harmony of all services and arms are necessary for the final victory. Within this concept, the army has come to play an increasingly important role. It has been developed into a highly mobile strike force with powerful tank and motorized rifle elements and is, in the words of Malcolm MacIntosh, the embodiment of the ability to 'strike first in the last resort'.

Since the mid-1960s, the size of the army has grown considerably. The number of line divisions has climbed from about 135 to around 180. The manpower of the motor rifle division also increased by 1000 and that of the tank by 500. The increase in the number of line divisions can be largely laid to the massive buildup on the Sino-Soviet border stemming from the ideological confrontation with the People's Republic of China which began in the late 1950s. Clearly, one role of the modern army has been to intimidate the Chinese as it has traditionally been used to intimidate Europeans. The utility of the army in these roles has grown in an era of strategic nuclear parity between the USSR and the US. The main thrust of the expansion was over by the early 1970s, however, and manpower increase since that time has been quite small. By the late 1970s, ground forces manpower stood at around 1.8 million.

Despite this size, the army is basically a cadre force which depends on major mobilization to reach its full potential. Line divisions are maintained in three categories of combat readiness

Above: The D-30 122mm howitzer is a standard Soviet field piece. It can fire a 48 pound shell to a range in excess of 15,000 yards.

Left: A soldier adjusts the sights on an 82mm M1937 mortar.

Opposite: An SD-44 85mm antitank gun which is fitted with an auxiliary propulsion system.

as measured in terms of available personnel and equipment. Category A units have at least 75% of their men and equipment and could be ready for operations within a few days. Category B units average about 50% in personnel with a few as high as 70% and have most of their equipment. These units would require weeks to become operational. Category C units have only 10-33% of their personnel and usually 50% or less of their authorized equipment, most of which is in storage and older models. These divisions would require months to become operational. Reservists from the local area fill out

these units except in thinly populated areas like Siberia and the Far East.

Less than a third of tank and motor rifle divisions are Category I and almost 60% of these are deployed in East Europe where all Soviet divisions are Category I units manned near full strength. The other major concentration is in the Far East where almost a third of the line divisions are Category I. Category II and III units are distributed over the various military districts except for the interior districts which have only a handful of divisions among them.

Beyond the Category III divisions is yet another layer of depth to the army's mobilization potential. There may be as many as 50 cadre or mobilization divisions stocked with older equipment and serviced by a small cadre in peacetime. Most probably these would be motor rifle divisions but would take as much as six months to become operational even for second-line duties. These cadre divisions probably represent a Soviet hedge against the contingency of a long war.

Category II and III units are the framework of the army which the Soviets can fill out as they see need. For the December 1979 invasion of Afghanistan, for example, the Soviets quietly mobilized several local low strength divisions and employed these in the operation. They were subsequently replaced by other units but their use meant that the Soviets did not have to with-

Above: Soviet troops dismount from BMP infantry combat vehicles during training. The troops are armed with RPG-7 grenade launchers and Kalashnikov automatic rifles held in the 'marching fire' position.

Opposite, top: BMP vehicles and troops are supported by Mi-24 Hind helicopter gunships during maneuvers. The BMP carries a 73mm smoothbore gun and also a launcher for Sagger antitank missiles although these are not shown here.

Opposite, bottom: A BMP infantry combat vehicle in desert camouflage. Originally designed for use on the nuclear battlefield in Europe, the BMP was used by the Egyptians in the 1967 Middle East War when it displayed a lamentable tendency to catch fire when hit.

Right: The SA-7 man-portable surface-to-air missile brings air defense down to the squad level in the Soviet ground forces. It would be particularly useful against helicopters and other low flying aircraft.

draw frontline units from other sectors nor signal their intentions by the obvious movement of forces.

The line divisions are motor rifle, tank and airborne. The seven airborne divisions are considered elite troops which are administratively part of the army but at least in peacetime report directly to the Ministry of Defense. About a third of the other divisions are tank but it should be noted that the motor rifle divisions have two-thirds as many tanks as a tank division plus a large number of BMP infantry combat vehicles which have the fighting power of a light tank. Both tank and motor rifle divisions have organic nuclear weapons and organic mobile air defense. Both also have a triangular structure. The motor rifle regiment has three motor rifle regiments plus tank and artillery regiments, each with three rifle battalions which in turn have three rifle companies. Soviet units generally have less personnel (but not necessarily less firepower) than comparable US units. The motor rifle division has about 13,000 versus around 16,000 for the US mechanized

Right: The PT-76 light amphibious tank mounts a 76mm gun and is lightly armored but highly mobile. It is typically used in the reconnaissance role.

infantry division, for example, and the Soviet rifle battalion about 450 to 830 for a US battalion. Many divisions and armies retain honorific designations earned from outstanding performance in World War II. Bestowed by Stalin, divisions are designated as 'Guards' while some tank armies have received the designation of 'Shock' for wartime exploits.

There are fifteen tank and fifteen motor rifle divisions deployed in East Europe in four 'Groups of Forces': the Group of Soviet Forces Germany which is the premier formation of the army, the Northern Group of Forces in Poland, the Central Group in Czechoslovakia whose five divisions are a legacy of the 1968 Soviet invasion, and the Southern Group in Hungary, also stemming from the 1956 intervention. About one fourth of the total strength of the ground

forces is deployed on the Sino-Soviet border. The estimated 106,000 Soviets in Afghanistan reportedly include six motor rifle divisions and the equivalent of an airborne division, although these began to be reduced in accordance with the Geneva Accord in August 1988, with an eventual run down to only a small number of advisers by February 1989. Contingents of army personnel can also be found in client states such as Angola, Ethiopia, Iraq and Libya.

Divisions are assigned to armies. The Combined Arms Army is the basic Soviet field army and typically has two to three motor rifle divisions and one or two tank divisions. Intended as an armor-heavy force to exploit breakthroughs, the typical tank army has three to four tank divisions and one motor rifle division. Armies also include independent artillery, air defense

Left: Shown here with Soviet naval infantry, the BTR-60P is typically armed with one 12.7mm and from one to three 7.62mm machine guns and has good amphibious capabilities.

Above: The BTR-50P armored personnel carrier has been in service with Soviet forces since the late 1950s. It typically carries 20 troops, 2 crew and 1 light machine gun.

and Scud nuclear missile brigades as well as reconnaissance, intelligence, signals, engineering and many other combat support and service elements.

Armies in peacetime are subordinate to the Groups of Forces in East Europe or military district commands in the USSR proper. The Group of Soviet Forces Germany, for example, has three Tank Armies and two Combined Arms Armies while the Carpathian Military District has one tank army and two Combined Arms Armies. In wartime, the organization would shift to the 'front' which is roughly equivalent to a US army group. A front could have three to four Combined Arms Armies, a Tank Army, a Tactical Air Army, and supporting forces. The Groups of Forces would presumably combine with the East European national

Forces to form fronts while the military districts would be the basis of fronts in the USSR. In particular, there are five important military districts in the Western USSR whose wartime roles have always been closely linked to the Soviet and East European forces in Central Europe. As fronts their role in wartime or major crisis would be to deploy forward into Central Europe. This has been a major aspect of Soviet military strategy since the early 1950s.

In contrast to its western counterparts, the Soviet army keeps its administrative 'tail' streamlined and centralized so as to maximize resources for its combat 'teeth'. The rear services are organized as a special service precisely to free the fighting soldiers for their main job. All units have a rear services unit under the control of the army's central rear service. The army service in turn is part of the Ministry of Defense's rear service headed by a deputy minister and which publishes its own service journal called *Rear and Supply*.

The army rear services also try to achieve a high degree of independence from the troubled civilian economy. Military state farms, especially in the Far East where the ground forces are at the mercy of the Trans-Siberian Railroad, grow much of the army's food and large unit gardens are also promoted. The army further maintains its own clothing and boot factories. In the important area of transport, however, the army is highly dependent on the civilian sector. The army (and other forces as well) would get most of their trucks in wartime or other contingencies through the autokolomka system. All civilian trucks are built to standard military designs and are part of military mobilization planning. The drivers themselves are more often than not reservists of the automotive troops, so the truck and its driver are called up together to support military logistics. This system had a severe impact on the harvest in 1968 when much civilian transport was mobilized to support the Czech intervention.

Warsaw Pact forces in East Europe are almost completely supplied from the USSR and thus depend on long, exposed lines of communication. Because of the lack of trucks, the Soviets depend mostly on railroads for their logistics as they did in World War II. But the high rates of advance envisioned for Warsaw Pact forces in wartime could cause them to outrun their supply lines, especially since these would be under sustained attack. The experience of the Czech intervention gives an example of the potential weakness of Soviet logistics. As Leo Heiman wrote at the time, 'During the first week of the occupation . . . a breakdown of

Above right: A T-55 tank crosses a river with the help of engineers and their ferry.

Right: The Soviets place great emphasis on successful river-crossing operations. One important item for these operations is the BLG-60 bridging tank seen here on a ferry.

Far right: A TMM 60 ton bridge. The Soviets consider river crossing under fire one of the most difficult of combat operations.

transportation and supply services threatened to paralyze the Soviet armies in Czechoslovakia . . . the situation was saved by airlift . . . Under actual combat conditions, . . . the Soviet forces would have lacked many essential items after the first twenty-four hours'. In short, the Soviet armored forces outran their rail-based supply and had not enough trucks to cope. And this occurred in a situation where there was no armed resistance.

Apart from the army proper, there are two other large, well-armed bodies of ground forces. The Ministry of the Interior (MVD) maintains an estimated 250,000 internal security troops and the KGB another 200,000 border guards. Though paramilitary, these forces have tanks, armored personnel carriers, helicopters and artillery and are fed by the same conscript system that sustains the armed forces. The KGB troops in fact bore the brunt of the border skirmishes with the Chinese in the late 1960s. In peacetime, these forces guard the borders and important civilian and military installations. In wartime, they would uphold the authority of the state, control the civilian and military populations, and secure rear areas. Their missions would be similar to those of the NKVD forces (ancestor of the KGB) in World War II which, as Albert Seaton has written, 'were not normally used in the forefront of battle, but formed the garrison of vital centres or were held back to round up stragglers or threaten Red Army units which were in danger of breaking'.

The Soviet Way of War

How the modern army would be employed in a future war is largely determined by how the Soviets see the circumstances of such a war. Historically, the Soviets have seen themselves surrounded by hostile capitalist states and supported by allies shaky at best. The Hungarian and Czech problems of the past, the current questions about Poland, and the outright defections of China and Yugoslavia from the Soviet orbit must surely give Soviet military planners cause for concern about the reliability of allies. The European and American military roles in the Russian civil war, deep Soviet suspicion of

Above & above right: Soviet soldiers practice nuclear/ chemical decontamination procedures. The Soviet forces are probably the most comprehensively equipped in the world for protection against nuclear/ bacteriological/chemical attack. Soviet forces also have a wide range of chemical and bacteriological weapons at their disposal.

the Allies in World War II, and the subsequent Cold War must in the worst case (which must always be the one considered by military planners) cause the Soviets to see a 'world in arms' against them.

And the Soviets could conceivably be outnumbered. Their potential enemies in the West are NATO and in the east China, Japan and the US. NATO (including US-based divisions) and China together would have about 260 divisions to array against the approximately 180 of the Soviets, a 3 to 2 advantage in manpower as Jeffrey Record has pointed out. Nor would full mobilization necessarily improve the ratio because the European members of NATO could muster some 3.25 million and the Chinese around 5 million trained reserves. These figures alone help to explain the Soviet penchant for a large army.

But beyond these rather questionable static force comparisons, the Soviets appear to have drawn several important lessons from their experience in World War II. That war showed the Soviets that the stakes were no less than national survival as the harnessing of the whole of national life to war brought complete destruction to the vanquished. In the Soviet case, the price of defeat would have been all that they have struggled to build since 1917. Thus the Soviets cannot afford to lose because national survival is at stake. 'The end of war is victory' as David Isby has tersely and aptly described the Soviet way of war. 'All else is nonsense'.

The vast human and material cost of the Ger-

man invasion in World War II further taught the Soviets never again to permit the battle to be fought on their territory. The basic Soviet vision of a future war with NATO is thus a powerful offensive staged from East Europe into West Europe where the battle is to be fought. Because NATO has greater military potential than the Warsaw Pact if given time to mobilize fully, the war must also be won quickly while Soviet forces are still superior. The army is thus oriented mainly toward Europe and structured for a quick, high-speed campaign across West Germany, the Netherlands, Benelux and France. In the Far East, the Soviets would probably launch an offensive on several axes into Manchuria and North China to strike at the most developed part of the country and move the combat away from Soviet territory.

The Soviets firmly believe that victory stems only from an offensive strategy. Victory is the 'the total defeat of the defending enemy and capture of vital areas of his territory' as V.Y. Savkin wrote in his widely read book *Basic Principles of Operational Art and Tactics*. The

goals of Soviet offensive strategy are thus unlimited and not just the defeat of an invasion or limited occupation of enemy territory. Soviet strategy is an offensive warfighting strategy as described by Soviet military writers: 'Victory over an enemy is achieved only by a resolute attack' and 'the offensive is the main type of combat action of Soviet troops'.

Defense is characterized as a 'forced and temporary form of combat' which even so requires strong counterattacks to prepare for the shift to the offensive. Soviet military treatises have been so forthright about their total offensive goals and warfighting doctrine that much adverse comment has been generated in the West. In recent years, this aspect of Soviet military doctrine has been played down as a result by Soviet commentators.

The simple outline of Soviet offensive strategy is to mass superior forces suddenly on a narrow frontage to overwhelm the defense, penetrate preferably in several places, and then loose powerful armored forces into the enemy rear. Once the enemy defenses have been penetrated, the Soviets envision very high rates of advance, in some cases 70 km a day. To accomplish this remarkable feat, they plan to use airborne and heliborne forces in advance of the attack and where appropriate to attack 'off the march'. The speed of the offensive is to be sustained by continuous operations, day and night, for as long as a month. No army has attempted such an ambitious program to date, so it is open to question how successful such very demanding operations can be.

The Soviets believe that the chances for the success of the offensive increase if the enemy can be prevented from regrouping, reinforcing or even resting. If the enemy is to have no respite, the attack cannot occur in stages but must

be relentless until victory is achieved. The tactic used to produce the continuous pressure of the attack is echeloning. The Soviets array their forces in a first, second and occasionally a third echelon if the enemy defenses are strong and deep. Each echelon has an assigned task, usually the same for the first and second echelons. When the attack of the first echelon begins to flag and it is unable to realize its task, the second echelon takes up the assault and the first withdraws from combat. Timing is critical because there can be no lag between commitment of the second and relief of the first. Reserves as forces withheld for contingencies are kept small in contrast to echelons. The Soviets employ echelonment at all levels from the tactical to the strategic. The Soviet Groups of Forces and East European national forces are the first strategic echelon in Europe and the forces in the western USSR the second.

The Soviet doctrine of the offensive envisions three basic types of action: the meeting engagement, pursuit, and the breakthrough attack. The most important is the meeting engagement which can occur during nuclear or conventional operations. The meeting engagement is simply mobile warfare in which the opposing forces encounter each other and attack on the move. From the Soviet side, the advance guard makes contact and attacks to pin down the enemy while the main force maneuvers to flank or rapidly envelop. If this maneuver fails, the advance guard and main force fuse to attack in concert.

The Soviets believe that at least the early phases of combat in Europe could well be characterized by important meeting engagements as Soviet advance forces encounter NATO units moving forward. But in a form of operation so dependent on speed and maneuver, the Soviets

Above: A group of T-64/72s tanks on maneuvers. The tank's smoothbore gun has an automatic loader which permits a rate of fire of up to eight rounds per minute. The T-64/72s has replaced the T-55 as the main battle tank of the Soviet Army.

could encounter problems in Central Europe. The Soviets have some tendency towards stereotyped maneuvers, as David Isby has noted, and could also face serious losses from uncertainty in fixing the position of the enemy. Because of heavy concentrations of mutually supporting forces and overlapping avenues of fire and defense, there may not be enough room for the kind of grand maneuver the Soviets apparently envision.

The pursuit is intended to maintain the pressure of the attack when the enemy is attempting to break off contact and withdraw. Frontal pursuit means an attempt to engage and breakthrough the rear guard while parallel pursuit is aimed at cutting off the enemy retreat. Best is a combination to catch and annihilate the enemy between two forces.

The operation for which the Soviets were famous in World War II was the breakthrough attack directed against well prepared defenses. Here were the immense artillery barrages, waves of tanks to smash through the defenses, and hordes of infantry. Losses were heavy and the infantry and artillery were not mobile enough to exploit the breakthrough properly with the armor. Since that time, the Soviets have come to believe that the breakthrough attack will not be a common form of action because of the time required for preparation and the danger of massing forces against a nuclear armed enemy. Soviet preference is to by-pass defenses when possible but otherwise to penetrate and force the enemy into withdrawal and the resumption of mobile warfare. The attack is to be mounted as soon as possible to reduce the enemy's defensive preparations. When the attack is ready, the advance guard begins to probe for a breakthrough. If one develops, the main force pours through for mobile operations in the enemy rear. This would be unusual, however, and typically a combined arms assault of armored infantry with artillery and air support is required. Vulnerable to prepared defenses bristling with antitank weapons, the tanks are withheld until the defenses are breached at one or more points, after which special Operational Maneuver Groups (OMGs) of highly mobile armor are committed to exploit the gaps. Another variant is for the advance force to engage in a holding attack while the main force tries to outflank or envelop.

Since the advent of nuclear weapons, Soviet offensive strategy has been indelibly colored by the specter of nuclear warfare. Nuclear weapons have profoundly affected Soviet thinking about warfare and thus Soviet approaches to war. 'Nuclear weapons are the most powerful means for the mass destruction of troops and objectives' wrote one Soviet. 'During the entire history of military art, no one weapon has such sudden and decisive influence on the nature of the offensive and on the conflict as a whole as did nuclear weapons. Their employment in battle . . . permits inflicting large losses in person-

nel and equipment on the enemy almost instantaneously, destroying, paralyzing and putting out of action entire regiments, divisions and even corps, and thereby changing the relation of forces sharply in one's favor . . .'

Because of these unique characteristics, the Soviets see nuclear weapons as integral to their way of war. This view stands in stark contrast to that of the West where nuclear use has typically been 'unthinkable' until very recently and more or less beyond the pale of serious military consideration for political reasons. The Soviets as a result have dealt more realistically with the problems of combat under nuclear conditions in terms of weapons design and various operational considerations, not the least of which is training. '. . . the chief influence on the methods of action undertaken by troops in any given situa-

Right: Cutaway artwork showing a 122mm self-propelled howitzer (based on drawings published in a Soviet magazine).

Below: The ASU-85 airborne self-propelled gun is an 85mm tube on the chassis of a PT-76 light tank. It is fully armored and is common in the Soviet airborne forces.

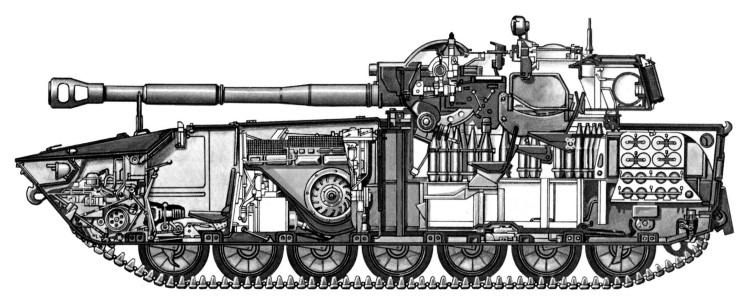

tion is the constant threat of the use of nuclear weapons' wrote I. Zavilov in *Red Star* in 1970. 'From this comes the main task – to train troops to operate both with and without the use of nuclear weapons, to achieve rapid transition . . . from fighting with conventional weapons to operations waged with nuclear weapons . . . The complexity lies in the fact that it is difficult to foresee at which stage of the operation nuclear weapons may be used. All this makes it necessary to train men for the successful execution of combat operations in all conditions.'

Although the Soviets believe that nuclear war could be initiated at any point by one side or the other, it is most likely to occur in situations in which NATO appeared to be preparing to cross the nuclear threshold to halt a successful Warsaw Pact offensive. In this case, the Soviets would attempt to preempt to forestall any radical change in the military situation unfavorable to them. Another possibility is using nuclear weapons to clear enemy defenses if the offensive has bogged down. In this way, offensive momentum and mobility could be restored.

Once the nuclear threshold has been crossed, the Soviets believe in 'mass employment of nuclear weapons' with the objective of destroying all enemy nuclear weapons, command and control, reserves, rear area installations, and front-line forces – basically, to clear the theater. Mass employment achieves full shock effect and is

Right: The AT-3 Sagger anti-tank wire-guided missile is still in wide use with the Soviet Army but is being supplanted by newer, more capable, weapons.

Below: The AT-4 Spigot is one of the newer weapons in the army's arsenal.

very much in keeping with Soviet artillery tradition which, as Martin Miller aptly wrote, 'has never been concerned with pinpoint accuracy and strict target selection but rather mass barrages intended to smash paths through enemy formations and rear areas for the ground units to exploit'. And the army has large numbers of tactical nuclear missiles and air-delivered bombs to use for this purpose.

Whereas NATO has historically seen the role of nuclear weapons as a deterrent to Soviet aggression and has emphasized their selective and controlled use, the Soviets see these weapons as a part of modern warfare and stress their warfighting role. Soviet writers ridicule western concepts of selective and controlled use as 'nonsense' and 'foolhardy'. The Soviets assume that the early use of nuclear weapons

and the ever present threat of use would be a basic fact of any war between the Warsaw Pact and NATO. The two most basic tenets of Soviet military doctrine are the importance of numerical superiority and the decisiveness of nuclear weapons in war. These weapons provide the army with the ultimate firepower to win. Numerical superiority and nuclear weapons are in fact related because the immense losses of personnel and equipment on the nuclear battlefield would require very large forces, yet another reason why the Soviets have invested in such a large army.

The Soviet fixation on the mass employment of nuclear weapons as the decisive factor in a future war has been both puzzling and disturbing to Westerners. Given that each side has thousands of nuclear warheads to employ in the European theater, much of that hapless continent would be devastated. As far back as the 1960s, studies by the United States Department of Defense estimated that 'Even under the most favorable assumptions, it appears that between two and twenty million Europeans would be

killed, with widespread damage to the economy of the area and a high risk of 100 million dead if the war escalated to attacks on cities'. The populations of East Europe and the Western USSR would also suffer human and economic losses beyond comprehension.

·Westerners have indeed wondered how the Soviet military could consider the mass employment of nuclear weapons in Europe a viable strategy for victory and have searched for any sign of movement away from this position. Some observers, such as Jeffrey Record, believe that the Soviets have become less rigid in recent years, citing as one example Marshal I.I. Yakubovsky's statement in *Red Star* that 'forces must be prepared to fight without using nuclear weapons, utilizing only the standard conventional weapons'. Other Soviet writers have also said that nuclear war is not inevitable but still highly probable. But the army's large investment in the 1970s to develop the capability for conventional as well as nuclear operations is the best argument for Soviet acceptance of the possibility that war in Europe might at least

have a conventional opening period.

However much the Soviet military believes in nuclear weapons as the ultimate tools of victory, it will not make the decision to cross the nuclear threshold. As the Soviet defense intellectual M.P. Skirdo observes, '. . . the decision to employ such devastating implements as nuclear weapons has become the exclusive prerogative of the political leadership. It is primarily the political, not the military, leaders who determine the necessity of employing mass destruction weapons, who specify the principal targets and when they are to be hit'.

The Army's Arsenal
In keeping with the emphasis on a high speed offensive, the primary weapons in the army's arsenal are the tank and the tactical nuclear weapon. The tank embodies a combination of mobility and firepower and the nuclear weapon devastating firepower to create prime conditions for high speed armored warfare. 'In offensive operations, tank troops will be the force which rushes to the ultimate goals' wrote V.Y.

The FROG-7 tactical rocket is the most recent version of this basic Soviet weapon and serves as part of the divisional artillery with the Soviet armies.

wrote Marshal of Tank Forces P.A. Rotmistrov. 'It plays the decisive role in the attack' while Savkin further observed, '. . . tanks are better able to withstand the effects of nuclear weapons, possess high cross-country ability and speed of movement off roads . . . With the fire of their guns and an armored blow, tanks are able to wipe from their path surviving remnants of existing enemy troops, deliver forceful attacks against their flanks and rear, and move to a great depth without halting.'

In 1980, the Soviets were estimated to have over 50,000 tanks of various models, about 3000 of which are thought to be in storage as war reserves. In fact, most of the army's tanks are in storage at any given time to protect them against wear and weather. The Soviets use training tanks, usually older models, to develop crew proficiency. This system keeps the top of the line equipment in near mint condition and leaves almost every tank deployable within a day. Crews, however, do not gain intimate fami-

Above: T-62 tanks in the snow. Soviet tanks generally have good cross-country mobility even in difficult conditions.

Top: T-62s in training. The T-62 is still widely deployed with Soviet forces even though production ceased many years ago because of less than satisfactory performance, shown especially in the 1973 Middle East War.

Main Battle Tanks

	T-54/55	T-62	T-64	T-72
WEIGHT (TONS)	36	37	35	41
SPEED (KM/HR)	50	50	50	60
MAIN ARMAMENT	100mm TANK GUN	115mm SMOOTHBORE	125mm SMOOTHBORE	125mm SMOOTHBORE
MUZZLE VELOCITY (MPS)	1,400	1,600	1,750	1,750

Savkin '. . . in the shortest line along routes laid by nuclear weapons'. Other weapons such as armored personnel carriers (APCs), artillery and antiaircraft weapons have become oriented toward supporting the tank. The army still also relies on Ivan – the man carrying a gun – but Ivan no longer walks. He is mounted and often fights from inside his armored personnel carrier or his infantry combat vehicle.

The Soviets see the tank as the decisive weapon in conventional battle. 'Armor is the basic maneuver element of the Soviet army'

liarity with their vehicles and lose much training time because there are not enough training tanks for every crew.

Soviet tanks compare very favorably with their Western counterparts. The Soviets historically have used heavier guns, made their vehicles lighter with lower silhouettes and better cross-country agility, and installed better nuclear-chemical-bacteriological defense systems. But they also carry less ammunition which could be critical in battle and where high speed operations in depth may outdistance logistics.

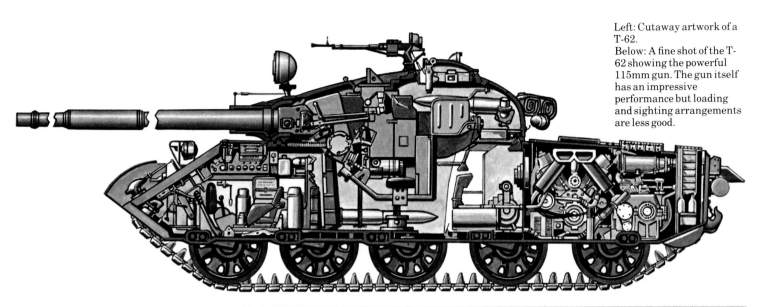

Left: Cutaway artwork of a
T-62.
Below: A fine shot of the T-
62 showing the powerful
115mm gun. The gun itself
has an impressive
performance but loading
and sighting arrangements
are less good.

Above: Motorised infantry
on maneuvers. The two
soldiers in the center are
using RPG-7 grenade
launchers, probably against
simulated anti-tank
defenses.

Right: A Czech M53 59 twin
self-propelled anti-aircraft
gun.

They also reportedly have a higher rate of breakdown. Until the advent of the T-64/T-72 series in the early 1970s, Western tanks also had advantages in fire control and optics.

The current Soviet tank force includes two generations. It is believed that the Soviets still have a number of World War II T-34s stockpiled, not least because some of these vintage weapons were shipped to Soviet clients such as Angola in the late 1970s. The succeeding T-54/T-55 series is probably still the most widely fielded tank in the Warsaw Pact and is reasonably well-armed, protected and mobile. The Soviets had apparently planned to upgrade their force with the T-62, the core of Egyptian and Syrian armor in 1973, but found it unsatisfactory. The T-62 ceased production some years ago but is still in service with Warsaw Pact forces. An entirely new family of tanks has been fielded in the 1970s in the T-64, T-72 and new T-80. These are advanced designs well able to compete with Western contempories. The new tanks have a notable tank fighting capability and are thought to reflect the lessons of the Middle East wars and the prospect of major meeting engagements between tank forces in Europe.

The Soviets believe that nuclear weapons are the instrument most likely to enable their army of tanks to mop up the enemy. When the time comes, nuclear weapons will be employed en masse with as many as a third of the army's warheads involved. The remainder are to be used in follow up operations as the need arises. The army has traditionally relied on tactical ballistic missiles and air delivered bombs but in recent years has had nuclear-capable artillery as well. The FROG (Free Rocket over Ground) unguided rocket and the Scud short range ballistic missile, improved over the years, have served as the army's main deliverers of nuclear weapons for over two decades. Each has a rather large, dirty warhead and rather poor accuracy as the Egyptians and Syrians found to their dismay in the 1973 war. These are old missiles with very serious operational drawbacks, and are in the process of being eliminated in accordance with the INF Treaty or replaced by more modern weapons.

Prior to the advent of nuclear weapons and still during conventional combat, the army relies on artillery for its main firepower. Indeed, the Soviets have had a longstanding, even passionate, love affair with the cannon, exemplified by Stalin's description of artillery as the 'god of war'. In World War II, the Soviets typically massed 150-300 guns per kilometer of frontage and carefully planned immense barrages to make possible the breakthrough attacks in the latter part of the war. The Soviets now believe that the rapid pace of the operations would prevent the massing of artillery resources which would also be vulnerable to NATO attack. The main mission of artillery is now the suppression of the formidable array of antitank weapons which

Above: The Kalashnikov in action. The original AK-47 design was based in part on the design of German assault rifles introduced late in World War II.

Left: The RPK-74 is a new light 5.45mm machine gun, now in service with the Soviet forces.

menace the Soviet armored offensive. Artillery thus plays a key role in the Soviet conception of combined arms operations. The enthusiastic espousal of nuclear weapons in the 1950s and early 1960s caused much of the army's artillery to be stripped away as unnecessary but since that time, the amount of artillery available at division level alone has more than doubled.

One of the lessons the Soviets drew from World War II was that towed artillery and marching infantry are too slow to keep up with high speed armored offensives. Although most Soviet artillery is still towed, the army began to introduce self-propelled pieces in the 1970s, with the intent of enabling their artillery to better support the mobile armored warfare they envision. The infantry too has been mounted, first in trucks and then in APCs. The APC is essentially a battlefield taxi which offers its passengers a modicum of protection from small arms fire. The Soviets were the first to introduce the infantry combat vehicle in the BMP in the late 1960s. Originally intended for the solely nuclear battlefield, the BMP has been incorporated into

The Kalashnikov family of automatic rifles in various models has been the standard weapon of the Soviet infantryman for over 30 years. The AK-47 and AKM models are in 7.62mm caliber while the new AK-74 model is 5.45mm.

combined arms doctrine and allows troops to fight from inside through firing ports in addition to having rather potent tank-killing power itself. The BMP has been extensively employed in Afghanistan and recently a new model – the BMP-70 – has been identified. The Soviets also rely extensively on the wheeled APCs of the BTR series.

Ivan is armed with the Kalashnikov family of automatic rifles: the AK-47, AKM and the new AK-74. The AK-47 (Automatic Kalashnikov) was designed in 1947 and entered service four years later. Essentially improved submachine guns, these weapons are simple, rugged and reliable but neither accurate nor long range. The soldier is taught to point the weapon and spray in a suppressive fire to keep the enemy down until dispatched by other weapons or the soldier is close enough to do the job himself. These simple tactics, as David Isby notes, are well suited to the training and competence of conscripts and conscript non-commissioned officers. The AK-47 has also been popular for

guerrilla and urban fighting because it is dependable and easy to maintain. Some US marines in Viet Nam reportedly used captured AK-47s in preference to the M-16 then being introduced. An estimated 40 million of the Kalashnikov family of weapons now have been produced.

The Army in the 1980s

The Soviet army has gone through a remarkable evolution from the victorious Red horde of World War II. It has been molded to fit the requirements of Soviet concepts of what a future war with NATO or China might be like. It has been outfitted with an up-to-date and effective arsenal of weaponry that generally is as good and in some cases better than that of the West. 'In the past, we counted on the superior quality of western weapons, equipment and technology to offset the decided advantage the Warsaw Pact enjoyed in quantity' General George Brown testified to the US Senate Armed Services Committee in 1976. 'That time is now past. The hard fact is that the Warsaw Pact has

Soviet infantry practice a dismounted assault from their BMP infantry combat vehicles with support from a Hind helicopter gunship.

Below: T-72 tanks rumble through Red Square in Moscow. The T-72 is basically an improved T-64 but an even newer tank, the T-80, is already entering the inventory.

achieved near qualitative parity with the West in general purpose weapons and equipment'.

The days when the Soviets had to focus their resources on a local, one front war are also over. The army is now deployed to deal with various contingencies, including major war in both the west and the east. In the 1980s, it may well be called upon to extend its readiness to the southern frontiers of the USSR, as suggested by its employment as an instrument of local Soviet policy in Afghanistan. It has become a far more sophisticated and flexible instrument for the

Soviet leadership and will become even more so in the future. This capability may well become an increasingly important factor in an era when both superpowers fear to brandish their strategic nuclear weapons at each other for fear of the ultimate miscalculation.

Above: The airborne forces have their own version of the Kalashnikov which is distinguished by its folding stock.

Right: All versions of the Kalashnikov share the same basic firing system, being gas-operated with a rotating bolt.

Right: The Scud-B tactical ballistic missile is believed to have a range of about 175 miles and, with conventional warheads, was employed to no effect by the Egyptians and Syrians in the 1973 Middle East War.

Below right: The T-72 tank is light compared to its western counterparts but packs a punch with its 125mm gun. It is considered to be a very competitive weapon by western analysts.

AIR POWER

Previous page: A Tu-95
Bear-C maritime patrol
aircraft being shadowed by
an American F-14 Tomcat
over the central Pacific in
1979.

Right: One of the first
bombers ever to be designed
was the *Russki Vityaz*
(Russian Knight) of 1913.
Carrying a crew of 7, it was
a four-engined plane with a
ski undercarriage.

Below: Perhaps the most
famous Russian plane of
World War II, the Ilyushin
Shturmovik, known as
the 'flying tank', was
comparatively slow but was
tough and maneuverable in
keeping with its ground-
attack role.

The publicity directed toward the expansion
and growth of Soviet military power is often
focused on the strategic, ground and seaborne
elements of the power equation, obscuring the
parallel growth in size and capability of Soviet
airpower. While individual aircraft, such as the
Backfire medium bomber, have found a niche in
the public mind, less note has been taken of the
evolution of Soviet air power into a modern multi-role strike force – a fully integrated and vital
member of the combined arms team for theater
conflict – reflecting growing Soviet requirements for flexible nuclear and conventional
capabilities over longer ranges. The expansion
and modernization of air transport forces have
also provided greater scope for peacetime operations in support of client states.

A primary force in the expansion of Soviet air
power has been the emphasis placed by the
Soviet military leadership on the enhancement
of conventional combat capability to complement the role of nuclear weapons. Nuclear
weapons remain pre-eminent, and manned aircraft continue to play a significant role in their
delivery and in defending against similar
strikes by the enemy. But for delivering nuclear
weapons, aircraft are viewed as running a poor
second to ballistic missiles. In defense manned
interceptors must share the ring with the
world's largest force of strategic and tactical

surface-to-air missiles. But the reverse is true
in terms of the delivery of the large amounts of
conventional ordnance required by modern
combat operations. Soviet attention to improving conventional capabilities is evident in the
current generation of combat aircraft. As one
Western analyst has observed, in contrast to
their predecessors, the current generation of
Soviet combat aircraft are first class multi-
mission platforms with advanced weapons delivery capability and avionics which are designed to deliver conventional weapons with
much improved accuracy even under adverse
weather conditions.

The Early Years
From its inception, the primary preoccupation
of the Soviet Air Force has been tactical support
of the ground forces. During the early years

Pe-2 light bombers under construction in an aircraft factory in the Urals during World War II.

following the Civil War, attention focused on the pursuit of a modern air force and aviation industry in cooperation with Germany. The Soviet desire to improve its air force and aviation industry meshed nicely with the German desire to maintain its knowledge of military aviation developments and a cadre of trained personnel. The German influence also tended to reinforce the Soviet predilection for focusing on tactical support operations rather than embracing the growing western school of strategic air bombardment. Operational control remained firmly in the hands of the Red Army Command and was exercised through the Military District Commanders. Soviet military doctrine called for integrated operations by all combat arms and most air units were directly attached to ground formations. Massive airstrikes closely tied to frontline operations were the order of the day.

The period from 1928 to the outbreak of World War II saw massive growth in the Soviet Air Force, in particular in aircraft designed to perform tactical support missions such as fighters and light bombers. The force had grown to some 4,000 aircraft by 1938. Firstline aircraft such as the I-15 and I-16 fighters and the SB-2 and SB-2bis twin-engine bombers were among the best of their era. However, continued problems in the aircraft industry and Stalin's preoccupation with numbers which kept obsolete designs in production inhibited the introduction of more modern types.

The Russians also pioneered the development of multi-engine, long-range bombers in the form of the four engine Muromets designed by Igor Sikorsky in 1914. In fact, however, the strategic bombardment arm of the Soviet air force has had neither a long tradition nor the prestige accorded other branches. There was periodic interest in strategic bombardment prior to World War II. In 1932, the USSR became the first post-1918 air force to fly a substantial force of four-engined heavy bombers in the form of the TB-3. Soviet medium and heavy bombers were formed into a separate command under the direct control of air force headquarters. But for a variety of reasons, the concept of strategic bombardment failed to take root in the Soviet military and the force began to atrophy.

The 1930s also gave the Soviet Air Force its first taste of modern air combat in Spain and against Japan in the Far East. The brief flirtation with strategic bombing led to the deployment of one of the largest fleets of heavy bombers in the world and the establishment of an independent heavy bomber force to parallel the essential tactical orientation of the air force. This development of long-range strategic airpower soon lapsed as its leading proponents fell in the purges and the Soviet leadership began to develop lessons from its involvement in Spain and the Far East. The generally ineffective use of bombers and the conversely heavy emphasis on ground-support operations in Spain seemed to disprove theories of the strategic bomber advocates and to reaffirm the traditional emphasis of tactical air operations. This thesis was

Right: On the first day of the German invasion in 1941 many of the Soviet aircraft were caught and destroyed on the ground.

Opposite: Soviet fighters sweep across the sky under the watchful eye of an air defense radar.

again affirmed in subsequent operations in the Far East and Finland.

As a part of the general reorganization of the Soviet armed forces following the debacle in Finland, the basic structure of the Air Forces was changed and the decision made to speed the introduction of modern aircraft. The air force was divided into five major components: Long-range Bomber Aviation (DBA) with long-range and medium bombers, an air-rescue component of the High Command, Front Aviation, Army Aviation and Corps Aviation. The later three were composed of tactical air regiments and divisions assigned directly to those army echelons for direct and indirect support of ground operations. By assigning air units directly to the forces they supported, the Soviet military leadership believed improved coordination would result. In fact the test of battle was to show that it seriously hampered centralized control and coordination of tactical aviation for major front-wide operations.

The Great Patriotic War

During World War II the Soviet Union continued to concentrate on refining the use of air power to enhance the striking power of the ground forces. During the war, operations in direct support of ground forces and air-combat operations aimed at attaining the air superiority required to allow ground attack units to perform effectively, accounted for nearly two-thirds of the nearly four million sorties undertaken by the Soviet Air Force.

On the first day of the German assault in 1941 the Soviets lost ten percent of their 12,000 aircraft. But most of these were obsolescent aircraft as the new generation of air combat fighters, ground attack and light bomber aircraft was only beginning to reach operational units. The first year of the war was a very hard uphill struggle to overcome Luftwaffe air supremacy. Like the Soviet air force the primary mission of the Luftwaffe was tactical air supremacy and support of ground operations, releasing the Soviets from major worries about strategic air defense. The aerial battle then was for tactical air supremacy between two ground support oriented air forces.

Soviet air doctrine stressed the importance of air superiority to protect friendly ground forces and to allow other air units to perform their missions. The Soviets stressed the key role of the air combat fighter in achieving air superiority. Emphasis was given to production of fighters and the best pilots were assigned to fighter units. Bomber units were generally poorly trained and concentrated on ground support and short range interdiction. Ground attack aviation, equipped with the famous Il-2 Shturmovik, became the second elite of the Soviet air forces and carried the burden of the tactical air war. Once the Soviets began offensive operations, ground attack aviation became the predominant element of the air war, functioning as flying artillery clearing the way for and supporting the rapidly moving tank armies. By 1943 the Soviet air force was able to attain

Below: An SA-2 surface-to-air missile in a field site. One of these high altitude missiles brought down the U-2 spy plane of Francis Gary Powers in 1960.

effective local air superiority in support of large-scale offensive operations and had closed the technical gap in aircraft design.

Increasingly as the war progressed independent air operations were employed as part of the preparation for offensive operations. These included fighter sweeps and strikes on enemy airfields to reduce enemy air strength and gain air superiority. These would be followed by pre- paration of breakthrough zones for the ground forces, support of advancing tank units, and strikes on enemy reserves, while fighters maintained a protective umbrella over friendly forces. Thus independent air operations became regarded as the center-piece of Soviet tactical air operations.

One of the major factors which contributed to the growing capabilities of tactical aviation was the recognition of the requirement for centralized control of major air formations to concentrate air power at critical points. The creation of air armies in 1941 combined front and army air units allowing the front to concentrate its air strength more easily. A reserve of air units was also created directly under the High Command. These reserves provided a centralized concentration of mobile firepower which could rapidly be focussed in critical sectors.

The Jet-Age Revolution

The end of World War II may be seen as a high-water mark for Soviet tactical aviation. While Frontal Aviation remained its largest component, the Soviet Air Forces like the other Soviet forces experienced a sharp decline between 1945 and the late 1960s. In the immediate post-war period Frontal Aviation was consolidated into 15 air armies and equipped with new aircraft such as the Il-10 Shturmovik introduced in 1945. The strategic imperatives in Soviet military policy were maintaining strong theater forces in Europe as a counterpoise to the United States and coming to grips with the development of nuclear weapons including both the development of air defense capabilities and a Soviet nuclear capability. The latter clearly re-

Below: The MiG-21 fighter first appeared in the mid-1950s and in its more modern models is still an important part of the Soviet fighter inventory.

Above: SA-3 SAMs, seen here on a four-rail launcher are a primary element in Soviet defense against air attack.

Right: An engineer captain adjusts equipment at an air defense site.

ceived priority at the expense of development of tactical aircraft.

The Soviets had a modest jet aircraft development program during the war and moved rapidly after the conclusion of hostilities to exploit German research. But the main thrust of fighter development was aimed at air defense requirements and resulted in the MiG-15 and MiG-17 fighters. For the next 20 years, the basic fighter aircraft found in Frontal Aviation were designed for the interception of high altitude bombers rather than air combat. Aircraft such as the MiG-17 were admirably maneuverable fighters but their heavy-caliber, slow firing cannon armament was better suited to their bomber intercept role than high-speed air combat. These clear-weather interceptors neverthless served as the backbone of Frontal Aviation's air combat fighter force. The wartime medium bomber force was replaced by a smaller force of twin jet Il-28 Beagle bombers. The ground attack element of Frontal Aviation languished as the Il-10 remained in service until the mid-fifties when it was retired without replacement. The ground-attack mission was transferred to fighter-bombers, in most cases fighter aircraft such as the MiG-17 displaced from air combat duties by more modern designs. Frontal Aviation was not completely re-equipped with first generation jet aircraft until the early 1960s.

In the years immediately following World War II the basic role of Frontal Aviation remained close air support of the ground forces. The mid-fifties saw a decline in the importance of Frontal Aviation due to what the Soviets have come to call 'the revolution in military affairs': the parallel development of nuclear

weapons and ballistic missile delivery systems. When the Soviet forces began to acquire tactical nuclear weapons in the late 1950s, Frontal Aviation found much of its former role eclipsed by the deployment of a range of battlefield missiles. Soviet military doctrine called for ground forces to do little more than mop-up after massive strikes by the Strategic Rocket Forces. Frontal Aviation was first and foremost to provide battlefield air defense to protect Soviet ground forces from enemy nuclear strikes. This was to be undertaken in close cooperation with the growing family of surface-to-air missiles. Fighter-bomber and light-bomber units were to deter flanking counter-attacks, strike mobile targets with nuclear weapons and generally support the ground forces.

Since the late 1940s, the standard air-combat fighters of Frontal Aviation have emerged from the Mikoyan design bureau: the MiG-15, -17, -19 and -21. All were basically clear-weather, short-range interceptors with internal cannon armament. The very small and maneuverable MiGs were mainly expected to provide point air

The Su-7 Fitter-A entered service with the Soviet Air Force in the early 1960s and became the standard Soviet tactical fighter bomber. A number are still in service.

The Fitter-C has variable-sweep outer wing panels which give some of the benefits associated with swing-wing aircraft. This type entered service in the early 1970s. Both Fitters shown on this page are in the colors of the Polish Air Force.

defense against western air strikes. Their short-range, high fuel consumption and low payloads made them unsuitable for more ambitious air combat operations. The primary air-combat fighter of the Warsaw Pact from the late 1950s to the present day is the MiG-21 Fishbed.

The ground attack element of Frontal Aviation from the late 1950s to the early 1970s was provided by a combination of obsolescent fighters and a new generation of fighter-bomber and light-bomber designs optimized for the de-

livery of tactical nuclear weapons. Such conventional air support as was required was provided by aircraft such as the MiG-17 which entered service as an interceptor in 1952 and finally left the Frontal Aviation fighter-bomber force only in the mid-1970s. As a fighter-bomber the MiG-17 is usually regarded by Western experts as marginal, being short-legged and having a limited ordnance capacity. However, reports from Egyptian sources indicate that during the 1973 war the MiG-17 was an effective close support aircraft, especially against Israeli motorized columns.

The second postwar generation of Soviet combat aircraft included two strike aircraft: the Su-7 Fitter fighter-bomber and the Yak-28 Brewer light-bomber. The design of both aircraft represented parallel development of interceptor types to perform the nuclear strike role. The Yak-28 is a swept-wing twin-engine aircraft derived from the Yak-25 Flashlight interceptor and developed in tandem with the Yak-28P Firebar interceptor. The Brewer-C was used to replace the Beagle in Frontal Aviation

The Yak-28 was introduced in the early 1960s as a two-seat attack aircraft. It is now considered obsolete and many have been withdrawn from service.

units. The Brewer-C carried its primary weapons load in a central fuselage between the main landing-gear units. Western experts feel that the presence of an internal weapons bay strongly suggests that its primary design role was tactical nuclear strike; the small cross section of the fuselage limits the internal load, but the internal bay may be necessary for the environmental control and arming of a nuclear weapon. The Brewer-C is equipped with a nav-radar system for all weather operations.

The Su-7BM Fitter became the standard strike fighter for all-weather weapons delivery in the early sixties. The Fitter has been described by some Western analysts as a rather 'shoddy' and inadequate ground-attack aircraft but this represents an unfair application of Western criteria. In combat service in the Middle East and India the Su-7 has earned a reputation as a rugged and reliable performer despite a limited radius of action (350-500 km) and small conventional ordnance load (2000 kg). The Su-7 was not designed for the deep interdiction role but is cast rather in the traditional

fighter-bomber roles. The result, as described by Egyptian pilots who have flown it, is one of the best aircraft yet available for high speed flight at low altitudes, being amenable to violent low-level maneuvering. This is a very desirable feature in an aircraft intended for the delivery of tactical nuclear weapons. The Su-7 also enjoys an extremely good rough field capability. In conventional conflict the Su-7 is of lesser value. Su-7s are seldom seen without twin auxiliary fuel tanks on the central fuselage pylons leaving only the four wing pylons for rockets and bombs. In both the nuclear and conventional ordnance delivery role the Su-7 is limited to clear-weather operations, being equipped with only a rudimentary weapon aiming system.

The Nuclear Deterrent

The Long-range Air Force was reconstituted as the semi-independent Long Range Aviation (LRA) in 1946, becoming reintegrated in the Soviet Air Force command structure the following year. The impetus for this rebirth came from a combination of recognition of the effectiveness

Right: An M-4 Bison bomber lumbers along with a US F-4 Phantom interceptor as escort. Intended as a strategic bomber, the M-4 has proved most useful as a tanker.

Main picture: An underside view of a Tu-16 Badger reconnaissance aircraft during an intelligence collection mission north of the UK.

of Western strategic bombing during the war and the pressing requirement to develop nuclear delivery systems of both medium and long range. Throughout the postwar period, the Soviet bomber force has pursued two parallel tracks, development and maintenance of a modest intercontinental capability and a much larger medium bomber force to strike targets in Europe and the Far East. The first Soviet strategic bomber was the Tu-4 Bull medium bomber, an unlicensed copy of the US B-29, slavishly copied down-to and including several design flaws. The Tu-4 entered service in 1948 and approximately 900 were deployed by 1950. An intercontinental heavy bomber, the Tu-85 was developed in prototype from the basic Tu-4 but was overtaken by developments in jet propulsion and never deployed.

Between 1952 and 1954, three aircraft were tested as replacements for the Tu-4. The Tu-16 Badger was chosen and entered service as the standard medium bomber in 1955. Comparable in both role and performance with the US B-47 Stratojet, Badger variants with improved en-

gines, weapons and avionics have remained the workhorse of LRA up to the 1980s, aptly described as 'a good basic airframe endlessly adapted to meet new requirements and carry new equipment'.

The requirement for an intercontinental nuclear delivery system led to the parallel development of two designs: the Tu-95 Bear and the M-4 Bison. Both of these aircraft, with modernization, continue, like their counterpart the US B-52, to be the backbone of their country's intercontinental heavy bomber force. The Tu-95 Bear is a direct descendent of the Tu-4 Bull and entered service in 1955. The Bear is unique in being the only turboprop-driven bomber ever to attain first line service with any country as well as being the only swept-wing turboprop aircraft in that same category.

The Bear was developed in parallel with and probably as a backup for the M-4 Bison turbojet-powered bomber. Like its medium bomber stable mate the Tu-16, the Bear remains the backbone of the Soviet bomber force as well as having been adapted for a variety of other roles.

A total of slightly over a hundred of the bomber variant were deployed before production ceased in the early 1960s. Production of one variant probably continued however.

The Bear's turbojet competitor was the Myasishchev M-4 Bison. The Bison or Molot, as it was unofficially known, fell short of the operating radius required for round-trip intercontinental missions, especially since LRA had yet to develop an aerial refueling capability. Although later models were fitted with more economical turbofan engines and in flight refueling capability, the M-4 gave way to the Tu-95 as the primary LRA heavy bomber.

The appearance of the Tu-95 in the mid-fifties caused considerable panic in US defense circles as existing all-weather fighters would have had considerable difficulty catching the Bear. But the development of surface-to-air missiles and radar controlled, missile-armed supersonic interceptors in Europe and the US spelled the end of the high-altitude bomber with freefall weapons. In any event, the Tu-95 and the M-4 were to be produced only in modest numbers as

the decision was made to assign primary responsibility for intercontinental strikes to the newly formed Strategic Rocket Forces.

The role of the Tu-95/M-4 force, aptly described by Thomas Wolfe as a 'token intercontinental threat', was to bridge the gap until a sufficiently large ICBM force could be deployed. This small intercontinental force did have its effectiveness increased by the introduction of aerial refueling and provision of air-to-surface missiles (ASMs). A large portion, perhaps half, of the Bison force was converted to aerial tankers and all heavy bombers were fitted with large flight refueling probes. The large lifting capacity of the Tu-95 enabled the provision of a standoff capability in the early sixties. About 50 Tu-95s became Bear-Bs with the AS-3 Kitchen ASM and a large nose radar. The AS-3 missile is one of the largest standoff weapons in the world and is derived from the Su-7 Fitter-A fighter-bomber. It is designed to carry a large thermonuclear weapon to a range of 650 km. The LRA intercontinental bomber force reached a peak in the mid-sixties with a total of about 200

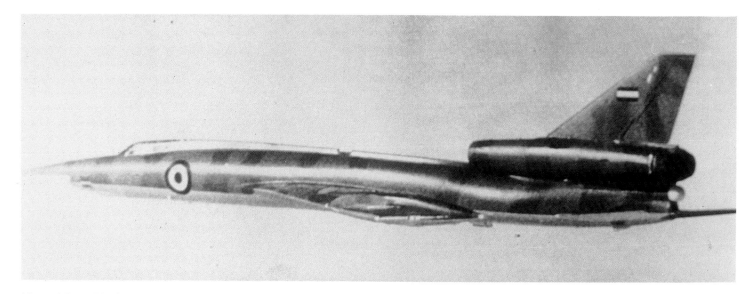

Above: A Tu-22 Blinder medium range bomber of the Libyan Air Force. The limited range of the Blinder proved disappointing to the Soviets which kept its production run small.

Right: Technicians perform maintenance on the engines and tail of a Tu-22 Blinder.

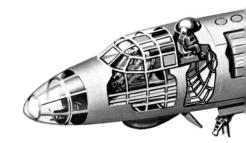

bombers and tankers.

While most theater nuclear delivery missions probably were absorbed by the SRF, the Soviets apparently saw a requirement to maintain a large medium bomber force for theater operations. While the LRA medium bomber force peaked in the early sixties, a substantial Badger force was maintained, augmented by a new supersonic medium bomber, the Tu-22 Blinder. The Blinder was developed in the late fifties as a replacement for the Tu-16 with greater speed and penetrability. The range of the Tu-22 was reportedly disappointing, however, and combined with changing requirements to lead to the production of a total of only approximately 170 Blinder-Bs. Some of these have seen service with the Libyan Air Force.

The Soviet Air Forces

Like its American counterpart, Soviet airpower is not concentrated in any single service but distributed among three mission-oriented services and a civil aviation authority. The Soviet Navy has a large land- and sea-based air army. The strategic air defense forces, termed PVO Strany, are an independent service operating over 2000 aircraft and approximately 12,000 missiles on 10,000 surface-to-air missile launchers at 1200 fixed sites. The Soviet Air Force reportedly ranks fourth in precedence among the five Soviet armed forces. The Commander-in-Chief, Chief Marshal of Aviation, P. S. Kutakhov, has administrative control over the three major functional commands: Frontal Aviation, Long Range Aviation, and Military Transport Aviation.

Frontal Aviation is responsible for supporting the ground forces and is under the tactical control of ground force commanders. It provides battlefield air superiority in conjunction with the army's anti-aircraft guns and tactical SAMs, nuclear and conventional battlefield strike, close air support and reconnaissance. Frontal Aviation has been the largest and most important component of the Air Forces since before World War II. Long Range Aviation (LRA) controls medium and heavy bomber aircraft, many armed with cruise missiles, probably assigned long-range strategic strike missions primarily in Europe and the Far East. They would also likely reinforce naval air forces in anti-shipping operations. Their major peacetime role is long-range strategic reconnaissance. Finally, Military Transport Aviation provides the Soviet armed forces with strategic and tactical airlift. It is backed up in this role by Aeroflot, the Soviet civil aviation authority which provides a ready reserve of transport aircraft.

Unlike the United States, the Soviet Union has no strong, independent advocate of the strategic effectiveness of air power, and, again unlike in the United States, such a policy has no historical roots. The Air Force is a part of a military heirarchy and doctrine in which the dominant role of air power is seen as the support of combined-arms theater operations. While the Soviets remain convinced that air power continues to be an important multi-purpose means of nuclear and conventional combat, its primary role is tactical. Strategic nuclear strikes, especially in intercontinental conflict, will be mainly the province of the missiles of the SRF and the Navy.

Frontal Aviation

Soviet tactical air power is concentrated in Frontal Aviation which, with over 5000 aircraft is the largest Air Forces command. Its order-of-battle includes air-combat fighters, dual-capable fighter-bombers, and light bombers, reconnaissance and electronic warfare aircraft as well as attack and transport helicopters. Approximately half to three quarters of Frontal Avia-

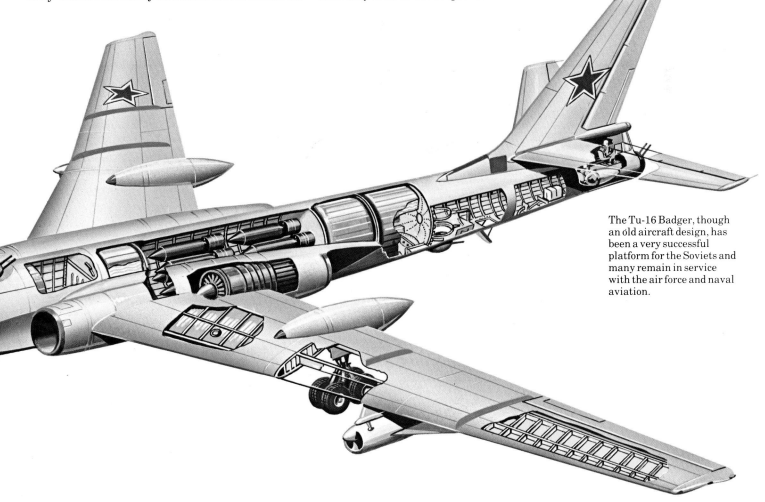

The Tu-16 Badger, though an old aircraft design, has been a very successful platform for the Soviets and many remain in service with the air force and naval aviation.

Three F-14 interceptors
warn off a Tu-95 Bear
reconnaissance aircraft
attempting to observe the
operations of the US carrier
Eisenhower in late 1982.

tion's aircraft are positioned for use in Europe, with the remainder in the Far East and to a lesser extent the southern and central USSR.

Frontal Aviation forces are organized into air armies under the operational control of the command of a group of forces or military district in wartime and a front in peacetime. The air army commander, normally a colonel-General of Aviation, functions as a deputy and air advisor to the front commander. During wartime, he and his staff would plan and implement air support operations under the supervision of the front commander but can exercise some initiative. In general, however, he lacks the freedom to plan and undertake the independent operations enjoyed by his Western counterpart.

The composition of an air army will vary with the demands of its wartime role. As Berman has

noted, an air army may be as large as the frontline 16th Air Army in East Germany with almost 1000 aircraft or as small as the 17th Air Army in the Kiev Military District with 100 aircraft. A large air army is composed of aviation divisions, usually including fighter and fighter-bomber divisions, and independent regiments of reconnaissance aircraft, helicopters and support units. Military Air Transport units are often assigned to Frontal Air Armies on a rotational basis. There are sixteen air armies or their equivalent including three or possibly four with Soviet forces in Eastern Europe. The 16th Air Army is not only the largest but also considered by Western analysts as the most potent and modern with the best trained pilots. Yet, as Berman has pointed out, there seem to be no clear priorities regarding which units receive

new equipment first.

Aviation divisions are usually commanded by a colonel - or major-general of aviation and consist of three air regiments, either all operating one type of aircraft or mixed by regiment. A regiment will normally consist of three squadrons with 10 to 15 aircraft each. This varies as some divisions have four regiments of four squadrons each. Squadrons normally include three flights of four aircraft. Flights of fighters and fighter-bombers usually operate in the traditional pattern of two pairs. This outline of unit structure is typical, but it is hardly inflexible and units will frequently vary to meet unique requirements.

The mid-fifties saw a decline in the fortunes of Frontal Aviation as it was relegated to providing battlefield air defense and limited nuclear

and conventional air support. However, modern Soviet military doctrine no longer envisions theater conflict as a post nuclear strike mopping-up exercise. Today's Frontal Aviation units, bolstered by LRA medium bombers, thus exist as a part of an air-ground strike force designed for large scale offensive operations. As John Erickson has observed, the shift in Frontal Aviation from primarily battlefield air defense to an emphasis on all-round air superiority and support for offensive operations is not a dramatic shift in Soviet doctrine but rather that after many years Frontal Aviation has acquired the means necessary to support that doctrine.

Western experts expect that at the onset of a conventional conflict in Europe, the Soviets would launch a massive independent air operation, including substantial Frontal Aviation

participation, against Western nuclear forces, command and control centers, airfields and air defense sites. Other Frontal Aviation units would continue to provide battlefield air defense and close air support. Since the mid-sixties the air defense burden has been shifting to the army's growing array of mobile SAMs and anti-aircraft guns, releasing Frontal Aviation air-combat fighters for other missions.

Frontal Aviation, with its multiple responsibilities and limited field maintenance capability, could be counted on for only a few major independent air operations at the onset of hostilities. Once these are complete and hopefully air superiority is attained attention would shift to interdiction and close air support operations. Some Western experts believe that close air support continues to run a distant third in Soviet priorities. This may be due to the strong growth in the firepower of Soviet ground force maneuver units over the last two decades obviating the perceived need for close air support. If the conflict should escalate to nuclear warfare, as many Western analysts see the Soviets' perception of the probable course of events, the basic missions of Frontal Aviation would remain the same. Frontal Aviation aircraft would probably be used to deliver nuclear strikes against mobile targets as well as airfields, command posts, and enemy lines of communications.

As Berman has noted, a doctrine aiming at air supremacy through conventional, large-scale air operations is one for which the Soviet air force will be better suited in the future. One major short-coming is that of training. Western analysts note that the Soviet air force operates its aircraft with less frequency than NATO and Soviet pilots annually spend only 60 percent as much time training as US pilots although their training may be becoming more intensive and increasingly realistic. Aircraft availability may be a significant factor. All Warsaw Pact forces use the same aircraft systems and all major maintenance is carried out at central depots rather than at the operational bases. Such a system meant that in the early seventies, the average Warsaw Pact aircraft spent 80 percent more time out of service than its average NATO counterpart. The system also limits tactical flexibility and unit mobility.

The bulk of Frontal Aviation aircraft are now the MiG-21 Fishbed and MiG-23 Flogger air combat fighters and the Su-17 Fitter, Su-24 Fencer and the MiG-27 Flogger-D fighter-bombers. In the last decade the capabilities of Frontal Aviation have increased fourfold in payload and two and one-half times in range, allowing them to strike critical targets deep in NATO's rear areas with conventional or nuclear weapons. Some Frontal Aviation regiments have 25 percent more aircraft than in the 70s.

The current generation of Soviet Mach 2+ air combat fighters includes the current versions of the MiG-21 Fishbed and its successor the MiG-23 Flogger. These aircraft have been fitted to carry the new generation of all-aspect air-to-air missiles (AAMs) as well as internal cannon armament to ranges up to 900 km and also incorporate improved avionics. The new generation of Soviet AAMs, such as the radar homing AA-7 Apex and the infrared AA-8 Aphid, represent a change in Soviet design philosophy, being primarily developed for the air combat role rather than air defense. Similarly, while the MiG-21/23 generation represents adaptations of what are basically interceptors, the next generation will probably reflect the requirements of the air combat rather than the air defense mission.

The current version of the MiG-21 Fishbed, of which almost 1800 of various versions remain in service, represents the third generation of this remarkable design which has evolved from a somewhat underpowered day-interceptor into a multi-role fighter. The MiG-21 through all its variants has been characterized as a rugged, simple and reliable aircraft, a pilot's airplane

Opposite: Two views of a Libyan Su-22 Fitter-J taken in August 1981. The Su-22 is the export version of the Su-17 and has considerably reduced equipment standards when compared to Soviet Air Force models. This example is carrying two AA-2 Atoll air to air missiles which are also Soviet-made.

When first introduced the MiG-21 was a short-range clear-weather fighter. It has been progressively updated but remains comparatively limited in range and payload and unable to compete with the most recent Western fighters in dogfighting performance. Some 1800 are still in service, including the Fishbed-N, with air to air missiles (Above) and the Fishbed-L (Left).

Above & top: Two views of the Su-17 Fitter-C. Western sources credit this aircraft with a payload of over 8000 pounds. Two 30mm cannon are also carried and maximum speed at low level is Mach 1.1.

with what those who have flown it in combat describe as very good air combat maneuverability, superior in many ways to western contemporaries such as the Mirage III. Progressively increased fuel loads have improved the aircraft's oft-criticized radius of action although it remains inferior to many of its western contemporaries. Early versions were also criticized for their austere weapons suite, a fault corrected in the current MiG-21bis Fishbed L/N with its GSh-23-mm cannon and provision for as many as four KA-13 or AA-8 AAMs as well as improved avionics. The MiG-21 remains a significant dual-capable component of Frontal Aviation and is likely to remain so for some time to come. Some Western analysts see indications that the MiG-21 will be used in roles emphasizing its low- and medium-altitude air combat maneuverability, other tasks it formerly fulfilled being absorbed by the MiG-23/27 family.

While the swing-wing MiG-23 Flogger is a considerable improvement over the MiG-21, it still represents more of a battlefield interceptor than a purpose-built air combat fighter. Development of the swing-wing MiG-23 probably began in the mid-sixties as a replacement for the MiG-21 and as a fighter in the class of the F-4 coupled with short runway requirements. The result was a divergence from the single basic design into two aircraft: the MiG-23

interceptor/air combat fighter and the MiG-27 fighter-bomber. The two air combat variants of the MiG-23 currently in service with Frontal Aviation in the air superiority role, offer 50 percent improvement in combat radius over the MiG-21 and a considerably larger and more powerful radar. The High Lark radar is reportedly comparable to that of the US F-4J Phantom and for the first time in a Soviet fighter, has a limited look-down/shoot-down capability. The normal air combat weapons load for the MiG-23 is two AA-7 Apex and two AA-8 Aphids and one GSh-23 23mm cannon. The MiG-23, however, reportedly lacks the simplicity and ease of maintenance and operation that marked its predecessor.

The design of Soviet combat aircraft often seems to take its cue from western trends and innovations albeit with a time lag. In addition, it should be remembered that new aircraft are manifestations of requirements formulated five to ten years before the aircraft is ever flown. As in the West, the lessons of various regional conflicts since 1967 have led to the requirement for an air combat fighter. A new Soviet air combat fighter, the MiG-29, has recently entered service with several frontline aviation units. The MiG-29 is reported to be similar to the US F-18 and to have a maximum speed of Mach 2.8 at altitude and Mach 1.5 at sea level. The aircraft is reputedly equipped with a look-down/shoot-down radar and the new AA-9 AAM as well as AA-8 Aphids and an internal GSh-23 23mm cannon. The Soviets are also testing, according to *Aviation Week,* the Su-27 fighter, believed to be the equivalent of the US F-15 Eagle or the F-14 Tomcat.

There are four basic fighter-bomber designs currently in service with Frontal Aviation. These include a small number of Su-7 Fitter-As, currently being retired in favor of a trio of modern all-weather aircraft: the Su-17 Fitter, the MiG-27 Flogger and the Su-24 Fencer. All three of these aircraft represent fulfillment of the Soviet requirement for longer-range multi-mission aircraft able to deliver nuclear weapons or large conventional ordnance payloads with improved accuracy under adverse weather conditions and to deliver the full range of Soviet precision guided air-to-surface tactical missiles such as the AS-7 Kerry command guided missile and the AS-10 laser guided weapon. The introduction of these new aircraft, combined with the improved secondary ground attack of Soviet air combat fighters, enables the Soviet air force to pose a credible conventional threat to targets all through NATO Europe. They remain, however, a generation behind their western counterparts, especially in critical areas such as electronic countermeasures.

The Su-7B Fitter-A clearly had a number of deficiencies, including short range with a limited ordnance load. It did offer excellent low-altitude handling characteristics, a stable weapons platform and an ability to absorb bat-

Left: The MiG-27 Flogger-D fighter bomber, has swing wings and Mach 1.6 speed.

Below: The MiG-23 Flogger-B is an all-weather interceptor which is becoming the mainstay of Soviet tactical air defense. It has different engine inlets and afterburning arrangements to the Flogger D and is accordingly considerably faster at high altitude.

Bottom: The Su-24 Fencer is the newest Soviet aircraft for nuclear and conventional attack to be deployed in numbers. Fencer became operational in 1974 and in addition to its external load it carries a twin-barrel 23mm cannon.

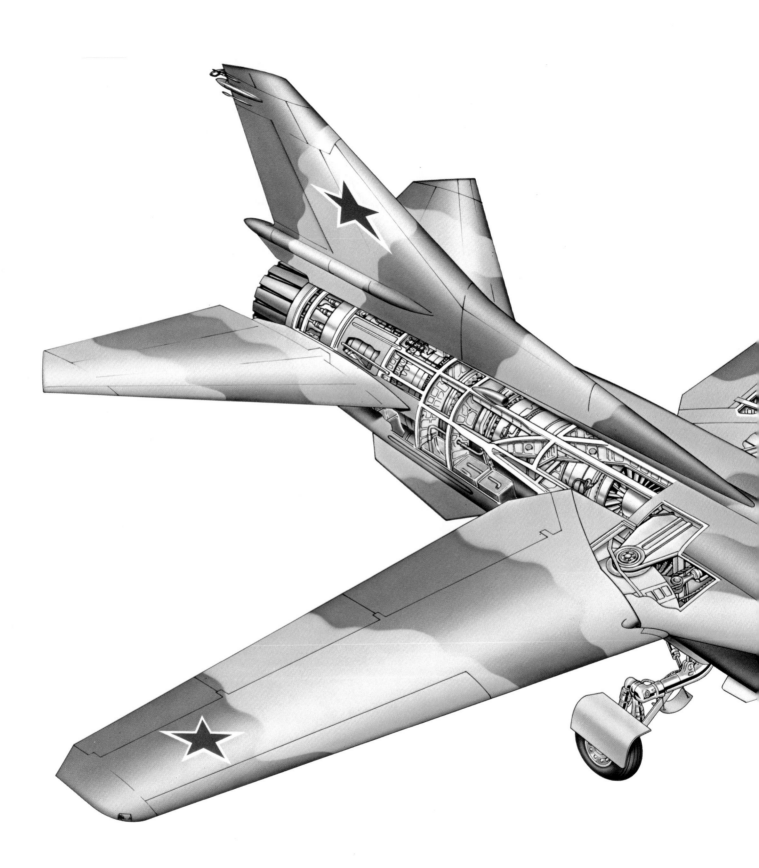

tle damage. Reportedly, an interim solution to the requirement to improve on the Su-7 was discovered in a Su-7 modified as a testbed for variable-geometry wing research. The result was unique among current service variable-geometry aircraft in being derived from an existing fixed geometry type. The Su-17 Fitter-C differs from the Su-7 in having a variable geometry outer wing and a more powerful engine, improving weapons payload and runway performance. The Su-17 also has a more advanced weapons delivery system. The Su-17 has been labeled by some Western experts as an object lesson in Soviet addiction to incremental design. Others recognize it as a cost-effective solution to the problem of providing an economical successor to a widely used aircraft without having to create a totally new logistics support system.

The MiG-27 Flogger-D is basically a modification of the MiG-23 design to improve low level subsonic ground-attack capability with heavier ordnance loads and better rough field performance. The aircraft differs from the MiG-23 in

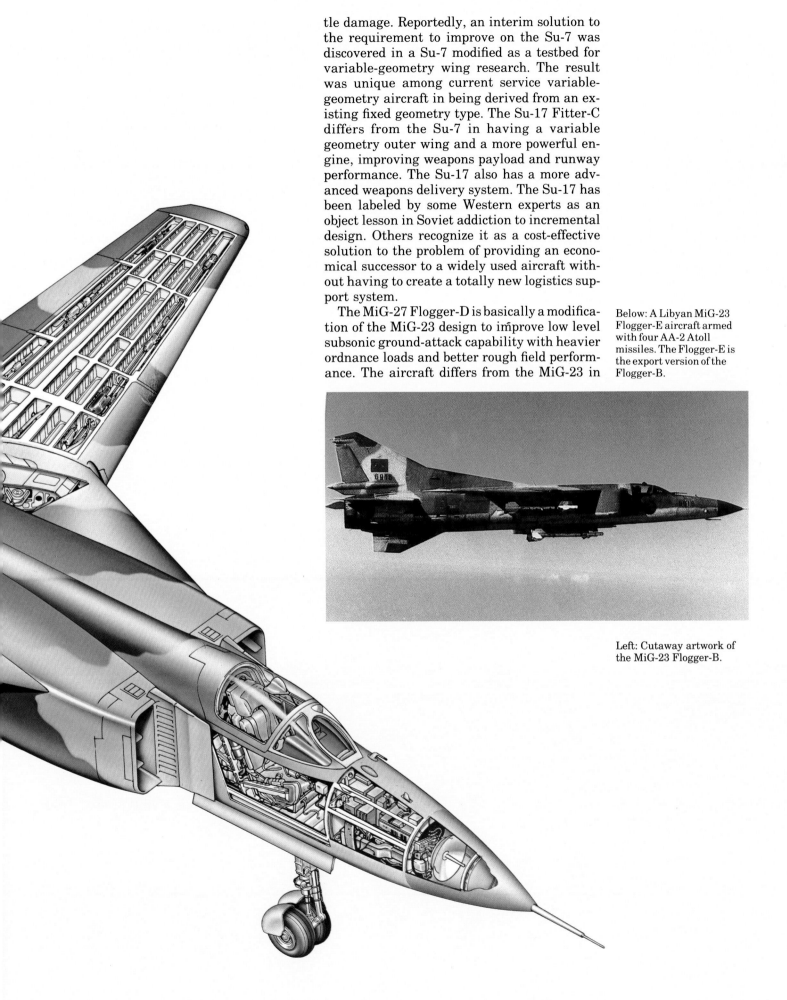

Below: A Libyan MiG-23 Flogger-E aircraft armed with four AA-2 Atoll missiles. The Flogger-E is the export version of the Flogger-B.

Left: Cutaway artwork of the MiG-23 Flogger-B.

having a mapping/terrain following radar, laser range finder, doppler radar and radar altimeter in a shallower nose which also offers an improved pilot field of vision ahead and below. The cockpit is heavily armored. The closest Western equivalent is the smaller Anglo-French Jaguar. The estimated payload of 3500 kg is small by Western standards but when combined with the aircraft's range and sophisticated weapons delivery capability, the result is a substantial improvement in Soviet ground attack capability.

The deployment of the Su-24 Fencer was a replacement for the Yak-28 Brewer light bomber, beginning in 1974, created considerable stir in the west. The Su-24, according to British authorities, can deliver a substantial conventional payload to UK targets from bases in East Germany. The Su-24 is a landmark Soviet aircraft, in many ways comparable to the multinational Tornado fighter-bomber. Pentagon officials credit it with a sophisticated pulse-doppler terrain avoidance radar as well as a nav/attack radar and 'the capability to deliver ordnance in all weather to within 180 feet of the target'. Equipment also includes a laser rangefinder and marked target seeker as well as an extensive array of active and passive ECM equipment. To operate this array of equipment the Fencer is the first Soviet aircraft to carry a weapons system officer, in a unique side-by-side two seat cockpit similar to the US F-111. Weapons pylons under the fuselage and inner

Bottom: Soviet armor engaged in a river crossing exercise receive air cover from two MiG-23 fighters.

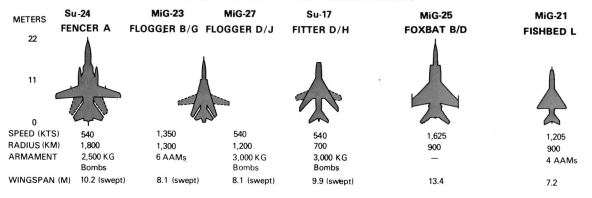

Frontal Aviation Ground Attack Aircraft

METERS	Su-24 FENCER A	MiG-23 FLOGGER B/G	MiG-27 FLOGGER D/J	Su-17 FITTER D/H	MiG-25 FOXBAT B/D	MiG-21 FISHBED L
SPEED (KTS)	540	1,350	540	540	1,625	1,205
RADIUS (KM)	1,800	1,300	1,200	700	900	900
ARMAMENT	2,500 KG Bombs	6 AAMs	3,000 KG Bombs	3,000 KG Bombs	—	4 AAMs
WINGSPAN (M)	10.2 (swept)	8.1 (swept)	8.1 (swept)	9.9 (swept)	13.4	7.2

and outer wings can carry a variety of stores including the AS-9 laser-guided missile as well as laser guided bombs.

The immediate future is likely to see the return of the Shturmovik in the form of the Su-25 ground attack aircraft. The Su-25 is a twin-engine, subsonic ground attack aircraft similar in concept to the US A-10 with an anti-armor gatling-type gun and 10 underwing and under-fuselage ordnance stations to carry a payload of 10,000 lbs. The aircraft has undergone combat evaluation in Afghanistan with emphasis on conducting integrated operations with helicopter gunships. The result is a potent close-air support and anti-armor team under the control of the ground commander.

The majority of Soviet helicopters are assigned to Frontal Aviation to provide airlift and more recently close air support to the ground forces. During the 1950s and early sixties Frontal Aviation fielded a number of medium and heavy lift helicopters such as the Mi-4 Hound and the huge Mi-6/10 Hook, at the time of its inception in 1957 the largest helicopter in the world. The Mi-4 was displaced by the larger turbine powered Mi-8 Hip as the standard Warsaw Pact medium transport helicopter in 1967. Comparable to the US S-61 family, the Mi-8 is reportedly a rugged, reliable transport which does however suffer from a vulnerable fuel system. A new heavy lift helicopter, the Mi-26 Halo is under development to replace the Mi-6/10. This huge aircraft has a cargo bay and payload capacity which is reportedly very similar to that of the US C-130 transport aircraft.

While most Soviet transport helicopters were provided with some light defensive armament, it was not until the late sixties and early seventies, drawing on the American experience in Vietnam, that the Soviet Union began to experi-

Above: An Mi-6 Hook heavy-lift helicopter in flight. The Mi-6 can carry up to 90 troops or artillery weapons, vehicles, supplies or armor.

Left & below: The Mi-24 Hind helicopter gunship is a formidable weapons system well respected by Western analysts. It is heavily armored and has been widely employed in Afghanistan. Both the Hind-E (left) and Hind-D (below) carry four rocket pods and a chin mounted Gatling-type gun. The Hind-E also has AT-6 Spiral anti-tank missiles in place of the earlier type's AT-2 Swatters.

Top: An Mi-24 Hind-A. The four rocket pods carry a total of 128 unguided 57mm rockets. The Hind has a maximum speed of around 200mph.

Above: An Mi-8 Hip twin-turbine transport helicopter, bearing Aeroflot markings, seen in service in Antarctica.

Opposite: A Tu-95 Bear bomber on a maritime reconnaissance flight.

ment with heavily armed helicopters in the air assault and close air support roles.

While adapting the Hip to the air assault role, the Soviets were developing their first helicopter with an integral weapons system and retractable landing gear in the Mi-24 Hind. The initial variant of the Mi-24, the Hind-A was a heavily armed assault transport with a crew of four and space for eight fully armed troops. It was armed with a nose mounted 12.7mm machine gun, two underwing stores carriers on each stub wing and up to four Swatter anti-tank guided missiles (ATGMs) on wingtip launchers.

The further development of the Hind into the Hind-D brought about the first true helicopter gunship with considerable close air support capability. The Hind-D's redesigned fuselage retains the troop-carrying capacity of earlier models but has a redesigned flight-deck with a crew of two seated under individual canopies and protected by thick titanium armor. Under the nose is a four barrel gatling-type machine gun as well as a sensor pack containing radar and low light TV. The latest version, the Hind-

E, mounts the AT-6 Spiral tube launched ATGM and increased armor.

The Hind series is an attempt to combine the roles of assault transport and anti-armor gunship in one platform and as such is an unsatisfactory compromise in many ways. It is large in size, making it vulnerable to ground fire. Its power-to-weight ratio is low compared to Western designs. Similar to the Mi-8, it is not likely to be agile. Western experts are also surprised at the lack of infrared signature suppression. The Hind-E is, however, a heavily armed and armored close-support aircraft with at least a limited air-to-air potential.

The Soviets place considerable emphasis on all types of aerial reconnaissance as a major means of gathering tactical intelligence. The MiG-21R and MiG-21RF constitute a large portion of Frontal Aviation-dedicated air reconnaissance inventory. Fishbed H is equipped with a centerline interchangeable pod carrying a variety of cameras, infrared and other sensors. The MiG-21R is complemented by the long-range, high altitude MiG-25R developed from the MiG-25 Foxbat-A interceptor. The Foxbat-B is an adaptation for photoreconnaissance while the MiG-25R Foxbat-D is reportedly devoted to electronic reconnaissance or ELINT with a large side-looking radar and other sensors. Both variants have a maximum speed greater than Mach 3 and a service ceiling over 85,000 feet. The Frontal Aviation reconnaissance force is rounded out by Yak-28 Brewer-Ds converted to photographic reconnaissance duties.

The Soviets have rapidly come to recognize the importance of electronic warfare, in particular electronic countermeasures (ECM) such as jamming and spoofing enemy radars and communications, to modern air and ground warfare. In addition to providing increased ECM capac-

An Ilyushin 18 Coot-A aircraft on an electronic intelligence gathering mission. The large pod under the fuselage contains electronic equipment.

ity including anti-radiation missiles to their combat aircraft, they have converted a small number of Yak-28 aircraft to Brewer-E ECM escort aircraft with an active ECM package in the weapons bay. There are also reports of an ECM variant of the Mi-4 Hound helicopter.

Long-Range Aviation

Long-range Aviation is comprised of long- and medium-range bombers, most equipped with standoff missiles, as well as aerial tankers, ECM and reconnaissance aircraft. The primary wartime mission of the LRA is long-range strategic air strikes predominantly in Europe and the Far East. In a conventional conflict, LRA medium bombers would probably play a significant role in theater-wide independent air operations. In a nuclear conflict, LRA bombers would complement the strikes of the SRF and ballistic missile submarines against military and industrial targets. A major wartime mission would also be reinforcing Soviet Naval Aviation in anti-shipping operations.

As presently constituted, LRA consists of three air armies, two deployed in European Russia and one in the Far East. The European armies reportedly contain 75 percent of LRA strength. Unit organization is based upon divisions, which are comprised of two or three regiments consisting of three squadrons usually with 12 aircraft each. The long-range bomber element of LRA is reportedly divided into detachments, rather than squadrons subdivided into flights.

Long Range Aviation currently has more than 740 strike and support aircraft, a level which has remained fairly constant over the last decade. This includes 175 long range heavy bombers: 170 Tu-95 Bear-As and Bear-Bs and five M-4 Bison-Bs. A further 40 Bisons are configured as tankers with a probe and drogue hose reel and possibly an additional fuel tank in the bomb bay. In addition to Bear-A/B strike aircraft, LRA operates Bear-E reconnaissance aircraft which are normally used for maritime reconnaissance.

The numerical backbone of the LRA medium bomber force continues to be the Tu-16 Badger with 272 currently in service. The majority of these are probably Badger-A freefall bombers with the remainder Badger-G air-to-surface (ASM) carriers equipped with two AS-5 Kelt or AS-6 Kingfish ASMs suitable for anti-shipping or land-attack missions. The Badger-A has also been adapted to serve in tanker, electronic warfare and reconnaissance roles. Badger-H/Js serve as electronic warfare aircraft, with the Badger-J functioning as an ECM escort aircraft with active jamming equipment in a canoe-shaped radome inside the weapons bay. Other Badger variants serve in the reconnaissance role including the Badger-E and F which are thought to be specialized electronic reconnaissance aircraft.

The Tu-22 Blinder B also continues to serve the LRA with the capability to deliver either the AS-4 ASM or freefall weapons. The Tu-22 is unique in being one of the few postwar medium bombers actually to drop bombs in anger. It was used by Iraq against Kurdish insurgents and on at least one occasion by the Libyans against Tanzania. Its stablemate the Tu-16 can claim a similar distinction in being one of few postwar bombers to launch cruise missiles in anger. Egyptian Tu-16s launched some 25 AS-5 Kelts against Israeli targets in the October 1973 war, obtaining three hits.

The latest addition to the LRA inventory, and one which has caused considerable stir in the West, is the Tu-22M Backfire, a twin turbofan swing-wing medium bomber. The Backfire is clearly a versatile, multipurpose aircraft capable of performing nuclear strike, conventional attack, anti-shipping and reconnaissance missions. Primary armament is reportedly one AS-4 Kitchen ASM semi-recessed in the underside of the fuselage or two AS-6 Kingfisher ASMs underwing. The Backfire can also reportedly carry the full range of Soviet conventional ordnance. The Backfire may also be equipped for aerial refueling.

Backfire development reportedly began in the mid-sixties, possibly, as the Soviets claim, as an improved Tu-22 variant, to meet a joint Naval Aviation/Long-Range Aviation requirement for a Tu-16/Tu-22 replacement. The design was evolutionary, combining existing turbofan engines, a general arrangement similar to the Tu-

The 1981 US Department of Defense Annual Report stated that 'Backfire undoubtedly has some intercontinental capability ... from Soviet home bases on a one-way, high-altitude, subsonic, unrefuelled flight with recovery in the Caribbean. With Artic staging, refueling and certain high altitude flight profiles, it can probably execute a two-way mission to much of the United States'.

The Soviets, for their part, continue to insist that the Backfire is a medium bomber intended for theater and maritime strike operations. Given the pressing requirement to replace the aging Tu-16 Badger force, the likely role of the LRA Backfire force is low-level strike in Europe and the Far East. The Backfire is the only Soviet aircraft which can cover most of NATO Europe at low-level from bases in the USSR. The Backfire also has extensive ECM and ECCM equipment to help it survive in the intense air defense environment of a conventional conflict in Western Europe. The new demands for high intensity conventional combat capability levied on Soviet air power cannot be met by the aging Tu-16 force. The low-level performance built into the Backfire also gives it a longer medium altitude radius of action which will improve LRA's maritime strike capabilities as well. In fact, the range of the Backfire may in part also result from the fact that the aircraft was de-

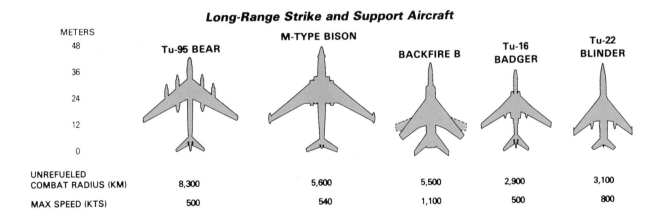

Long-Range Strike and Support Aircraft

METERS	Tu-95 BEAR	M-TYPE BISON	BACKFIRE B	Tu-16 BADGER	Tu-22 BLINDER
UNREFUELED COMBAT RADIUS (KM)	8,300	5,600	5,500	2,900	3,100
MAX SPEED (KTS)	500	540	1,100	500	800

28 Fiddler interceptor and a unique semi-variable geometry wing. The prototype, Backfire-A, first flew in 1969. The slightly redesigned Backfire-B entered service in 1975. Approximately 178 are currently in service with LRA with the nominal production rate of 30 per year probably being equally divided between Naval Aviation and LRA.

As one Western analyst has observed, 'It was inevitable that any bomber with variable sweep and turbofans would have very long subsonic range, and thus some strategic potential, as a corollary of improved low-level and loiter performance'. The appearance of the Backfire-B with a reported combat radius of 3400 miles, as well as an inflight refueling capability provoked considerable speculation in the West about the aircraft's intercontinental capabilities.

veloped to meet SNA requirements as well as those of LRA.

The assignment of the Backfire to theater and maritime roles is buttressed by recent press and official reports of the testing of a large, variable geometry heavy bomber. This aircraft has been given the name Blackjack and is allegedly similar in design to the US B-1 but larger and was still under development in 1988. According to *Aviation Week* it is expected to have a combat radius of 4000nm and a 36,000lb payload with a Mach 2.3 dash speed. This aircraft will probably be deployed in modest numbers to replace the Bears and Bisons in the intercontinental and maritime strike and reconnaissance roles. It will probably be armed with an air-to-surface missile with various warheads for nuclear and conventional missions.

Military Transport Aviation

The provision of military airlift support to the Soviet armed forces is provided by Military Transport Aviation (VTA). In addition to its military role, VTA provides peacetime strategic airlift in support of Soviet friends and clients. Of approximately 1500 fixed-wing aircraft in VTA, there are about 700 short-range transport aircraft, about 700 medium-range transports and about 100 long-range transports. VTA is organized into divisions, regiments and smaller independent units. While the number of assigned aircraft vary, VTA squadrons normally have 10 fixed-wing aircraft or 12 helicopters. In a combat situation, VTA is capable of moving one airborne division at long-range, and two-to-three divisions for short distances. Western analysts believe VTA's capacity to move troops and cargo has increased over a third since 1970 even though in this time its complement of aircraft has declined.

The backbone of VTA remains the medium-range An-12 CUB, a four-engine turbo-prop transport with the classic lay-out and performance of a military freighter: a high wing, landing gear inside fairings, a flat, low-level floor, and a rear loading door with integral ramp. The An-12 is able to carry up to 20 tons of cargo or 100 paratroopers. The An-12 is slowly being displaced by the larger Il-76 Candid turbofan powered transport. The Candid can carry twice the payload over five times the range, 40 tons of cargo or 140 troops a distance of over 3000 miles. Delivery of the Candid began in 1974, with a total of 370 in service by 1988. Long-range heavy lift capability is provided by a

small force of 55 An-22s which can carry up to 80 tons, including various tactical missile systems and armored vehicles including the T-62 tank. The An-22 Cock is a large four-engine strategic freighter modelled closely on the An-12 with an excellent short range and rough field performance. The An-22 first flew in 1965 with a total of 100 produced before production ended in 1974.

National Air Defense Forces

The threat posed by western nuclear armed heavy bombers forced Soviet recognition of need for an integrated air defense system. In 1948 various air defense units were combined under a single headquarters, which in 1954 attained the status of an independent service called PVO Strany. PVO Strany remains responsible for defending military targets and industrial areas in the Soviet Union against all forms of air attack. PVO-S currently is comprised of four major arms: the interceptors of the Air Defense Fighter Command (IA-PVO); the surface-to-air missiles of the Anti-Aircraft Missile troops

Left & main picture: The Tu-22M Backfire bomber seen here in an air-to-air photo and in an artist's impression, can carry a payload of some 12,000 pounds and can attain a speed of Mach 0.9 at low level.

Left: An Il-76 Candid transport in service with Aeroflot. The Il-76 is also widely used by the Soviet armed forces. The Il-76 is similar in size to the US C-141 but can operate from shorter, rougher airfields.

Right: The Il-76 is powered
by four Soloviev turbofan
engines. Unlike the C-141
which is its nearest Western
equivalent it is not fitted for
air-to-air refueling.

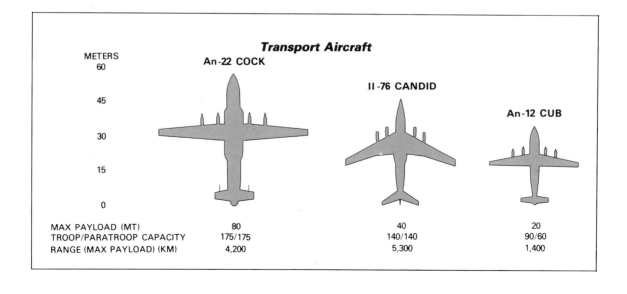

Transport Aircraft

METERS	An-22 COCK	Il-76 CANDID	An-12 CUB
MAX PAYLOAD (MT)	80	40	20
TROOP/PARATROOP CAPACITY	175/175	140/140	90/60
RANGE (MAX PAYLOAD) (KM)	4,200	5,300	1,400

Below: A US Navy F-4 Phantom inspects an An-12 Cub military transport aircraft in a flight over the Indian Ocean in 1980.

Above: Close-up of the tail
turret of an An-12 Cub. The
turret is manned as the
picture shows and
armament is normally two
23mm cannon.

Main picture: An An-12
seen at Keflavik Airport in
Iceland. Although the Cub
is being superseded by the
Il-76, some 400 remain in
service.

(ZRV); the warning and control systems of the
Radar Technical Troops (RTV); and finally the
Anti-Space Defense Troops (PKO) which are
reportedly charged with defense of the homeland against space threats, possibly including
foreign space reconnaissance systems.

PVO-S headquarters in Moscow exercises
centralized control over sixteen air defense districts, of which six are in the Warsaw Pact countries and the remainder in the Soviet Union. It
is most likely that control centers subordinate
to the respective districts coordinate detection
and tracking radars, select and commit

weapons systems and closely manage local air battles.

Early warning and control systems manned by the RTV cover the entire Soviet land mass with over 5,000 surveillance and ground control intercept radars currently deployed. Although lagging behind the West in sophisticated electronic components, the Soviets are reportedly increasingly deploying more modern phased array radars to replace older mechanical systems. Early warning is typically provided by 'Tall King' surveillance radar systems with range-, azimuth-, and height-finding radars feeding into the central control center. Although the decision to commit missiles or interceptors in a specific circumstance will be made by the control center, long standing Soviet practice has been to engage attacking aircraft at maximum control range with interceptors, to harass them en route with a controlled mix of fighters and surface-to-air missiles (SAMs) and to rely on SAMs for point defense of target areas.

Two strains of PVO interceptors have evolve over the years and continue to be evident in th current inventory: large, long-range intercep tors and medium-range fighter-interceptors. In the late 1960s, two new long-range high-altitude interceptors were introduced – the Tu-28 Fiddler and the MiG-25 Foxbat – as well as the long-range SA-5 Gammon SAM to counter the threat of long-range stand-off missiles launched from high-flying Western bombers. In the same period the Mach 2.5 Su-15 Flagon interceptor armed with two AA-3 Anab AAMs, became the primary PVO interceptor. Approximately 700 Su-15s remained in service complemented by 120 Yak-28s and MiG-25s. The subsequent advent of a low-level threat led to the introduction of a modified Su-15 and PVO deployment of the MiG-23 with its limited look-down/shoot-down capability and the recent deployment of a modified MiG-31, the Foxhound, with a new look-down/shoot-down radar system. The Foxhound will likely be followed into PVO service by a variant of the Sukhoi or Mikoyan advanced fighters currently under development. The USSR maintains more than 2000 interceptors and may have reorganized some interceptor units and placed them under the operational control of military district and groups of forces commanders.

The troops of the ZRV man over 12,000 surface-to-air missile launchers throughout the Soviet Union. About 2500 are SA-2 launchers, a high-altitude, long-range command guidance missile in service since 1959. The SA-5 is a radar homing system primarily deployed in the Moscow-Leningrad area for long-range, high-altitude interception. There has been specula-

The An-22 Cock is the only long-range transport in service with the Soviet Air Force and Aeroflot. It has been extensively used to ferry arms and material to Soviet clients in Asia and Africa.

The Su-15 Flagon has seen wide service with Soviet air defense forces since the 1960s. Although many Su-15s have been replaced by MiG-23s, Western experts believe that the Su-15 will see many more years of service.

The Tu-28 Fiddler is the world's largest fighter and is equipped with air-to-air missiles and has Mach 1.5 speed. It is apparently deployed to protect the Soviet northern periphery from air attack.

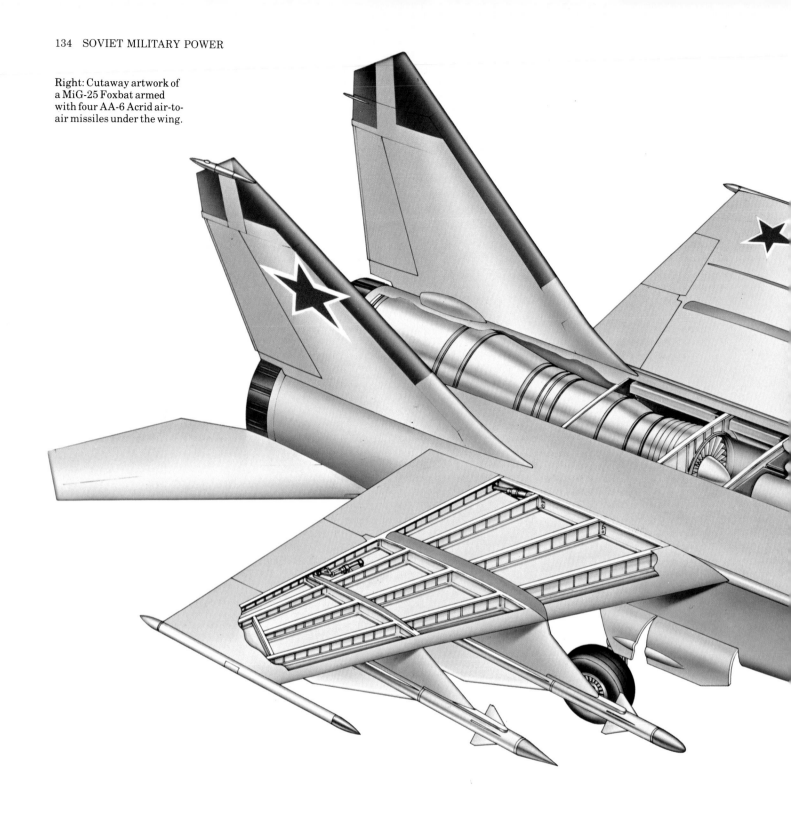

Right: Cutaway artwork of a MiG-25 Foxbat armed with four AA-6 Acrid air-to-air missiles under the wing.

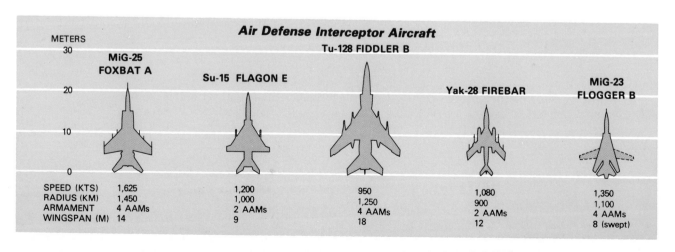

Air Defense Interceptor Aircraft

	MiG-25 FOXBAT A	Su-15 FLAGON E	Tu-128 FIDDLER B	Yak-28 FIREBAR	MiG-23 FLOGGER B
SPEED (KTS)	1,625	1,200	950	1,080	1,350
RADIUS (KM)	1,450	1,000	1,250	900	1,100
ARMAMENT	4 AAMs	2 AAMs	4 AAMs	2 AAMs	4 AAMs
WINGSPAN (M)	14	9	18	12	8 (swept)

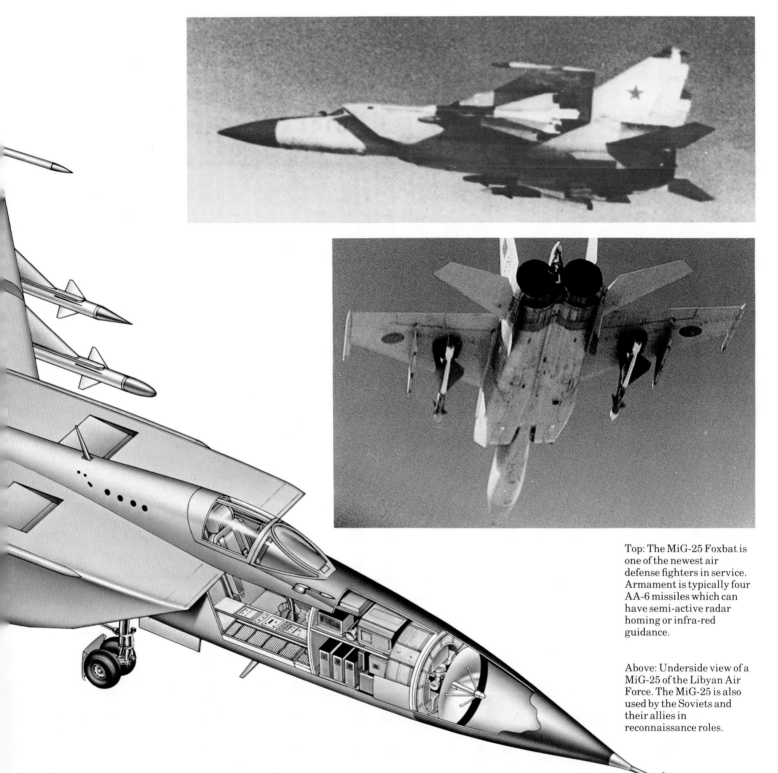

Top: The MiG-25 Foxbat is one of the newest air defense fighters in service. Armament is typically four AA-6 missiles which can have semi-active radar homing or infra-red guidance.

Above: Underside view of a MiG-25 of the Libyan Air Force. The MiG-25 is also used by the Soviets and their allies in reconnaissance roles.

tion that the SA-5 may have an ABM capability. Low altitude coverage is provided by the SA-3 Goa system, a command-guided missile mounted on a mobile, multi-rail launcher. To meet the low-level cruise missile threat, the Soviets are currently deploying the SA-10 SAM reportedly looking to engage targets below 300 feet.

Peacetime Occupations

The major peacetime occupation of Soviet air power is to prepare for its wartime roles. The fielding of large combat-ready forces is central to the Soviet doctrine of deterrence. Soviet leaders have, however, often sought to turn their growing military capabilities to the pursuit of foreign policy objectives. The utility of Soviet air power in this role has grown with its expansion and modernization. Developments related directly to a power projection capability such as the provision of inflight refueling capability for tactical aircraft which would permit their rapid overseas deployment have not, however, been pursued. While Soviet airlift capability has been greatly expanded, there are not indications of a desire to match the global strategic airlift capability of the United States. The ability of the Soviet Union to flex its aerial muscle at greater distances is not at issue. The question is rather whether these developments

The Tu-126 Moss early warning aircraft, with 36 foot rotating radome and nose-mounted refueling probe, is considered distinctly inferior to similar Western aircraft because of its supposedly limited ability to detect low-flying aircraft.

mark a conscious Soviet policy thrust or rather limited exploitation of the additional capabilities of the latest generation of Soviet aircraft.

Soviet political leaders have often turned to military forces to further their political objectives in the postwar era. Soviet air power has been used to support Soviet territorial claims in East Europe and elsewhere and to provide tangible evidence of Soviet support to various clients. In Korea, Soviet pilots flew missions with North Korean forces, gaining considerable combat experience as a by-product. Soviet air units were also deployed to China during the 1958 crisis over the islands of Quemoy and Matsu. Soviet tactical air units also provided tradi-

tional air support to the Soviet intervention in Czechoslovakia and also recently in Afghanistan. Soviet combat air units have been used in more peaceful 'show the flag' operations including exchange visits with Finnish and French air force units.

The largest peacetime deployment of Soviet combat air power outside of Eastern Europe came early in 1970 with the arrival of Soviet surface-to-air missile units and air-combat fighter units to stiffen Egyptian air defenses. The probable objective was to deter mounting Israeli deep penetration raids over the Nile delta. There were also reports of small numbers of Soviet interceptors operating out of six Soviet

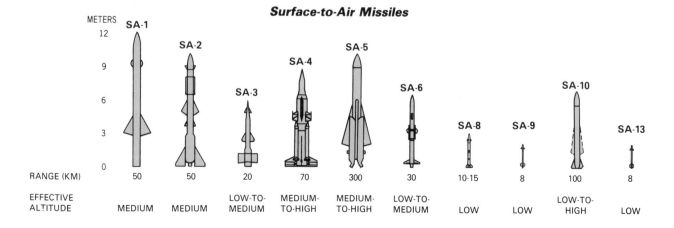

Surface-to-Air Missiles

	SA-1	SA-2	SA-3	SA-4	SA-5	SA-6	SA-8	SA-9	SA-10	SA-13
RANGE (KM)	50	50	20	70	300	30	10-15	8	100	8
EFFECTIVE ALTITUDE	MEDIUM	MEDIUM	LOW-TO-MEDIUM	MEDIUM-TO-HIGH	MEDIUM-TO-HIGH	LOW-TO-MEDIUM	LOW	LOW	LOW-TO-HIGH	LOW

Above: The SA-8 Gecko missile is typically mounted on a wheeled vehicle which also carries its targeting radar. Although it is one of the most modern Soviet SAMs, the SA-8 did not fare well against Israeli forces in Lebanon in 1982.

Right: The SA-9 Gaskin tactical SAM is mounted on a BRDM scout car chassis and uses a box launcher for its infra-red homing missiles.

Top: The SA-6 Gainful SAM is mounted on a tracked vehicle with three launchers. These missiles were badly beaten by Israeli pilots in 1982.

Above: The SA-4 Ganef is a mobile strategic SAM intended to provide wide area coverage for Soviet theater forces.

Right: SA-3 Goa missiles are deployed at over 400 sites in the USSR and Warsaw Pact countries to provide point air defense for certain strategic areas. Both two-rail and four-rail launchers are in service.

controlled air bases as a component of a Soviet operated air defense system. The Israeli raids ceased shortly after Soviet combat air patrols began. But as Soviet patrols moved closer to the Canal, they were met by a calculated Israeli response in the form of an aerial ambush which cost the Soviet's five MiG-21s. The Soviet response was a careful and cautious shift from combat air patrols to surface-to-air missiles. According to one Western analyst, by the time of the cease-fire in August, Egypt had been turned into a model Soviet air defense district with all radar and missile sites operated by Soviet personnel.

The Soviet Union has made use of its client states as air bases to pursue other peacetime interests, especially reconnaissance and probing of Western defenses. On a regular basis Soviet long-range aircraft probe the defenses of neighboring countries and shadow Western naval forces. Access to overseas facilities allows the Soviets to plug gaps in their peacetime surveillance systems. Since April 1970, Soviet Bear-D aircraft have been reconnoitering the US East Coast based in Havana. Soviet reconnaissance flights have also been used to symbolize Soviet concern over political or military developments in adjacent areas. MiG-25 Foxbat reconnaissance aircraft flying at high altitude

Above: An SA-2 Guideline strategic SAM shown on its launcher in a revetted field site.

Right: An SA-2 in the ready-to-launch position.

reportedly began violating Iranian airspace in 1973, primarily as an expression of concern over growing Iranian military capabilities.

More direct support to Soviet overseas political pursuits has come in the form of willingness to provide advanced combat aircraft and air defense missile systems to foreign customers and the use of airlift rapidly to resupply client states. The Soviet Union had, by the early 1980s, exported more aircraft of just one type, the MiG-21, than all the tactical aircraft the NATO allies had operational in Northern and Central Europe. Since the Soviet Union began exporting military aircraft outside the Warsaw Pact in the mid-1950s one or more models have gone to over 40 countries. Often these aircraft are accompanied by training teams of Soviet pilots and technicians. Major consumers are Middle Eastern states including Iraq, Syria, Libya, and Egypt, Latin American nations such as Cuba and more recently Peru, and Asian states including Vietnam and India. India, in particular, has been a major consumer of Soviet aircraft to the extent of large scale licensed production of the MiG-21.

The peacetime utility of Soviet air power has been strongly enhanced by the development of air transport capabilities. This capability has allowed the rapid resupply of client states with critical arms as well as mounting humanitarian disaster relief expeditions. The 1973 October War prompted a Soviet airlift of arms to Egypt and Syria of greater proportions than the Soviets had previously attempted. Early in the

effort there were 60 to 90 flights per day. Overall the Soviets flew 930 missions and delivered 15 million tons of material, which, while only a fraction of the US airlift to Israel, remains a very credible performance. What has been described by Western analysts as virtually an air bridge between the Soviet Union and its new found friend Ethiopia was mounted between 7 November and 31 December 1977, an operation at its peak involving some 225 transport aircraft using seven different routes simultaneously. This massive effort which extricated the Ethiopians from the threat of defeat by dissidents in Eritrea and the Ogaden is further evidence of the effectiveness of Soviet air logistics.

Airlift capability, developed to support wartime air mobility requirements, also confers on the Soviet military the potential rapidly to intervene in peripheral areas such as Afghanistan or the Middle East using either its own considerable airborne forces or those of its allies such as Cuba. In 1968, the first units deployed in the Soviet invasion of Czechoslovakia were airborne units airlifted into Prague to secure the airfield and vital communications installations. During the 1973 Middle East conflict, the Soviet Union threatened the deployment of airborne forces to support Egypt if the Israelis failed to observe a ceasefire. Credibility of the threat was signaled when Soviet transports were diverted from resupply operations and routine domestic flights to areas of the USSR where airborne units could be rapidly loaded. The light Soviet

airborne formations which could have been moved to Egypt would not have posed a serious military threat to the heavily armored Israeli forces but would have provided a symbolic deterrent.

Soviet air power has experienced a dynamic growth, especially in Frontal Aviation, as the air force has evolved to meet the requirements of nuclear and conventional combined-arms combat. According to the US Department of Defense, the USSR produced an average of almost 1300 combat aircraft per year between 1976 and 1980. Large scale production of SAMs also continued with some 50,000 produced in 1980 alone. The pace of this effort will probably slacken only slightly with the introduction of the next generation of SAMs and aircraft in the early 1980s, including the MiG-29 Fulcrum multi-role fighter and the SA-10 SAM.

But air forces have always been and remain a supporting service with no primary mission of their own. Despite the development of a new strategic bomber, the Blackjack, the main emphasis is still on tactical aircraft as important members of the combined arms team. The introduction of the new generation of tactical aircraft in the coming years will not, however, erase the traditional technological dominance enjoyed by Western air forces. NATO remains almost a generation ahead of the Warsaw Pact in fighter and ground attack aircraft because the modernization cycles of the two alliances are not synchronized, and this advantage will remain.

Top left: Operators in an air defense control center. Soviet air defense tactics emphasize strict control of missiles and interceptors rather than the Western practice of allowing pilots some individual initiative.

Top: SA-2 SAMs in transit. The SA-2 has been operational since 1959 and is used by some 20 countries.

Above: Soviet soldiers conduct maintenance on SA-2 missiles. Versions of the SA-2 were widely used in the Vietnam War but US electronic countermeasures rendered them relatively ineffective.

NAVAL POWER

Right: Peter the Great built the first Russian Navy.

Second right: A modern reconstruction of the barque *Neva*, the first ship built by Peter the Great, reflecting Soviet interest in Russian naval traditions.

Previous page: A Foxtrot class submarine with a Kashin class guided missile destroyer in the background.

In addition, as Jurgen Rohwer has noted, the actual course of development, as revealed by the appearance and number of various ship classes, is reflective of the discontinuities in the role that Soviet strategy assigns to seapower. Thus ships designed for one mission have often entered service to face a totally different set of requirements and operate in roles for which they appear unsuited.

The final justification of any warship or navy is its ability to fulfill its combat mission. The basic rationale of the Soviet Navy remains, as Admiral Gorshkov has said, as a component of Soviet general warfighting capabilities. While a

Since the mid-1950s, the Soviets have made a concerted attempt to expand their efforts to exploit the sea for political, economic and military ends. In just over three decades, the Soviet ocean-going merchant marine has grown from an insignificant, coastal-oriented fleet to fifth place in the world in total ships and to serve the state as a hard-currency earner and a secure means of communication with friends and clients. The Soviet Union operates the world's largest fishing fleet, owing its growth to a decision in the late forties that fisheries were a very cost effective protein source for an agriculturally backward country. Finally, the Soviet Navy has emerged as a dynamic and credible component of Soviet global warfighting capability as well as a tool of political influence.

The growth of Soviet naval power, however, has excited the greatest concern in the West. From a postwar miscellany of obsolescent and lend-lease warships, the Soviet Navy has grown to a formidable force which many Western analysts view as a potentially serious rival to the dominance enjoyed by the US Navy since 1945. But the evolution of Soviet naval power has been far from a steady, purposeful march. The Soviet Navy, under the paternal guidance of Admiral of the Fleet of the Soviet Union, S. G. Gorshkov, for over 25 years until 1985, has to fight continual battles for resources as well as recognition of the importance of sea power in meeting the growing array of Soviet military missions. But Soviet military doctrine and policy remain dominated by the Army and to a lesser extent the Strategic Rocket Forces (SRF). The Navy is still clearly a junior service and at times has been required to adopt systems and tasks that, as Michael MccGwire has aptly observed, violate traditional naval assumptions and force the Navy to develop 'radical' solutions.

clear policy for the employment of naval forces in pursuit of peacetime political objectives has emerged, warfighting requirements continue to be dominant in Soviet naval programs as evidenced by the continued emphasis on submarines. The latest generation of Soviet surface combatants, such as the *Kiev* and *Kirov*, has greater endurance and conventional combat capability than its predecessors and in some ways presents the image of an incipient capability to project power into the Third World. But providing increased conventional capabilities for the Navy parallels developments in the ground and air forces and reflects the evolution of Soviet doctrine for fighting a general war. The Soviet Navy has graduated to an increasingly significant role in that doctrine as the Revolution in Military Affairs has gone on.

The Tsarist Legacy

The Soviet Union did not suddenly stumble onto seapower with the advent of Admiral Gorshkov. For the last 200 years, as Michael MccGwire has noted, Russia's fleet has historically been third

Left: The battered wreck of the battleship *Slava* lying in Moen Sound in the Gulf of Riga in 1917 after an action with German dreadnoughts. The Russian Navy was largely unable to disrupt German control of the Baltic during World War I.

or fourth largest in the world although its effectiveness has never matched its size, in part due to accidents of geography. Tsars from the time of Peter the Great developed naval forces to assist the army in its campaigns in the Baltic and the Black Sea. Three times between 1768 and 1827, Russia successfully deployed sizeable forces to the Mediterranean to operate against the Turks. But the isolation of those squadrons from their homebases highlighted a continuing problem for Soviet naval policy planners – the vulnerability to blockade of Russia's access to the open ocean. In order to reach the open ocean, Russian forces must pass through various geographic choke points, such as the Dardanelles, all controlled by foreign powers. In 1863, five Russian warships visited New York and another group visited San Francisco, partly to improve Russian-American relations during the American Civil War, but primarily to have a force of commerce raiders safely in friendly ports on the open seas as war was then a distinct possibility between Russia and Great Britain.

Through the nineteenth century, Russia increasingly found herself confronting threats from maritime powers and was forced to maintain forces in four widely separated areas, thus preventing mutual support. Russia remained predominantly a land power, however, with the only realistic threats to her security by land. Naval forces were required to defend against seaborne assaults and to contest attempts by maritime powers to dictate events in areas adjacent to Russia. Many of the latter, in fact, involved attempts to break out of the narrow seas, such as the Black Sea, and gain open ocean ports. In 1878 the absence of Russian naval opposition allowed the appearance of the

Below: The battleship *Oslyabya* which was sunk by the Japanese in the Russian debacle at Tsushima in 1905.

Above: A petty officer instructs sailors in the characteristics of various classes of ship in a picture taken between the two world wars.

Russian-Soviet naval history displays a number of clear breaks which mark fundamental changes in basic strategic doctrine. As Jurgen Rohwer has observed, this has commonly alternated between a so-called 'young school' which pursues a defensive strategy to undermine an opponent's control of the sea by employing advanced technologies aboard large numbers of small, relatively inexpensive platforms. In the 20th century this involved submarines, aircraft and torpedo craft. This was opposed by adherrents of the classical Mahanian style battlefleet intended to wrest control of the seas. The major difficulty with the latter has been the huge resources required to maintain four battlefleets, especially with huge and more pressing demands for ground forces.

Towards the end of the nineteenth century, Russia joined the race for classical naval power and began a major capital ship program. The majority of the new ships was deployed to the Mediterranean and the Far East, marking the shift in the Russian maritime horizon beyond the Baltic and Black Seas. This flexing of Russian muscle came to an abrupt end with the demise of two Russian fleets under Japanese guns at Port Arthur and Tsushima in the Russo-Japanese War of 1904-5.

With the demise of its fleet, the Russian Navy was compelled to make a fresh start, reverting to a defensive, narrow seas orientation. As Russian concern focused on the threat from Imperial Germany, the Austro-Hungarian Empire and Turkey, Soviet naval doctrine focused on protecting the seaward flanks of Russian armies in Europe and the Caucasus and defending the seaward approaches to the Gulf of Finland. In 1910 a large building program began the return to a classical battle fleet but only one destroyer was completed by the outbreak of World War I and further expansion plans were shelved.

In the Baltic, the emphasis in Russian war-

British fleet to force a halt to the march of a victorious Russian army on Constantinople. But as Michael MccGwire has pointed out, naval forces were seen as an expensive defensive necessity rather than as a preferred instrument of overseas policy.

While clearly a junior and often neglected service, the Russian Navy nevertheless had no lack of innovators. The traditional Russian spirit of technical and conceptual innovation and a readiness to adopt new but unproven technological advances, are traits which persist to the present. In particular, considerable interest was shown in the application of mines and torpedoes to the problems of coastal defense and naval operations in confined waters. Russian designers also pursued development of the submarine. As with its American counterpart, the Russian navy focused on the twin missions of coastal defense and commerce raiding for much of the nineteenth century.

time operations was on the use of light forces to contest German naval superiority. Russian forces proved especially adept at offensive and defensive mine warfare. The situation was reversed in the Black Sea where the Russian Navy was able to achieve ascendancy over Turkish forces through extensive use of offensive mine warfare and destroyers supported by larger units. The Russian fleet then turned to the traditional tasks involved in supporting the seaward flanks of the army: providing gunfire support and amphibious landings while screening friendly forces against similar operations. The Russian tradition of technical innovation continued with the *Elpidifor* class, possibly the first purpose-built amphibious ship, for large-scale landings in the Black Sea. The Black Sea fleet also made extensive use of aircraft while in the Baltic, the Russians launched the *Krab*, the first submarine specifically for minelaying.

Any military force will reflect the inherent tensions of the society from which it is drawn, and the Imperial Navy was no exception. The Tsarist Navy was generally ill-led and poorly trained, its morale weakened by the wide gulf between officers and men. Prolonged periods of inactivity enforced on the Baltic Fleet's major surface units led to a general deterioration of men and material and increased revolutionary disaffection. The result was the effective collapse of the Navy as its officers were removed and many of its sailors drafted for service ashore with the revolutionary forces.

Stalin's navy

The Foundation of the Red Navy dates from Lenin's decree of 11 February 1918 but in fact, Soviet maritime power was starting over from scratch. The navy's limited participation in the Revolution was similar to its participation in previous wars, defending the gulf of Finland and protecting the maritime flanks. Emphasis

Below: The Soviet battleship *Marat* seen at the British 1937 Coronation Naval Review. The *Marat* was damaged beyond repair while serving as a floating battery during the siege of Leningrad in World War II.

Top: Loading a torpedo aboard a Soviet warship just prior to World War II.

Above: The Soviets built large numbers of *Shchuka* class submarines for coastal defense.

on mine warfare continued with over 7000 mines being laid between 1918 and 1920. The Navy also formed a number of improvized river flotillas to support the armies.

The Civil War and the resulting intervention by the Western Powers underscored for the new Bolshevik leadership their vulnerability to the threat of amphibious landings. Given the existing situation, the new Red Fleet had to look to a defensive posture emphasizing submarines, mines, torpedo boats, and aircraft. The young fleet was in desperate straits in the aftermath of the Revolution, with only the Baltic Fleet sur-

viving. The ships that remained – two battleships, a cruiser, 18 destroyers and nine submarines by 1924 – were in a bad state of repair, lacking not only spare parts but also ship repair facilities.

Robert Bathurst has suggested that the design of the Soviet fleet at this time was a function of four factors: the complete collapse of the country's industrial infrastructure; the heightened sense of a threat from a hostile west; the hope for an international Communist movement directed from Moscow; and concern about the Navy's political reliability as a result of the 1921 uprising of dissident Baltic Fleet sailors at Kronstadt. Concern about the Navy's political reliability also probably stemmed from its exposure to foreign contagion as it went about visiting foreign ports.

While both Lenin and his successor Stalin wished for a navy capable of supporting their political objectives, harsh reality dictated otherwise. A sample of the desire for a high seas fleet was an ambitious plan for the construction of eight battleships, 16 cruisers and over 60 destroyers. In fact it was only after extensive shipyard development in the early 1930s that the Soviets could begin construction of large submarines and destroyers. Naval building programs were integrated into the five year economic programs with first priority given submarines, then torpedo boats and finally destroyers. The plans for this new 'young school' fleet also exceeded the industrial capacity of the nation as, for example, the 1933 plan called for a totally unrealistic figure of 369 submarines to be completed by 1937. In fact, while construction of surface units lagged, the submarine construction program continued at a steady pace with a total of 66 units in service by the end of 1937. By the time World War II got underway, the Soviet Union had the largest fleet of underseas craft in the world.

While practical reality dictated a primarily coastal defense orientation, the yearning for classical naval power never disappeared. The majority of the military hierarchy saw the future conflict as essentially a land conflict and believed the Navy's mission must be rooted in the requirements of the army. A small school felt otherwise and, according to Jurgen Rohwer, did not wish to exclude the possibility that a suitable fleet 'could itself fulfill the main objective during some phases of the war in one theater or another'. Despite the liquidation of most of the proponents of the limited or defensive school in Stalin's purges, their perspective continued to dominate actual Soviet Naval operations. The opposing oceanic school was making headway toward the end of the decade. Following the Spanish Civil War, in which the Soviets were unable to protect their merchant ships carrying supplies to their loyalist allies, Stalin apparently was increasingly influenced by classical concepts of seapower.

The third Five Year Plan, inaugurated in 1938, assigned a much higher priority to shipbuilding. As with previous plans, it carried an air of unreality. Including ships from the preceding plan not yet completed, it called for the construction of ten 59,000-ton battleships, six battlecruisers, 14 cruisers, 12 flotilla leaders and 96 large destroyers by 1942. As Michael MccGwire had noted, 'it would have been a fleet of short-legged ships, sailed by inexperienced seamen under the command of novice admirals'. Submarines were also not neglected with 27 large, 89 medium, and 80 small submarines planned. Infrastructure improvements were also made including upgrading existing shipyards and building large new facilities in the North, the Pacific and on the Volga River. But the dictator's desires could not instantly conjure up industrial capability, and a great deal of foreign assistance was sought. The Italians were particularly active, producing a destroyer leader and design assistance and plans for destroyers, cruisers and even battleships. Common design influences are evident in Soviet and Italian warships even to the present.

The Soviet Union at the end of the 1930's had a modest defensive fleet tied to the requirements of its army but much greater aspirations. Its defensive concepts were strongly influenced by evolving Soviet military doctrine, including defense in depth. Coordinated attacks by air, submarine and surface units with special emphasis on underseas craft were the order of the day.

With war clouds looming, the reality of Russia's military position reasserted itself. On 19 October 1940, construction on all large ships was halted and work on submarines, torpedo boats and destroyers accelerated. By June 1941, a total of three battleships, two battlecruisers, 14 cruisers, 11 destroyer leaders, 71 destroyers and 297 submarines had been laid down of which four cruisers, seven flotilla leaders and

The *K.21* was a large fleet submarine operating against the Germans in World War II.

Above: Sailors man an anti-aircraft machine gun against German planes.

Below: The World War II submarine *Naradovolets* in an Arctic anchorage.

30 destroyers as well as 206 submarines had been completed. These modest forces were stretched between four fleets, all of which confronted substantial challenges from potential opponents.

The Great Patriotic War

Against superior German forces in the Baltic, the Red Fleet followed a strategy similar to that of its Tsarist predecessor in 1914. As Robert Bathurst has observed, the history of naval operations in the Baltic during the first few months is a story largely of retreat, escape and evacuation. The fleet's surface units were effectively bottled-up in the innermost corner of the Bay of Kronstadt, serving in support of the defense of Leningrad. Attempts to use the fleet's submarines to interdict German supply lines proved a costly failure. The Black Sea fleet, while the superior surface force, suffered greatly from German air power. The fleet carried out resupply and evacuation operations while the ground forces were in retreat, and amphibious operations after the turn of the tide in 1942. The fleet's submarines had only limited success operating against German sea lines of communications. In the north the Soviets were confined to limited operations against German convoys and in the final stages served as escorts for allied convoys. A senior British naval officer

responsible for liaison with the Northern Fleet reportedly described Soviet seagoing efficiency as poor and tactical behavior as erratic.

As Michael MccGwire has observed, the Second World War confirmed the USSR's traditional belief that ground forces were the basis of her security and assured the continued domination of the defense hierarchy by military leaders. But by 1945, her most likely opponents were maritime powers who had just demonstrated considerable skill in large-scale amphi-

Above: Destroyers of the Baltic Fleet at Kronstadt.

Top: Present-day Soviet sailors on parade in Red Square.

The *Sverdlov* class cruiser *Alexander Suvorov* takes part in an exercise in the Philippine Sea with a Kotlin class destroyer in the background. Despite their somewhat dated design the *Sverdlov* class ships caused great concern to Western analysts when they appeared in the years after World War II.

bious operations at great distances from their own shores. The possibility existed of amphibious operations against the vulnerable Baltic and Black Sea coasts, both areas offering the potential invader the opportunity to outflank the USSR's newly acquired forward defenses in Eastern Europe. At the same time, the impetus of wartime development had greatly increased the scope of Soviet investment in its Far Eastern and Northern ports, making those areas vulnerable to attack as well.

The Soviet Navy's performance in the war has been described as valiant but inept, performing its primary mission of protecting the flanks of the land armies with inadequate equipment, training and doctrine. One bright spot was the appreciation of the value of naval air power in the narrow seas and its growing strength throughout the conflict. The end of the conflict saw the Soviet fleet a hodge-podge of foreign and domestic designs. By May 1945 over half of the surface fleet had been sunk and the surface ship building program had been destroyed along with most of the construction and support facilities of the western fleets. The submarine

force fared better as the submarine building yards remained in Russian hands and the Soviet Union emerged from the conflict with an even larger subsurface fleet than that with which it entered the conflict.

The war also brought a much needed technical boost to the Soviet fleet. Warships transferred from the Western allies introduced new technologies such as radar and sonar. The defeat of the Axis powers allowed the Soviets to increase the size of their postwar fleet with former Japanese and German warships, but more importantly it provided access to advanced naval technology in areas such as submarine design and construction.

Postwar Recovery and Renewal

The Soviet Navy's postwar recovery may be dated from Stalin's 1944 decision to resume his pursuit of a bluewater battle fleet with a program to construct a fleet of 175 destroyers, 24 cruisers, eight battlecruisers, four aircraft carriers, and a whopping 1200 submarines, albeit mostly medium and small coastal boats. The naval air forces were also to be modernized and expanded. Such grandiose plans were not only beyond the means of the shattered Soviet economy but with most of its experienced cadres siphoned off first by the prewar purges and subsequently the war, it is doubtful such a fleet could be manned. The immediate requirements of coastal defense dictated that priority be given to submarines and light forces, and a building program was initiated.

By 1950 the first postwar Soviet submarine design was ready for service in the form of the 1300-ton Whiskey class medium-range patrol submarine. Approximately 240 Whiskeys were built between 1951 and 1957. The Whiskey has been characterized as probably one of the most advanced submarine designs in the world at the time. The Whiskey design was accompanied by the larger Zulu class, a 2200-ton long-range patrol submarine of which 25 were built between 1951 and 1955 and the Quebec class of 740-ton coastal submarines. The numbers of first generation postwar diesel-electric submarines actually built fell far short of planned forces as the evolution of Soviet doctrine led to curtailed production runs. However, the Whiskey and Zulu class submarines, direct descendants of the German U-Boats, caused a considerable stir in the West which feared a renewed Battle of the Atlantic. In fact, only the Zulus were well suited to mercantile warfare. The prewar defensive strategy of defense in depth by coordinated air, submarine, and surface ships strikes remained in vogue.

The results of postwar surface ship construction programs also began to make their appearance in the late 1940s and early 1950s. Designs were conventional and initially of prewar origin including the 19,000-ton *Sverdlov* light cruisers with 12 six-inch guns and the 3500-ton *Skoryy* class destroyers of which 70 were built between 1949 and 1954. The first postwar design was the Kola class, a 1600-ton escort ship. This class was followed in 1955 by the 3600-ton Kotlin class of 19 ships. These were the last conventional all-gun destroyers in the Soviet navy, production being cut back from a planned total of forty ships.

The defensive capability of the naval air forces was also strengthened in the immediate postwar period to a total of 4000 aircraft by the mid-1950s. Over half were fighter aircraft to provide air cover for bases and ships while the remainder was a small number of Badger medium bombers, Beagle twin-jet torpedo bombers and a miscellany of reconnaissance, anti-submarine warfare and liaison aircraft. It was not until the mid-1950s that the introduction of long-range heavy bomber aircraft gave naval aviation truly long-range reconnaissance and strike capability.

Gorshkov's Navy

In the view of many Western analysts, when Stalin passed from the scene in March 1953, his aspirations for a traditional western-style high

seas fleet died with him, a victim of scarce resources and more importantly, the Revolution in Military Affairs. The Revolution in Military Affairs in the context of the Navy meant a period of doctrinal turmoil as it sought ways to deal with new technologies and establish its new role in a hierarchy dominated by the military. In practical terms it meant the application of the parallel development of nuclear weapons and propulsion as well as guided missiles and electronics to new and traditional missions for naval forces.

The evolution of the modern Soviet Navy cannot be divorced from the career of Admiral Gorshkov. Appointed to head the Soviet Navy in January 1956 at the age of 45, Gorshkov proved to be a skilled bureaucratic warrior, able to extract from the army-dominated defense establishment the resources for the creation of, in his own words, 'a powerful ocean-going Navy'. As several Western analysts have noted, the 'front' for Soviet naval leaders has been the political arena and the major visible weapon has been the printed word, especially those of Admiral Gorshkov. While occasionally addres-

Above: The helicopter carrier *Moskva* takes on fuel from the oiler *Boris Chilikin*.

Top: Close up view of twin 57mm gun mountings on the *Boris Chilikin*'s foredeck. These dual-purpose automatic weapons have since been removed from the *Boris Chilikin* (the photograph dates from 1971) but remain in service in Kresta class cruisers and other ships.

Bottom left: An Osa II class missile attack boat. The Osa class boats are armed with surface-to-surface missiles and 30mm guns.

Main picture: The Soviet Kotlin class destroyer *Besslednyi* seen from the deck of the USS *Walker* shortly before the two ships collided. Such collisions are not uncommon. Soviet captains often maneuver their ships very aggressively when observing Western exercises.

Top: A Nanuchka class guided missile patrol boat at sea in 1982. The Nanuchka boats carry two triple SS-N-9 surface-to-surface cruise missile launchers and a retractable SA-N-4 SAM system in the forecastle.

Above: One of the most unusual-looking ships in service anywhere, the space tracking ship *Kosmonaut Yuri Gagarin.*

sing the desirable fighting qualities of a modern navy, Gorshkov seemed more intent on justifying an expanded naval role in modern war, both absolutely and relative to other arms, rather than matters of tactics, doctrine or even operating policy.

One of Gorshkov's interesting weapons has been the creative adaptation of Russian and general naval history to educate his superiors and argue his general thesis that:

1) The Navy should be accorded greater prominence in the Armed Forces structure due to the strategic significance of its ballistic missile submarines and the growing maritime threat as well as the Navy's unique peacetime capabilities.
2) The necessity for the Soviet Union to have a 'balanced' fleet integrating the various types of platforms, including surface ships, as the sine qua non for any great power to achieve naval strength.

The admiral's battles within the military hierarchy, in the end, revolved around the acquisition of resources to pursue his balanced fleet. As Gorshkov himself has written, the Navy must be seen as a component force within the framework of total armed forces requirements which are themselves a part of the politically-directed planned economy. At the same time, the admiral advanced the growing im-

portance of naval forces and the growing cost of increasingly complex naval systems as the rationale for a larger naval slice of the resource pie. This argument has apparently not been totally successful since, while the Soviet Navy has been able to make qualitative improvements and additional resources have been allocated to ship construction, there have been quantitative reductions in force levels. Gorshkov finally stepped down from office in December 1985, to be replaced by Admiral Vladimir Chernavin and, despite the problems, he still inherited a modern and versatile force.

Missions, New and Old
Sometime in the mid-fifties the primary seaborne threat perceived by the Soviet leadership shifted from fear of amphibious assault to the problem of countering nuclear strikes from the sea, initially from carrier aircraft. The Soviet political and military leadership, over the objections of some naval officers, saw the solution in the new technologies embodied in long-range cruise missiles carried by surface ships, submarines, and aircraft. But as Michael MccGwire has noted, much of the Soviet naval effort over time has been thwarted by improvements in Western systems, especially aircraft and subsequently missile ranges, forcing Soviet units to operate further from home in increasingly hostile environments. Another factor has been the evolution of Soviet warfighting doctrine from the idea of immediate and full-scale nuclear conflict, essentially war of a single salvo, to a more flexible view which includes the possibility of a period of conventional hostilities and continuing operations after the big salvo.

The Initial Problem
The anti-carrier warfare problem was addressed with a strategy which envisaged engaging enemy carrier groups with coordinated cruise-missile attacks, a wide variety of platforms providing the relatively large numbers required. In part this aspect was the product of the heavy military emphasis on combined arms, another example of a positive aspect to the doctrinal dominance of the military. The concept also embraced the idea of area defense, involving an inner zone where local superiority would allow sea control and an outer zone where enemy operations are contested and disrupted. This traditional Soviet concept was extended to meet the new threat. To secure effectively the inner zone, it would be necessary to seize the natural defensive barriers at the entrance to each fleet operating area, all of which were held by members of the NATO alliance. Interdicting NATO nuclear delivery systems in the outer zone became substantially more difficult as those delivery systems gained increasing range. As Michael MccGwire has observed, a comprehensive answer requires the ability continuously to track the enemy's nuclear delivery platforms, a difficult task when dealing with carriers, all but

impossible against ballistic missile submarines. But the Soviets pressed on with their typical incremental approach to the problem, doing what they could with what was available while putting in hand a series of short to very long term development programs.

Missions Evolve

Even before the new cruise missile platforms were fielded, it became clear that the next generation of threats from the sea would pose new and more challenging problems. The next generation of carrier-based aircraft would have substantially increased ranges, forcing the Soviet combined-arms strike groups to venture further afield, perhaps beyond range of land-based fighter cover. A partial reponse was to produce surface platforms with better anti-aircraft capability. But the role of the large surface ship was under revision as new and more pressing requirements developed. The anti-carrier role became increasingly a submarine and aircraft mission.

In January 1960, Nikita Khrushchev revealed a major shift in Soviet defense policy with the formation of the Strategic Rocket Forces (SRF) and its dominant position as the principal arm of the Soviet military. Research was to be concentrated on landbased ballistic missiles, at the expense of other programs, including the Navy's incipient nuclear-powered ballistic missile submarine program. But this policy soon fell by the wayside as Soviet planners became concerned with the development of a credible warfighting capability in the face of the planned deployment of large numbers of US strategic systems. Two major roles emerged for the Soviet Navy: to provide seabased strategic missiles as a secure, survivable warfighting reserve to complement the SRF; and, to develop the capability to threaten the West's ballistic missile submarines.

Western naval analysts such as Norman Polmar have expressed the view that the priority accorded the development of SSBNs over the last 15 years makes it clear that the strategic nuclear strike mission has become the primary one for the Soviet Navy. From 1967 through 1981, Soviet shipyards have completed 68 SSBNs and construction of new ships and the development of new missiles continues. The Soviet SSBN force reportedly contains 40 percent of Soviet strategic missiles and roughly one-quarter of total missile warheads. In his 1976 book, *Seapower of the State*, Admiral Gorshkov put it rather well 'because the introduction of nuclear weapons in the Navy has imparted to it the capability of effecting the outcome of a war, i.e., a strategic capability, the main goal of the Navy has become the execution

Top: Over the last decade the Soviet Navy has increased its range and regularly deployed ships to distant areas. Seen here at anchor in the Mediterranean is a squadron including Kotlin and Kashin class destroyers and various support ships.

Above left: An Amur class repair ship at anchor on a foreign station. Soviet ships seem to spend much of their time on distant stations at anchor with major electronic systems shut down.

Above: An Agr class radar picket ship, formerly a minesweeper of the T-43 class.

Main picture: A Ka-25 anti-submarine helicopter flies past a *Moskva* class helicopter carrier. Visible in front of the helicopter are the ship's two RBU-6000 antisubmarine rocket launchers. These weapons are carried by many classes of Soviet warships.

of strikes against the enemy shore and the protection of one's own territory against such strikes by the enemy'.

As John Herzog has noted, every navy in the world has its high value ships, those designed to carry out the navy's most essential mission and much of the rest of the fleet is built with their support in mind. The Soviet Navy has but one true high-value unit – the SSBN. Whatever the role of Soviet SSBNs in strategic strike planning, the Soviet Navy must protect them as they would become clear targets for Western anti-submarine warfare (ASW) forces once the war began. Given the strength of Western ASW forces, the first generation of modern Soviet SSBNs, the Yankee class, were probably an interim solution, since the range of their SS-N-6 missiles, 1600nm, required patrol areas close to the American coast, in the face of coordinated air, surface, and subsurface ASW forces. The solution, paradoxically enough, lay in the geographic choke points which in the past had inhibited Soviet naval power and which now served as the boundary of the inner defense zone. The development of long-range SLBMs, beginning in 1973 with the 4200nm range SS-N-8 aboard the Delta class, allowed the Soviets to pursue a strategy of creating SSBN sanctuaries in areas north of the Greenland-Iceland-UK gap, such as the Barents and Norwegian Seas and in the northern Pacific.

One of the major roles for the other elements of the Soviet fleet is to maintain the security of the inner defense zone as an SSBN sanctuary. This is achieved by a traditional combined arms defense employing airborne, surface and sub-surface platforms. The Soviets now had to prepare for the kind of sustained operations necessary to achieve command of a large sea area, requiring long endurance, large weapons loads, and an underway replenishment capability. These requirements were magnified as Soviet military doctrine shifted to a more flexible view of conflict, with the possibility of initial conventional combat. Further, this mission is greatly facilitated by control of the adjoining coast, strengthening the requirement for amphibious forces to seize critical choke points.

While the primary threat to Soviet SSBNs comes from NATO's fleet of nuclear powered attack submarines (SSNs), the threat posed by the ASW potential of Western carrier groups and surface forces as well as long-range ASW aircraft such as the British Nimrod could not be

Below, far left: An officer gives instruction in seamanship aboard a Soviet vessel.

Below left: A Kashin class guided missile destroyer, Nanuchka class missile patrol boat and a Kotlin class destroyer at anchor in the Mediterranean.

ignored. The Soviet Navy must therefore be prepared to complement its anti-surface and anti-carrier warfare capabilities with an effective defensive ASW capability, melded into a coordinated combined arms sea control effort. This is the new role to which much, but by no means all, of the growing surface fleet became oriented. Soviet writers, including Admiral Gorshkov, frequently refer to the supporting role that both surface ships and aircraft must play to ensure the success of submarine operations. It is one of Admiral Gorshkov's principal rationales for this burgeoning blue water surface fleet.

The Threat

While the Soviets' early entry into the SLBM arena undoubtedly also sensitized them to the threat posed by their Western counterparts, the scope of the US SSBN programs of the early sixties may have caught them by surprise. Michael MccGwire has postulated two overlapping concepts in the Soviet response, area defense and long-range interdiction. Set at 1500nm based on the range of the Polaris A-2 SLBM and centered on Moscow, the arc of threat took in the Norwegian Sea and the Eastern Mediterranean. These areas were only marginally beyond the inner defense zone established by natural geographic barriers, but in 1964 the

introduction of the Polaris A-3 with a range of 2500nm now extended the threat out into the Atlantic from beyond Greenland to the African coast abreast of the Canaries and across the Arabian Sea between the Horn of Africa and Bombay.

The likely Soviet response to the growing distance at which they would have to deal with the Western SSBN threat was to extend their outer defense zone. While attempts were put in hand to develop the means to contest the use of these areas by Western nuclear strike forces, the typical Soviet attitude of 'meanwhile get out there and do what you can with what you have' became evident. The need to go out after Western SSBNs probably accounts for much of the initial impetus for increased out-of-area operations in areas such as the Mediterranean and Indian Ocean. As the inherent difficulties and limitations of conventional ASW operations became evident and the requirements for ASW forces for securing the inner defense zone grew, this rationale for surface units forward deployed probably has been displaced by an awareness of the benefit of political presence operations and the need to support anti-carrier warfare missions, particularly with support to submarines. Some anti-SSBN mission rationale also probably remains given the Soviet principle of never allowing the enemy a free ride and making use of the not-very-good just to complicate the opposition's life.

The anti-SSBN mission continues to command considerable Soviet attention, with considerable resources reportedly being devoted to the problem. Western analysts believe that two areas of effort are the trailing of SSBNs and the development of wide-area search systems, possibly space-based may be among those being pursued. The requirement is to be able to provide immediate targeting data at the onset of a nuclear exchange. There is considerable speculation that if a space-based system was to be developed, it might be used to target SRF missiles against the SSBNs. Analysts believe that western surface forces in areas such as the Mediterranean have been targeted by SRF missiles for some time with targeting data provided by space-based and air reconnaissance as well as surface 'tattle-tails'. Similar strike missions have been postulated for Soviet SSBNs. The Soviets currently employ two types of satellites for ocean surveillance: ELINT or electronic intercept platforms that can detect and locate electronic signals from ships and radar ocean reconnaissance satellites (RORSATs) which use active radar to detect ships.

Traditions Live On

While strategic strike operations evolved to become the Soviet Navy's premier wartime mission, it has not been allowed to forget its responsibilities in the narrow seas to defend the coast and support the army. This remains a strong component of mission of sea control operations

An Osa class patrol boat equipped as a radio-controlled target.

A Komar class guided missile patrol boat. This class was the first Soviet type of missile boat. They caused a sensation in Western naval circles when an Israeli destroyer was sunk by the Styx missiles of Egyptian Komars in 1967. However, they are now regarded as having many limitations.

in the inner defense zone and in some cases beyond. Throughout the postwar period, significant numbers of gun-armed cruisers and destroyers were maintained, presumably to provide support for the army. This mission plays a major role in operations in all four fleet areas but it is of primary importance to the Baltic and Black Sea fleets. The major mission of these fleets is to control the waters of these narrow seas with airpower and light forces such as light frigates, guided missile corvettes and fast patrol boats. Amphibious forces would support the army with flanking operations and the seizure of key maritime choke points. With renewed Soviet emphasis on conventional offensive operations, it is likely that support to the ground forces will receive even greater attention.

Support to the land campaign may also extend to the outer defense zone to include interdiction operations against Atlantic lines of communication to prevent or delay the arrival of critical reinforcements. This could include submarine and air strikes against shipping as well as air strikes and mining operations against ports. While perhaps not the favorite mission of naval officers, it is likely to be a favorite of the military men who dominate the General Staff, undoubtly ensuring the allocation of what they consider adequate resources. Western analysts believe, however, that regardless of the significance attached to NATO sea communications, some anti-shipping operations will be mounted at the onset of hostilities as a means of pinning down NATO forces.

Organization, Tactics and Effectiveness

The Navy is subordinated to the Ministry of Defense, within which its Commander-in-Chief Admiral Chernavin holds the political position of Deputy Minister of Defense. The Navy is overseen by its own Main Naval Staff and a number of functional directorates such as shipbuilding and rear services as well as a Chief of Naval Aviation. The operating forces are divided among four fleets, the Northern, Baltic, Black Sea, and Pacific as well as an independent Caspian Sea flotilla. Surface ships and submarines within each fleet are grouped into squadrons and brigades. Ships will be formed into combined arms task groups for operations. Naval aviation, which uses air force rather than naval ranks, is subordinate to a Naval Aviation commander, with units within each fleet organized into specialized regiments, e.g., strike, reconnaissance, ASW, of 28 to 30 aircraft. Each regiment consists of three squadrons, and there may also be independent squadrons.

The central tenet of Soviet naval operations, as indeed of all Soviet military operations, is strong centralized command and control. This is required to implement successfully a combined arms strategy with a large number of dissimilar high speed units, including the use of missiles and offboard sensors for targeting. The fundamentally defensive orientation of Soviet missions imposes the requirement for: reconnaissance and surveillance, command and control to bring superior forces to bear, and a sufficient mass of forces to ensure effective strikes. Also a

A merchant ship with two Turya class hydrofoil patrol craft carried on deck. A few of this type of attack and anti-submarine craft have been transferred to Cuba.

Below: An Echo II cruise missile submarine. Twenty-nine of this class were built during the 1960s. A number have had their original of SS-N-3 missiles replaced by longer-range SS-N-12s.

Center: A Victor class nuclear powered attack submarine. Production of the latest Victor III variant is continuing.

key element in Soviet tactics is surprise. The combination of centrally collected intelligence and centrally controlled attack forces of all types continues as the basis of Soviet Naval practice according to Western naval analysts, although a trend toward increased authority for the on-site commander has been noted. Surface strike operations normally involve attacks delivered simultaneously, often along several different axes to overwhelm target defenses. Weapons are launched at maximum range. High speed for concentration in response to new command requirements also becomes a desirable quality.

Contemporary Soviet ASW tactics, at least for defensive and barrier penetration operations, developed along similar lines, as Western analysts such as Norman Polmar and Norman Friedman have noted. In search and attack operations, all ships in a defending area would be linked to shorebased computer centers which coordinate operations. These computers were eventually put to sea onboard the current generation of large ASW ships which are designed to assume ASW group command functions. Aircraft and nuclear attack submarines are an integrated part of the team as are conventional attack boats when barrier operations are called for. Much less is known about Soviet offensive ASW tactics for combating Western SSBNs.

Current Soviet forces could prove very effective in targeting and striking any Western surface forces attempting to penetrate their inner defense zone. Soviet ASW capabilities continue to lag, however, and their effectiveness against Western SSNs and SSBNs is questionable. The key to an effective ASW capability is a truly effective wide area search system which most Western analysts believe the Soviets currently lack. Current limited Soviet ASW capabilities represent evidence of commitment to a problem which is unlikely to lapse but rather be marked by marginal, incremental advances which may or may not keep pace with Western technological improvements. A breakthrough in submarine detection technology would not, however, be sufficient. That development would have to be integrated into an effective ASW system with new equipment and operating and training patterns, not an easy or rapid course.

Submarines

The submarine force has always been the dominant branch in the Soviet Navy. The advent of

nuclear power and submarine-launched ballistic missiles has served to further the primacy of the submarine arm. Western naval analysts believe that despite his adherence to the concept of a balanced fleet, Gorshkov exhibited a distinct bias for submarines – especially ballistic missile submarines – as the Navy's most effective weapons. Throughout his writings, he gave submarines the highest praise of any units in the Soviet Navy.

Research on a submarine nuclear power plant began in the late 1940s. The first Soviet nuclear submarine was the 360-foot, 4200-ton November class attack submarine, the first of which was completed in 1958. The Novembers, of which 14 were built between 1958 and 1962, were noisy and generally a poor design but they put nuclear power to sea. The Novembers were probably intended as general-purpose torpedo-attack submarines. Michael MccGwire suggests, however, that they may have been one of the Soviet Union's first strategic delivery systems, intended to fire nuclear-tipped torpedoes into US ports.

Above: A Ka-25 helicopter in flight near a Foxtrot class submarine.

Left: A Juliett class diesel-electric cruise missile submarine. For firing the launch tubes for the SS-N-3 missiles must be elevated from their normal position flush with the casing. As in the Echo class firing must be done while the boat is surfaced.

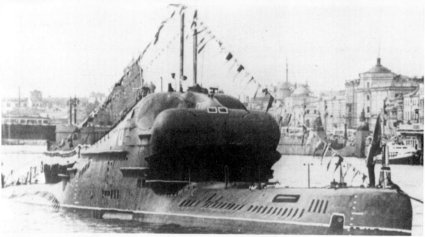

Top: The Golf II diesel powered submarines carry three SS-N-5 missiles. They are also armed with ten torpedo tubes.

Above: A Whiskey Long Bin cruise missile submarine. A small number of these converted boats remain in service, probably for training purposes.

Ballistic Missile Submarines

The period of the late 1940s and the entire decade of the 1950s was marked by massive Soviet programs to combine the fruits of the Revolution in Military Affairs – nuclear weapons and guided missiles – into effective delivery systems. This was felt in the naval arena in the combination of ballistic and cruise missile delivery systems with the nuclear submarine to produce the immediate ancestors of the core of the modern Soviet Navy. The Soviets launched their first ballistic missile submarine, the first of six Zulu class submarines modified to carry two SS-N-4 surface launched ballistic missiles with a range of 350nm in 1955, two years before the first US SSBN began construction. In 1958 came the first of 22 Golf class conventional submarines with three SS-N-4 missile tubes in an enlarged sail. Also in 1958 came the first Soviet SSBN, the 6000-ton Hotel class also with three sail-mounted SS-N-4s and a hull and propulsion plant similar to the November. In common with other first generation Soviet nuclear submarines, the Hotels were noisy and unreliable as was their surface launch missile system. Only eight Hotels would be built, reflecting the 1959-60 decision to vest the strategic, in particular the intercontinental, strike role in the SRF at the expense of the Navy.

The Khrushchev policy which denied the Navy a strategic strike role was short-lived however, because, of all the problems which faced the Soviets in 1961, the simplest was to provide sea-based strategic forces. The Soviets were committed to achieving a production rate of 10 nuclear submarines per year with deliveries to start in 1967-68. It was therefore possible to provide six ballistic missile submarines annually for the next decade although this change did cause disruption in the shipyards as the new classes of SSBNs were considerably larger than the attack submarines they displaced. In the interim, plans were set in hand to modernize the recently completed Hotel and Golf classes. Between 1963 and 1967, the Hotel class was modified to carry the SS-N-5, a submerged launch SLBM with a range of 700 miles. After the conversion of the Hotels, half of the conventionally powered Golf class was similarly modified, being christened the Golf II.

The limited range of the SS-N-5 and the limited payload and reliability of the Hotel and Golf boats and their small numbers meant the Navy's contribution to the strategic strike mission was limited. But a clear commitment to put

more strategic weapons to sea was evident. In late 1967, the capabilities of the SSBN force were significantly enhanced with the entry into service of the first of the Yankee class. An 8000-ton submarine with 16 missile tubes, the Yankees were initially armed with the liquid fueled SS-N-6 Mod 1 SLBM with a range of 1300nm and a single warhead in the megaton range. The Mod 1 was progressively replaced by the Mod 2 with a 1600nm range and subsequently the Mod 3 with a two to three warhead arrangement. Beginning in 1969, Yankees took patrol stations in the Atlantic near the US Coast, providing target coverage as far west as the Mississippi River. Increased numbers allowed the establishment of a Pacific patrol in about 1971, extending coverage from the California coast to the Rocky Mountains. A total of 34 Yankee class submarines was built between 1967 and 1977.

In 1973, the first of the Delta series appeared, equipped with long-range SLBMs which allowed them to strike US targets from the sanctuary of home waters. A total of 18 Delta Is entered service between 1973 and 1977, complemented by four Delta II SSBNs with four additional SS-N-8 launch tubes in a lengthened hull. In 1975, the first two boats of the even more powerful Delta III class entered service, armed with 16 SS-N-18 SLBMs, reportedly an improved version of the SS-N-8.

Cruise Missile Submarines

By 1954, test firings of a cruise missile with a range of 150 nautical miles were being carried out and by 1958, the 220nm range SS-N-3 surface launched cruise missile with either a nuclear or conventional warhead was being fitted in a pair of cylindrical launchers on six Whiskey class submarines, primarily for at-sea testing. A more efficient conversion put four SS-N-3 launchers in a remodeled fin on a lengthened Whiskey hull to produce the seven ships of the Whiskey Long Bin class beginning in 1960. The November/Hotel generation of nuclear submarines was completed by the Echo nuclear-powered cruise missile submarine (SSGN)

Above: A Charlie class cruise missile submarine under way in the South China Sea.

Top: Delta I class boats carry the 4800 nautical mile range SS-N-8 ballistic missiles.

Left: Whiskey class submarines were built in the years after World War II and their design made use of German submarine research. Despite their age some remain in service. The example shown here is one of four converted around 1960 to serve as radar pickets.

Below: A Delta III nuclear powered ballistic missile submarine seen in 1981.

Above: Artist's impression of the massive Typhoon class missile submarine. The first of these 25,000 ton boats was launched in 1980 from the Severodvinsk Shipyard on the White Sea.

Right: An Alfa class nuclear powered attack submarine. The Alfa class are believed to be the fastest and deepest diving submarines in service with any navy. Their pressure hulls are constructed of titanium which contributes to their deep diving performance.

range. The primary mission of Soviet first generation SSGs and SSGNs was undoubtedly anti-surface ship warfare but the systems may also have had a secondary shore strike capability similar to their US counterparts with the Regulus cruise missile system.

In 1968, the Charlie class SSGN entered service, forming with the Yankee class SSBN and the Victor SSN the third generation of Soviet nuclear submarines. In addition to its torpedo tubes, the Charlie I carried eight launch tubes for the submerged-launch SS-N-7 cruise missile which had a range of 35 miles. The short range for the SS-N-7 removed the need for mid-course guidance and Western experts assume an autonomous control system exists for these missiles. The undersea launch capability of the Charlie I's missile armament made it a much more effective member of the combined arms anti-surface team.

There is also some evidence of the Soviet desire to use SSBNs in a tactical role against carriers and potentially submarines. The SS-N-13 SLBM had a range of 300nm and mid-course and terminal guidance. As with most long-range tactical missile systems in the Soviet inventory, initial targeting data and guidance would have to be provided by some other platform, since the Yankees, the platform which most Western analysts associated with the system, probably lack on-board sensors of sufficient range. The SS-N-13 was reportedly cancelled in

Soviet submarines in an Arctic base. The vessel nearest the camera is probably a Foxtrot class diesel-electric attack submarine.

equipped with the SS-N-3 beginning in 1960 with the Echo I. The five Echo I SSGNs were each armed with six SS-N-3s but lacked the guidance radars for the system which were included in the 29 Echo II SSGNs, which had eight SS-N-3 launchers as well, entering service from 1963. The Echo Is may have been stopgaps assembled from redundant Hotel class components when that program was cut short. The Echo program also had a conventional parallel in the 16 Juliett SSGs with four SS-N-3s, built between 1962 and 1967. The SS-N-3 has an effective range well in excess of the ability of submarine based sensors to provide the required mid-course targeting guidance, an example of the Soviet willingness to make use of a second platform to target a weapon while the launching platform remains out of retaliation

Crew members stand to attention as a submarine sets out on patrol from an icy northern port.

the early 1970s probably due to technical difficulties and Soviet unwillingness to reallocate SLBM launchers, constrained by SALT, away from strategic strikes.

Attack Submarines

The Soviet Navy did not immediately follow-up on the November class. Following a hiatus, the submarine arm of the coordinated ASW team was significantly enhanced by the introduction of the Victor SSN series. The 4300-ton Victor I, with eight 553mm torpedo tubes and 30+ knot speed, was succeeded in 1972 by the slightly larger Victor II class. A total of 23 Victor I and IIs are currently in service.

While embracing nuclear power, the Soviets have not neglected conventional diesel-electric designs. In 1958, the Soviets also completed the first of 67 Foxtrot submarines, a follow-on to the Zulu class, as a long-range conventional attack boat. While only 60 of the Foxtrots were completed for the Soviet Navy over a 10 year period, the size of the program reflected continuing Soviet interest in the type. As Arthur Bakes has

noted, the conventionally powered counterparts to Soviet nuclear-powered attack, cruise missile and ballistic missile submarines might be thought of as 'second-rate' designs in the traditional Soviet fashion, not so much as programs to flesh out force levels due to resource constraints but rather conscious designs to produce a lesser ship for less demanding, specialized missions such as barrier operations. At the same time resource constraints undoubtedly did play a role, the construction of nuclear submarines being enormously more expensive especially in terms of scarce resources such as skilled labor. An easily fabricated boat, a Foxtrot can be built in a floating drydock in about 90 days using relatively unskilled labor. The Foxtrot was followed by the four ships of the Bravo class which were configured to serve as 'hard' ASW torpedo targets for training other fleet units. Other unique specialized submarines include the two India class which carried two small salvage/submarine-rescue submersibles in wells on the after casing. Several older conventional attack submarines have reportedly been converted to serve in the oceanographic research role.

Soviet Submarines Today

A total of eight classes of submarines are currently in series production in the Soviet Union. The construction of SSBNs has tailed-off as the Strategic Arms Limitation Talks (SALT) ceiling of 62 modern SSBNs was reached and the transition was made to the gigantic 25,000 ton Typhoon class armed with the 4000nm range MIRVed SS-N-20. There is no clear reason why the Typhoon, which became operational in the mid-1980s, is so huge. The US *Ohio* class carries 24 missiles on a hull with a displacement two thirds that of Typhoon. The Soviets are also continuing production of the Delta III SSBN armed with 16 SS-N-18 missiles. A total of 14 have been built to date.

Four classes of general purpose nuclear submarines are currently in series production. The Victor III SSN and the Charlie II are lengthened and improved versions of submarines introduced in 1968. The Victor III is a 6000-ton long-range, high speed (29 knot) ASW platform probably armed with the 20nm range SS-N-15 nuclear tipped ASW missile (similar to the US SUBROC) or the SS-N-16 armed with a homing torpedo, both fired from standard torpedo tubes. The Charlie II is armed with the improved submerged launch SS-N-9 cruise missile with a conventional or nuclear warhead. Twenty-two Victor IIIs have been built since 1978 while only six Charlie IIs have been built since 1973.

The two remaining types are unique and interesting boats which have caused considerable comment. The 3700-ton Alfa class SSN has undergone a considerable development period with the prototype being completed in 1972 and subsequently scrapped. Probably intended as a fast, highly automated ASW platform, the Alfa

Nuclear Ballistic Missile Submarines and Missiles

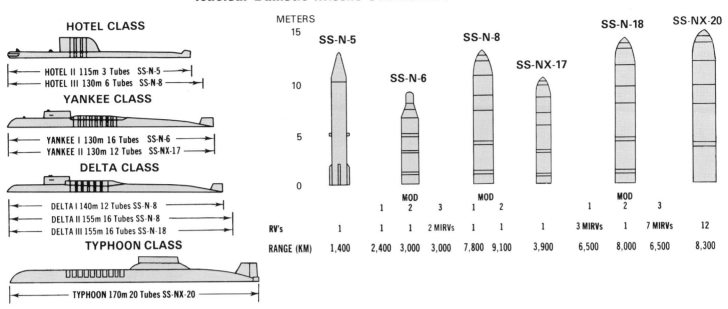

HOTEL CLASS

HOTEL II 115m 3 Tubes SS-N-5
HOTEL III 130m 6 Tubes SS-N-8

YANKEE CLASS

YANKEE I 130m 16 Tubes SS-N-6
YANKEE II 130m 12 Tubes SS-NX-17

DELTA CLASS

DELTA I 140m 12 Tubes SS-N-8
DELTA II 155m 16 Tubes SS-N-8
DELTA III 155m 16 Tubes SS-N-18

TYPHOON CLASS

TYPHOON 170m 20 Tubes SS-NX-20

	SS-N-5	SS-N-6			SS-N-8		SS-NX-17	SS-N-18			SS-NX-20
MOD			2	3		2			2	3	
		1			1		1	1			
RV's	1	1	1	2 MIRVs	1	1	1	3 MIRVs	1	7 MIRVs	12
RANGE (KM)	1,400	2,400	3,000	3,000	7,800	9,100	3,900	6,500	8,000	6,500	8,300

may have been designed with SSBN trailing operations in mind or with the intent of combining it with some offboard area search system, the boat's high speed allowing it to respond rapidly to contacts. The Alfa's 40 knot underwater speed reflects a drag-reduction hull form and possibly a new compact high technology powerplant and allows it to outrun as well as out dive (up to 2000 feet due to its titanium hull) any quarry or pursuer, except possibly the latest American torpedoes. The difficulty of working with titanium may also be a significant factor in this submarines's slow production rate of about one a year since 1979.

The likely successor to the Charlie II class SSGN is the huge 13,000-ton Oscar class armed with 24,300nm range submerged launch SS-N-

19 cruise missiles, as well as torpedoes. The first Oscar was launched in 1980. The size of the Oscar and its heavy weapons load – three times the number of missile launch tubes found on the Echo II or the Charlie II – may represent a response to the increased ordnance requirements of a more flexible warfighting doctrine which allows for the possibility of a period of conventional combat but still requires constant readiness for nuclear combat. The range of the SS-N-19 suggests the possibility that the Oscar is intended to replace the aged Echo IIs.

Finally, the Soviet Union continues to produce conventional attack submarines for use in barrier and closed sea operations in areas such as the Baltic. The 3200-ton Kilo class may be intended as a medium-range replacement for

The aircraft carrier *Kiev* seen in the Mediterranean in 1976. As well as aircraft and helicopters the *Kiev* carries a comprehensive armament of surface-to-surface and surface-to-air missiles.

Main picture: A Kamov Ka-25 helicopter silhouetted against the setting sun. The principal versions in service are the Hormone-A, which mainly carries anti-submarine equipment, and the Hormone-B, which provides mid-course guidance for surface-to-surface missiles like the SS-N-3 and SS-N-12.

Below: The helicopter cruiser *Moskva* under way in 1982. The *Moskva* and her sister ship *Leningrad* usually operate 18 Ka-25 helicopters.

along the US coast, flying from Cuban bases. Variants of the Tu-16 Badger, about 100 planes are the medium-range component of the SNA sea surveillance force.

The SNA strike responsibility initially rested on a large force of Tu-16 medium bombers dating from the 1950s. Some of these aircraft were converted to carry the Kipper air-to-surface missiles (ASM) (Badger-C) or later two Kelt or Kingfisher ASMs (Badger-G). The Tu-16 was complemented in the early 1960s by the Tu-22 Blinder, a supersonic medium bomber which was originally intended to displace the Tu-16 but whose performance proved disappointing. Only a small number of freefall bombers entered service with the SNA. In 1974, the Tu-22M Backfire entered service with SNA, providing the service with a modern supersonic, long-

Above: Yak-36 Forgers parked on the flight deck of the carrier Minsk, a picture taken in the western Pacific late in 1982. The Forger is believed to be a less capable aircraft than its nearest Western equivalent the British Harrier. Unlike the Harrier the Forger can only operate in the vertical take-off mode which restricts range/payload when compared to the short take-off run normally used by the Harrier.

Right: Admiral of the Fleet of the Soviet Union and Deputy Minister of Defense Sergei Georgiyevich Gorshkov, the father of the modern Soviet Navy.

the Whiskey class of which some 60 remain. The Tango class of 3700-ton long-range patrol submarines has been in production since 1972.

The general purpose submarine force has also been reinforced by several interesting conversions and modifications. As new Delta class SSBNs have been launched, Yankee class boats have had their missile tubes disabled and may be converting to SSNs in order to comply with the SALT ceiling of 950 SLBM launchers. In the late 1970s three Golf class SSBs had their missile tubes removed and advanced communications gear installed to become submersible command ships.

Soviet Naval Aviation

Second only to the submarine force in Soviet naval strategy, Soviet Naval Aviation (SNA) has continued to grow and modernize. Remaining primarily a landbased force, it has continued to make use of modified medium and heavy bomber aircraft for its twin major missions of sea surveillance and reconnaissance and ASW and ASUW strike operations. SNA maritime reconnaissance is a critical component of the Soviet ocean surveillance system. The primary Soviet long-range reconnaissance aircraft are the Tu-95 Bear-C/D/E variants of the Tu-95 strategic bomber with a range of almost 9000nm in the reconnaissance role. The Bear-D, of which approximately 50 remain in service according to Western sources, also fulfills anti-shipping missile control missions with the aid of the 'Puff Ball' radar housed in a large ventral dome. The radar displays the target location and the missile launch point, the presentation being data-linked to the launcher. These aircraft often undertake ferret missions

range air-to-surface missile (ASM) carrier armed with one or two AS-4 or AS-6 ASMs. The parallel introduction of the Backfire into SNA and LRA is interesting as in the past, priority was usually given to LRA.

The Soviet Navy also deployed large shorebased airborne ASW forces. The Il-38 May is a turboprop medium-range maritime reconnaissance and ASW aircraft adapted from the Il-18. The aircraft's systems include radar, MAD, expendable sonobuoys and an internal weapons bay. The 50 Mays in service are complemented by about 100 twin-engine Be-12 Mail amphibians with a maximum range of 2000nm. Long-range airborne ASW is performed by the Tu-95 Bear-F which first appeared in 1973 and is a sophisticated ASW variant of the earlier bomber. The F variant was probably developed to give the navy a plane with the range to reach the Polaris operating areas. A large force of landbased helicopters has also been deployed in the ASW role since the late 1950s. The most modern part of this force is the Haze, an ASW variant of the Mi-8 Hip transport helicopter.

Seabased Aviation

As the ranges at which Soviet naval forces would be required to operate and the requirements of protracted combat grew, so did the requirement for seabased aviation.

The Soviet Navy's entry into the field of seabased aviation began in earnest with the laying down of the first of what may have been a planned total of twelve *Moskva* class helicopter carriers. Many Western analysts believe they were intended to extend the area of operations for shorebased ASW helicopters, in the form of 14 to 18 Hormone-As, a twin turbine helicopter with a unique super-imposed co-axial rotor which entered service in the mid-1960s as the Navy's standard all-weather search and attack ASW helicopter. The *Moskva* also had a capability for self-defense with two twin rail launchers for the long-range SA-N-3 surface-to-air missile (SAM) as well as a twin rail launcher for the SUW-N-1 a nuclear tipped ASW weapon developed from the Army's FROG unguided artillery rocket. Western experts believe both ships handle well in heavy weather and are capable of helicopter operations under adverse conditions. But the Mediterranean has been the major operating area of these ships, suggesting they may not be up to the rigors of service in the Northern seas. The first and name ship of the class entered service in 1967.

It was likely that the design decision on the *Kiev* class of light aircraft carriers – Tactical Aircraft-Cruiser (TKA) in Soviet terminology – was taken in the mid-1960s with the first and name ship of the class being delivered in the mid-1970s. The *Kiev* marks a new milestone for Soviet naval aviation with its air wing of 23 Hormone-A/B helicopters and 12 Yak-36 VTOL fighters. The Yak-36 Forger is the SNA's first seabased tactical fighter, with a maximum speed of 800mph and a range of 150 miles. The Forger is limited to clear weather delivery of the 2200 lbs of gun pods, rockets and air-to-air missiles it can carry. The Forger is clearly a limited system, probably representing another example of the Soviet willingness to deploy a 10 percent solution while further development of a better answer goes on. In addition to its aircraft the *Kiev* class also carries a comprehensive cruiser type armament, all on a rakish 36,000 ton hull with four gas turbines and a top speed of 32 knots.

An Il-38 May maritime patrol aircraft drops a sonobuoy while being shadowed by a Corsair from the carrier USS *Midway*. Soviet sonar equipment is believed to be less advanced than that in service in western navies.

Naval Aviation in the 1980s

The real story of the 1980s for Soviet Naval Aviation has yet to fully develop – the reported construction of a 50,000 to 60,000 ton nuclear aircraft carrier equipped with catapults and arresting gear to operate conventional fixed-wing aircraft. Some Western analysts believe construction may have already begun and delivery may be expected late in the 1980s. Some analysts see either a modified Flogger-D or a new fighter as leading candidates for employment on the ship. The appearance of a traditional aircraft carrier would mark a departure in modern Soviet naval planning, especially given the frequent criticism levelled at the aircraft carrier by Soviet naval theorists. But much of this criticism has been reversed in the past few years as Admiral Gorshkov and his associates have come to see a role for such a platform in their naval doctrine. The primary role of such a platform would probably be to improve the air defense capability of Soviet forces operating in traditional roles such as SSBN screening and support of the ground forces. This will include the ability to interdict Western airborne ASW systems as well as increase the number of Soviet airborne ASW assets at sea. Admiral Gorshkov and his political superiors are also probably not averse to the benefits of such a platform in the peacetime presence role.

The Surface Fleet

The Soviet Union today maintains the world's largest fleet of major surface combatants to provide what Admiral Gorshkov has referred to as 'combat stability' for his primary fighting

Main picture: The forward superstructure of the helicopter carrier *Moskva* showing the two twin launchers for the SA-N-3 missiles with one of the two controlling radars farther aft.

Bottom left: The *Moskva* with a US Navy Neptune patrol aircraft in the foreground. Although both pictures on this page show the pennant number 857 this is misleading since the pennant numbers on Soviet ships are changed from time to time.

Above: Kara class guided missile cruisers are powered by gas turbine engines which give a maximum speed of 33-34 knots. The first of the class to be seen publicly by Western observers was the *Nikolayev* which entered the Mediterranean from the Black Sea in March 1973.

forces. Anti-submarine and anti-surface warfare ships are integrated supporting components of the combined arms teams which secure the inner defense zone and hunt western nuclear strike platforms. In addition to being necessary elements of a 'balanced fleet', surface ships are the best suited for peacetime showing the flag operations in support of state interests. In addition to major surface combatants, the Soviet Navy operates more small combatants – missile, torpedo and patrol boats as well as minesweepers – than the remainder of the world's navies combined. It is these forces which are critical to controlling the narrow seas and supporting the Army.

Soviet surface forces are a mixture of new construction reflecting the doctrine in the most recent period, modernized ships reflecting an attempt to modify existing platforms to meet new missions and threats, often as a stopgap and older ships made obsolescent by age or by the march of doctrine and technology. The rapid evolution of technology and doctrine, combined with a gestation period of up to almost a decade from concept to commissioning, often results in a ship design for a mission or threat which no longer exists and which is then assigned new missions for which it may or may not be equipped simply because it is a 'hull in being'.

Khrushchev's interpretation of the Revolution in Military Affairs almost spelled the end of large surface ships in the Soviet Navy. Khrushchev saw Stalin's large building program as the ideal place for budget cuts. He viewed large surface ships as rendered obsolete by missiles and nuclear weapons and heaped scorn on them as useful only for carrying admirals on state visits – a role apparently not then accorded the priority it is now. To implement his new view of naval power, Khrushchev fired the current navy commander and replaced him with Sergei Gorshkov. While the immediate large scale reduction in shipbuilding was in part related to resource cuts, it must also be remembered that in his new role, Gorshkov faced one major problem: the surface ships extant in the mid-1950s were not of the type which could present a viable counter to Western carriers. In the absence of air superiority capability, it was simply impossible for the Soviet Navy to challenge Western carriers. But it was conceivable that missile technology could provide 'transient air super-

iority' in the form of cruise missiles for strike missions and SAMs for self-defense. But the missiles had to be developed and put to sea.

The rapid deployment of cruise missiles and SAMs at sea is an example of the ability of Soviet designers rapidly to adapt existing platforms as a means for 'getting something out there'. By 1958, the SS-N-1 cruise missile, reportedly an army missile adapted for naval use, was at sea on board the Kildin class, a conversion of the conventional Kotlin design. These were followed by the 4600 ton Krupny class, also probably a conversion of a conventional gun destroyer design, of which a total of eight were built with the first appearing in 1959. The Krupnys carry two cumbersome hanger/launchers for the SS-N-1, each with a total of six missiles. The missile had a range of 150 miles

and required mid-course guidance. The ships were limited by their radars and their lack of any long-range air defense.

Meanwhile, work began on two new classes of large surface ships designed for anti-carrier warfare. The first of these were the Kynda class guided missile light cruisers which entered service from 1962 to 1965. The Kynda, the first of which Khrushchev described as a 'floating coffin' at her commissioning, is a heavily armed but apparently short-legged ship with the SS-N-3 long-range cruise missiles in two trainable quadruple launchers as well as eight reloads. It also carried one twin rail launcher for the Soviet Navy's first SAM, the SA-N-1, an adaptation of the landbased SA-3 Goa medium-range SAM. While the Kynda lacked a helicopter to provide mid-course guidance for its SS-N-3, that could

Above: The Kresta II class cruiser *Marshal Voroshilov* seen in 1979. All ten of this class were built in the Zhdanov Shipyard in Leningrad.

Top: A *Sovremennyy* class guided missile destroyer. The name ship of this class began trials in the summer of 1980 and entered full operational service about twelve months later.

Left: Eight SAM Kotlin
class destroyers were built.
These ships have a missile
launcher fitted in place of
the aft gun turret that other
Kotlins carry.

Below left: A Kashin class destroyer in Pacific waters in 1973. A number of ships of this class were refitted during the 1970s with improved equipment including a variable-depth sonar installation.

Main picture, below: Some 72 Skory class destroyers were built in the early 1950s. Their main armament was four 130mm guns. A very few remain in service.

Bottom: Sailors relax on the fantail of a Riga class destroyer escort. As well as their guns, this class carry antisubmarine torpedoes and rocket launchers. Built in the 1950s, many have been transferred to Soviet allies.

be provided by a variety of other platforms in the strike group. While designed to operate within range of landbased aircover, the Kynda's air defense capability would be complemented by a specialized SAM destroyer, the Kashin.

The Kashin is a rakish 4000 ton ship with the distinction of being the first class of warships in the world to rely entirely on gas turbines for propulsion. Western analysts believe the initial intended mission of the Kashin was to provide defense for the Kyndas against possible air strikes from Western carriers. To this end they were armed with two twin-rail SA-N-1 launchers and two rapid-fire twin 76mm gun mounts as well as short-range ASW weapons for self defense. In point of fact the Kashins, of which approximately 20 were built between 1963 and 1972, proved a handy general purpose design, despite the loss of one ship of the class to an internal explosion which claimed the lives of nearly 300 of her company.

Even before the Kyndas were completed, it was clear that the next generation of Western carrier-based aircraft would have substantially longer range, forcing the Soviet combined arms strike groups to venture further afield, perhaps beyond landbased fighter cover. The response was in part to develop a follow-on design better suited for distant operations. This took the form of the Kresta I program, the first of which was begun in 1964. The 7500 ton Kresta I shipped two twin SA-N-1 launchers and a Hormone-B helicopter to provide guidance for its four SS-N-3 cruise missiles. The loss of four cruise missile launchers and all reload capability was probably an acceptable tradeoff given the nature of Soviet warfighting doctrine. But the entire role of surface ships was being rethought in the early 1960s. The Kynda program was terminated after only four units (some Western analysts also attribute this to design faults, including instability). Its successor the Kresta I was also held to only four units.

In 1966, an ASW version of the Kresta class was laid down, emerging in 1969 as the 6000 ton Kresta II class large ASW ship (BPK). In the latter half of the 1960s, the Soviets introduced a new nomenclature which added to the tradition-

Far right: Detail of the superstructure of a Kresta II class cruiser. Among the equipment shown is (top) the aerial for the Top Sail air search radar.

Near right: Silhouettes and displacements of the newest Soviet warships.

Major Surface Ships

KIEV

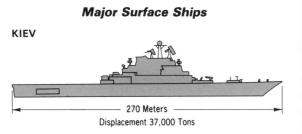

270 Meters
Displacement 37,000 Tons

KIROV

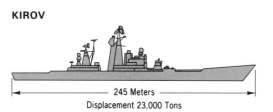

245 Meters
Displacement 23,000 Tons

MOSKVA

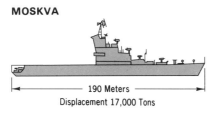

190 Meters
Displacement 17,000 Tons

UDALOY

160 Meters
Displacement 8,000 Tons

SOVREMENNYY

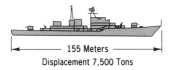

155 Meters
Displacement 7,500 Tons

al categories the terms ASW cruiser, large ASW ship and small ASW ship, assigning the bulk of their new construction and modernization programs as well as existing types such as the Kashin to this category. The Kresta Is were even subsequently redesigned as BPKs, reflecting the new strategic role of the surface fleet: anti-submarine warfare.

The main armament of the Kresta II ASW ships is the SS-N-14, a winged missile with an ASW homing torpedo payload. A total of eight

are carried in two large launchers. In addition the ship carries a Hormone-A helicopter. Two twin SA-N-3 SAM launchers and assorted automatic weapons provide air defense. A total of 10 Kresta IIs entered service between 1970 and 1978. The Kresta II was paralleled by the Kara class the first of which was laid down in 1969. The Karas, handsome rakish vessels of 8000 tons, have been described as 'Kresta IIs tailored to fight where the threat to their existence, particularly from the air, is higher but where the need for endurance is less'. To basic Kresta II armament was added heavier AA gun armament and two twin-rail SA-N-4 point-defense SAM systems. The new blue-water ASW fleet is rounded out by the handsome 3000 ton Krivak class frigate, incorporating ASW systems such as the SS-N-14 with self-defense capability in the form of two SA-N-4 launchers and gun systems in a hull designed both for speed and good seakeeping.

Older, obsolescent platforms were also made to play their part. The Kashin was redesignated an ASW ship and, according to Michael McGwire, its production extended by five units. Eight units of the Krupny class were modernized with ASW and SAM systems comparable to the Kashin from the cancelled Kresta I program. SA-N-1 systems from the cancelled units of the Kynda class were used to improve fleet air defense in eight SAM Kotlin conversions. In the early 1970s the first ship of a Kashin modernization program appeared with improved ASW capability in the form of a variable depth sonar and helicopter handling facilities and a limited anti-surface capability with four SS-N-2C cruise missiles.

The Surface Fleet in the 1980s
A total of seven classes of major surface combatants are currently under construction in the Soviet Union. The *Kiev* class carrier, the Krivak and Grisha class frigates have been in production since the early 1970s. But two new cruiser classes and two new destroyer classes embody the new generation of Soviet surface combatants. In general they represent the Navy's commitment to heavily armed high endurance

A Krivak class frigate takes on fuel from a tanker. Later Krivak class ships have the twin 76mm guns replaced by single 100mm mountings.

ocean-going combatants to meet peacetime and wartime requirements for distant operations as well as the variety of high intensity combat operations envisaged in a more flexible war-fighting doctrine. In the early 1970s Soviet warships tended to mount more launchers than their US counterparts but to carry less ammunition, suggesting conformity with a doctrine for a preemptive first strike in a short intense conflict. More recent figures, however do not justify continuation of that assumption. The movement of some command and control functions to sea may also account for size growth. In general US Navy studies have shown that Soviet sur-

face combatants are well armed and fully fitted-out with sensors. One of the interesting facets of Soviet weapon and sensor suites is the practice of providing each ship with redundant and complementary single task weapon and electronic systems, such as radars, to perform each individual mission. The Soviets also provide alternative modes for operating equipment such as local control for gun mounts. For example, the 30mm Gatling gun system installed on many Soviet combatants for cruise missile defense has both a radar and manual control as well as a possible electro-optical backup in contrast to its US counterpart which has only a

single automated firing mode.

The premier ship of the new generation of Soviet warships is the 23,000 ton *Kirov* class battlecruiser, the first of which entered service in 1980. The nuclear-powered *Kirov* has been pronounced by Western analysts as the most impressively armed surface warship in the world with a capable combat system which provides an in-depth capability for all modes of warfare. These include the reloadable SS-N-14 ASW missile launcher, a first for a Soviet ship; vertical launch silos with a total of 96 SA-N-6 SAMs complemented by two SA-N-4 point-defense systems; 20 launch tubes for SS-N-19

cruise missiles and assorted gun systems. Targeting information for the SS-N-19 can be provided by the three Ka-25 Hormone helicopters or via satellite communications systems. The ship's extensive electronics suite probably includes elaborate command and control systems. While the ships are capable of extended independent operations, they are more likely to function as the core of Northern and Pacific fleet combat groups providing support to smaller units as well as a centralized, survivable command and control center. The second cruiser design under construction is a little known 10,000 ton ship, apparently oriented toward air defense

Above: A fine view of the Krivak class ship *Bodry* taken in the English Channel in 1968. The large box on the foredeck is the quad SS-N-14 launcher while the two light colored areas are the tops of retractable SA-N-4 surface-to-air missile launchers.

and surface strike with the SS-N-12 SSM and the SA-N-6 as well as ASW with the SS-N-14. Three are reportedly under construction in the Black Sea.

While the design of the new cruisers suggests a trend away from specialized ASW platforms to general purpose ships, the opposite is the case with destroyer programs. The *Sovremennyy* is a 7600 ton gas turbine powered ship oriented toward surface strike operations with eight SSM launchers in two quad mounts and provision for a Hormone-B helicopter for targeting. The ship is also armed with two single rail SA-N-7 SAM launchers. It further has two twin 130mm gun mounts of a new fully automatic, water-cooled model, the largest caliber gun mounted on a Soviet warship since the late 1950s. The 130mm mounts probably represent the intention to maintain a gunfire support capability for amphibious landings and other army-support operations. The overall ship design is reportedly derived from the Kresta I and II series built at the same yard and uses the same hull form and propulsion. Construction of a large surface-strike oriented platform, the first since the Kresta Is in the late 1960s, is probably a form of response to the threat posed by the growing number of western cruise missile equipped ships. The advent of systems such as Harpoon and Tomahawk may bring renewed attention to such operations.

The ASW counterpart to the *Sovremennyy* is the *Udaloy*, a 6700 ton destroyer armed with two SS-N-14 quad mounts and two Helix-A ASW helicopters. The ship's armament is rounded out by two 100mm guns and provision for an as yet unidentified point-defense SAM. The *Udaloy* is built on the ways formerly allocated to the Kresta II and is probably intended as a successor to that platform.

Amphibious Forces
The Soviet Union maintains a modest force of 93 amphibious ships, including one *Ivan Rogov* landing ship dock (LPD) which is capable of transporting a battalion of naval infantry, helicopters, amphibious armored personnel carriers and air cushion vehicles. The balance of the

Opposite: The Soviet Navy is one of the largest users of hovercraft in the world. There are three classes in service: Gus, Lebed and Aist.

Main picture: Soviet Marines dismount from a Gus class air cushion vehicle.

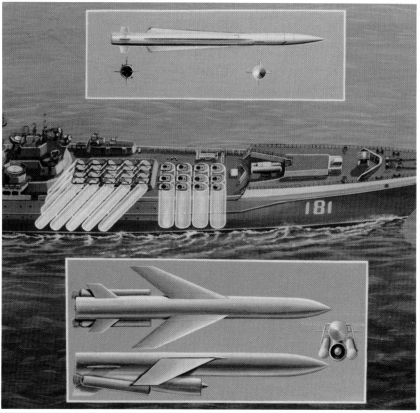

ocean-going amphibious fleet includes approximately 30 LSTs and as many as 45 smaller medium landing ships. This is something less than an impressive capability when divided among four fleet areas.

Amphibious ship construction for the Soviet navy reportedly is nil with only the protracted completion of the second ship of the *Rogov* class

Top: Artist's impression of the nuclear-powered *Kirov*. Apart from aircraft carriers the *Kirov* is the largest surface warship to be launched since the battleships of World War II.

Left: Detail of the forward parts of *Kirov* showing the oblique launch tubes for SS-N-19 and the vertical tubes for SA-N-6. Forward of these is the twin SS-N-14 equipment.

currently underway. Amphibious lift can of course be provided by the Soviet merchant fleet. There are many modern advanced design merchant ships uniquely suited for amphibious operations including over 40 roll-on/roll-off (RO/RO) vehicle carriers with large stern access ramps which can supposedly be extended through the use of pontoon bridges, as well as five self-sustaining barge carriers of two distinct designs. Soviet amphibious forces do make use of a large number of air cushion assault craft such as the 200 ton Aist class which are ideal for short-range operations in narrow seas such as the Baltic.

The amphibious assault forces available to the Soviet Navy consist of approximately 12,000 to 15,000 naval infantrymen (marines) distributed among a brigade in the North and Baltic Sea Fleets, and one regiment in the Black Sea Fleet, and one regiment in the Pacific Fleet possibly subordinate to a division headquarters.

Below: Missile hatches on the foredeck of the *Kirov*. Also shown are four of the ship's eight 30mm Gatling-type guns and (left) the tops of the retractable SA-N-4 mountings.

Naval infantry regiments/brigades have a strength of about 2000 men and are probably organized along the lines of a Soviet Army motorized rifle regiment. The primary mission of the naval infantry is to support the army's maritime flank by mounting small scale amphibious operations and serving as the spearhead of larger operations involving army units. Soviet amphibious operations would probably also include what Western analysts call breakout operations to secure maritime choke points such as the North Cape and the Baltic exits to

Main picture: The *Kirov* heels to port during a high speed turn. Her nuclear-powered engines may give *Kirov* a speed as great as 35 knots.

assist the Navy in its strategic missions. While the primary role of the Naval Infantry is to provide amphibious landings in support of the army in areas contiguous to the Soviet Union, small units have been deployed on Soviet amphibious ships in home waters in a political presence role. The potential interventionary capability of these units, at most a small battalion, is limited by their size, lack of tactical air support and logistical problems.

The Soviet Navy of the 1980s
The powerful ocean-going Soviet Navy of today is directed toward the achievement of three major wartime missions while making use of available resources in the complementary peacetime task of presence in support of state interest. The wartime missions of the Soviet Navy are:

1 To maintain a secure nuclear strike force in the form of its SSBNs to complement the warfighting capabilities of the SRF.

2 Sea denial operations to blunt nuclear strikes by Western martime forces against the Soviet Union and its allies.

3 To control the narrow seas and undertake short-range power projection operations in support of the land campaign.

The Soviet Navy remains very much a junior partner and a component force within the total framework of Soviet warfighting capability. The wartime requirements facing the Soviet Navy do not, however, include the overseas deployment of large scale conventional military forces and there is no evidence of the development of such a capability. But as a by-product of developing platforms to meet new requirements, the Soviet Navy has also developed the capability to deploy naval forces out-of-area to lend their presence to the support of Soviet political interest. While a clear policy for the employment of naval forces in pursuit of peacetime objectives has evolved, clearly defined warfighting requirements are dominant in all the platforms currently under construction.

The widespread global deployment of the Soviet Navy in the 1960s and 1970s combined with the appearance of ships such as the *Kiev* sparked considerable speculation about a global conventional power projection role for the Soviet fleet. Admiral Gorskhov's 1964 order for his fleet to go to sea and stay there stemmed from a requirement to go where the potential strategic threats lie: distant areas including the Mediterranean Sea and Indian Ocean, as well as a recognition that sustained deployments in harsh environments such as the Northern Seas in wartime required sustained peacetime sea training. But as the Soviet ensign moved to

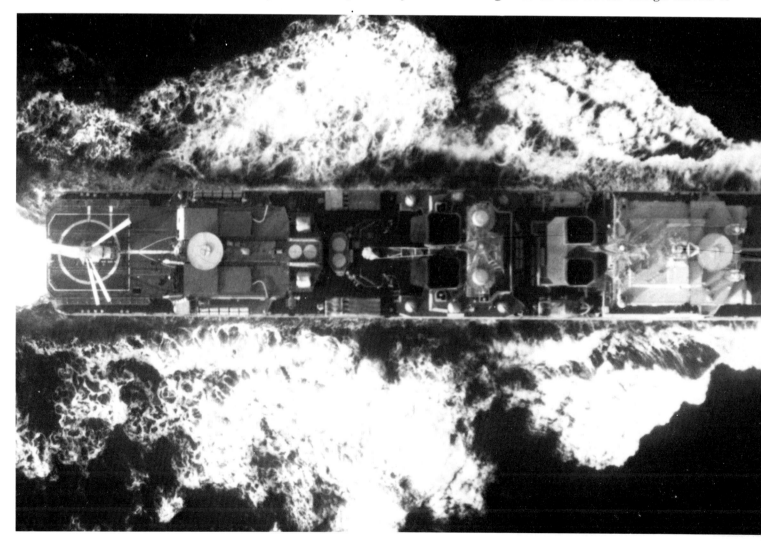

distant waters, an appreciation grew of the political benefits that such presence could provide, whether simple cruising or deploying ships to supplement a client's air defense or sealift, most recently in Ethiopia. These benefits come at minimal cost since no real large conventional power projection capability must be paid for. While the Soviet Union has fielded larger, longer-legged combatants, they remain clearly oriented toward the Navy's main missions in a general war. And while building larger combatants, the Soviet Union has not developed the extensive specialized service forces required for large-scale conventional power projection.

The Soviet Navy is a large and capable force, although, overall, it remains technologically behind the US Navy. The Soviets remain hard at work and Admiral Chernavin continues to be able to extract sufficient resources to continue a balanced shipbuilding program. But while the Soviet Navy is now an accepted member of the team, albeit a junior member, if a resource crunch should hit the Soviet military, the Navy may not continue to fare as well. Given the retirement of Gorshkov, it is likely that the Navy would face this new test without the valued political skills of its greatest leader. Even so, the Navy can look back over two decades of large-scale investment in ships, aircraft, weapons, sensors and related naval hardware as having produced a highly capable and in many ways innovative fleet, a fleet which has gone to sea, honed its skills and made its presence felt in every ocean around the world.

Above: A Helix helicopter seen aboard the destroyer *Udaloy* in 1981. The Helix was first publicly reported in the West at that time. Although it seems to use the same rotor system as the Ka-25 Hormone it is appreciably bigger and presumably carries a new powerplant.

Left: A fine vertical view of the *Udaloy* under way, taken a few weeks after the picture above.

THE SOVIET

FIGHTING MAN

Armed forces are national institutions. Who serves for how long under what conditions and with what motivations is reflective of the society and its political values. Nowhere is this more true than with the USSR which, bar the Peoples Republic of China, maintains by far the largest standing military forces in the world. These forces are manned mainly by temporary civilian soldiers led by a highly professional and highly politicized corps of career officers. Overall, the military obligation to the state touches all citizens in one form or another because the Soviets believe they must train their society in peacetime for the contingency of future war.

The Soviet Nation in Arms

'All male citizens of the USSR, regardless of race, or national identity, religion, educational, residence, social or property status, are obligated to perform active service in the ranks of the Armed Forces' state both the military law of 1967 and the 1977 Soviet constitution. One of the strongest military traditions in the USSR is conscription as the base of the armed forces. Conscription long antedates the advent of Soviet rule, however, since selective conscription involving only certain social classes was introduced in 1699 and universal military service in 1874. After a brief flirtation with a volunteer system, the early Bolsheviks also turned to conscription.

Military obligation in the USSR goes far beyond a specified period of active service. At the core of Marxism-Leninism is the 'nation-in-arms' concept. The state must have the capacity to defend the socialist revolution from the capitalists and to export the revolution when suitable and timely. The concept of the 'militarization of the entire population' was formally expressed in 1925 by M.V. Frunze, then head of the Red Army. In Frunze's view, victory in the next war would require far more than the regular army. The advent of strategic bombardment in World War I presaged the need for civil defense formations in the rear and the labor force manning the war economy would have to be treated as part of the military force structure. The farsighted Frunze had recognized what has now come to be called 'total war'. The next conclusion was that organizing the country for war meant training the country for war, a concept known as 'mass military literacy' in Soviet terminology. Communist party control through cells in every sector and level of Soviet society has traditionally facilitated the implementation of this concept of popular militarization.

Although the original ideal was the 'military and society woven into a single, seamless political garment,' the Soviets early on fixed on a traditional standing army as the result of mili-

Previous page: Soviet Navy enlisted personnel stand at attention on parade.

Below: BTR-60 APCs maneuver at speed. These amphibious vehicles can reach a speed of 50mph on land and 6mph on water.

tary reality but also began to develop structures for 'militarizing society'. These have now developed to the point that many western students see the USSR as in a state of semipermanent mobilization.

The current pattern is large standing forces which the Soviets work hard to maintain in a reasonable condition of combat readiness, no easy task during the nearly four decades of peace since World War II. Beyond this immediate and formidable bulwark, the Soviets recognize that any more than a very short war would require additional large numbers of personnel and reserves of equipment. The Soviets plan to expand the military rapidly with large numbers of trained reserves and thus they have developed an extensive training system to provide these reserves.

The Soviets have never used a 'boot camp' approach as does the US. Prior to 1967, conscripts spent a 'quarantine period' of up to six weeks in small induction centers where they were instructed in the basics of military life and discipline and then assigned directly to operational units. The 1967 military law brought about important changes in training procedures. The term of active service was reduced from three to two years for all services except the air and naval forces which went from four to three. The extra service, as William Odom has pointed out, was not dropped but pushed back into civilian life, particularly to the ninth and tenth grade levels of secondary school. A standard military program of marching, rifle training, individual and squad tactics, and instruction in military terminology, regulations and history was made mandatory for all male students. The conscript who has completed this program is posted directly to an operational unit and receives the rest of his training on the job. The extent of this program has given rise to a variety of problems and it well may be many more years before the Soviets can be satisfied with the results. In recent years, only about half the conscripts have completed the program before induction.

The mandatory secondary level program is in addition to the extensive programs in military skills training sponsored by youth and other mass political organizations. The most important is sponsored by the DOSAAF (Voluntary Association for the Army, Navy and Air Forces), a major mass organization staffed by retired and reserve military officers. The 1967 military law shifted the DOSAAF from a focus on general skills and indoctrination to specialist training that the future conscript can use during his active service. Since 1967, there has been major expansion in DOSAAF facilities and budget. The shift in focus is undoubtedly related at least in part to what the Soviets term the 'technical imperatives of modern weaponry'. The military newspaper *Red Star* reported in 1972 that the number of military specialties in the army had increased from 400 in the 1950s to 2000 in 1972.

The Soviets are clearly concerned to improve the technical preparation of the conscript and Soviet writers do refer to improved levels of technical preparation.

Many Western analysts denigrate the value of this premilitary training but it does involve large portions of the future conscript population. For any army that is 80 percent conscripts on two year hitches, this training can be important because it instills at least the basics of military discipline with whatever skills as a bonus. Conscripts are inducted in the fall and spring which turns over up to 25 percent of the personnel in units semiannually. Units thus have two training cycles a year running from basic skills to large unit maneuvers. Units can teach skills but the Soviets believe that recruits must arrive already disciplined.

The current system gives the Soviets a mobilization base of eight to nine million reservists with active duty within five years. These can be mobilized behind the standing forces and have been so in military exigencies such as Czechoslovakia in 1968 and Afghanistan in 1979. The changes in military service and training stemming from the 1967 military law reflect a clear Soviet desire to draft more males every year and thus increase the number of veterans with recent service in the mobilization base.

Soviet emigrés and published public opinion

Bottom: A PMP floating bridge bay being launched from a Tatra truck during a river crossing operation.

Below: The BTR-50PU armored command vehicle carries extensive communications equipment.

Above: Infantry drive home an attack during training.

Above right: Physical fitness and agility exercises play as great a part in Soviet training schemes as in most armies.

Above, far right: Well camouflaged Soviet infantry negotiate barbed wire obstacles while one of their number gives covering fire with his AK-47.

Right: T-72 tanks and infantry advance during an exercise. The infantrymen are in the 'marching fire' pose commonly seen in pictures of Soviet troops.

data suggest that the fact of conscription is generally accepted by the populace and that conscripts have at least some idea of why they must serve and what is expected of them as soldiers. This acceptance, as Ellen Jones suggests, probably stems from 'legitimacy through longevity' (the draft has been in effect since Tsarist times) and the fact that few are able to escape their military obligations. The authorities also undertake a variety of programs to promote acceptance of service. These include personal letters from serving soldiers to future conscripts and letters to servicemen's families from their commanders.

For a state with such emphasis on broad military obligations, women play a surprisingly modest role in the military. Women can be drafted in wartime but are banned from combat. In peacetime, women can be conscripted if they have special skills such as medical training or volunteer. The majority – currently probably less than 10,000 – are enlisted because women cannot attend officers schools and have little other opportunity for advancement. But the world's first and to date only female cosmonaut is a Soviet and the Soviet air force boasts several female test pilots. Large numbers of young women outside the military, however, get some military training through the DOSAAF and Komsomol (Young Communist League).

A last major means by which the Soviets organize society for war is civil defense. There is a civil defense hierarchy in the regular military which almost constitutes a sixth service. Every factory, collective farm, school, hospital or other facility is required to have a civil defense organization. Civil defense exercises are frequent and sometimes large enough to be the sole occupation of an entire large city for a whole day. Civil defense provides yet another massive

system of peacetime military education and some ability to maintain administrative control of the civilian sector in wartime. Many western writers question the potential effectiveness of civil defense in wartime for the USSR (and for the US as well) but the Soviet authorities, if not their citizenry, take it very seriously and invest substantial sums.

The Political Context of Military Service

The Soviets have thus created an almost cradle to grave network of military obligations for their citizenry. The state reaps a number of important non-military benefits from this system. The mass military is often tapped for labor for civilian construction projects and the harvest. The vocational and technical skills which veterans bring to the civilian labor force are also significant. But most important in official eyes is the role of the military as, in the words of the late Minister of Defense Marshal Grechko, 'a unique nationwide university which is completed by practically all young men who are citizens of the Land of the Soviets'. Next to the

A Victor class nuclear powered fleet submarine seen in the South China Sea. Modern submarine hull forms tend to give enormous wakes on the surface but are extremely efficient in submerged operations.

A Krivak class frigate seen from an American carrier aircraft in the Arabian Sea in 1980. Soviet forces have been deployed in increasing strength to the Indian Ocean in recent years, a worrying development in the eyes of Western analysts.

educational system, the military provides the state with its most important opportunity to attempt to mold its varied citizenry into the 'new Soviet man', its ideal patriot whose sole loyalties are to the Communist Party, the Soviet state, and 'proletarian internationalism at home and abroad'.

The primary mission of the military is to support the policies of the Communist Party which has always attempted to maintain absolute control over the armed forces. This is accomplished through a network of agencies which virtually blanket the military. The most important are the Main Political Directorate, the KGB (Committee on State Security), and the Communist Party itself with its auxiliary organizations.

The primary political agent of the Party in the military is the Main Political Directorate which functions as a department of the Party bureaucracy. The MPD is the heir of the military Commissars, that cadre of party loyalists inserted into the military to ensure obedience to the Party. The Commissars disappeared for good early in World War II but the requirement for party oversight has continued and even increased. The main function of the MPD is to coordinate party and its youth auxiliary Komsomol activities.

The MPD extends Party control down to the company level through the agency of the Zampolit – the Russian contraction for deputy commander for political affairs. By Party directive, the line commander and the Zampolit work toward the common goal of an effective military unit with joint responsibility for unit political activity and training. The primary function of the Zampolit is the political training of all personnel, including officers. He is also responsible for military education in the sense of integrating the political and combat aspects of training.

Political training is a major feature in the landscape of military life. According to Soviet sources, 90-100 minutes of the working day and two and a half to four hours of non-working days are devoted to political training for both officers and enlisted men. The time is mainly filled with classes designed to instill 'a scientific world view and high moral, political and combat qualities'. The main themes are the responsibilities of servicemen, the historic role of the armed forces, the achievements of the Communist Party, and the differing roles of communism and capitalism in contemporary affairs. President Brezhnev's three volumes of memoirs first published in 1978 were compulsory reading in political education classes. In effect, Brezhnev was, until he was discredited, the ultimate Zampolit.

The Soviets believe that training must harden the soldier ideologically as well as physically. Thus the highly repetitive daily barrage of propaganda (which occurs even on field maneuvers) is intended to mold the individual into a highly patriotic, industrious, moral and informed soldier who is a good communist and

hates bourgeois ideology and capitalist imperialism. In fact, there is abundant evidence that the average soldier is bored with the content and anesthetized by the dosage. The manifest ineffectiveness of political indoctrination in the military is a genuine source of concern to the Party whose reaction in recent years has been to mandate increased dosages of the same medicine rather than try other prescriptions.

The Zampolit has other duties which include basic education such as teaching Russian to ethnic minorities, morale, discipline and personal problems, and, most importantly, smoothing the transition of conscripts from civilian to military life. He serves as the senior Party member in the unit and conducts a continuous propaganda effort to explain and support Party policies and programs. He heads the unit Komsomol and oversees its recruitment, training and program development. At higher levels of command, the Zampolit is deputy chairman of the unit's military council with the commander as chairman. The military council makes decisions about operations, training programs and logistics for the guidance of commanders.

Some students rooted in the relatively apolitical military tradition of the West profess to see continuing conflict between the line officers and the political officers. Although conflict certainly did exist in the days of the military Commissars and dual command, the relationship in recent years has in fact evolved into mutual dependence. The party has consistently brooked no reduction in the role of the political officer and has made the careers of the regular military dependent on cooperation. The line commander needs the Zampolit's support both for unit success and career advancement. The Zampolit evaluates the political conformity and participation of regular officers in fitness reports, a very significant factor in a system where promotion and posting are treated as political matters. But the Zampolit in turn needs the support and cooperation of the commander to fulfill his duties successfully and advance in his own service. The line commander and the political officer thus tend to avoid conflicts which would damage careers, a tendency reinforced by considerable pressure from above.

In the past, the Soviets also encouraged interchangeability of command between line and political officers but this too has changed in recent years. When necessary, a subordinate line officer fills in for the commander. Political officers appear to remain within the MPD both functionally and as a career pattern.

A Ka-25 Hormone-A anti-submarine helicopter in flight. A fine view of the two contra-rotating rotors by which this type is powered.

Right: An eager *praporshchik* (warrant officer) reads *Malaya Zemlya* (The Far Lands), one of the three volumes of the late President Brezhnev's autobiography.

Below: Future non-commissioned officers receive classroom training. Most of those shown are two-year term conscripts whereas in Western armies NCOs are almost invariably long-service volunteers.

Opposite, top: The Soviet Army is not unusual in believing that bayonet drill helps instill aggressiveness and that the bayonet is not outmoded in modern war.

Opposite, below: Airborne forces on maneuvers. The infantry are armed with Kalashnikov automatic rifles and RPG-7 rocket launchers while the supporting armored vehicles are ASU-85 assault guns which can be air-dropped or carried by Mi-6 or Mi-10 helicopters.

over the military is membership in the Party itself or the Komsomol. The Party is the source of all power and influence in the state and membership and party work are considered crucial for officer career advancement. But Party membership is not automatic and standards of admission, already high, have been raised even higher in recent years. Even so, some 80 percent of all officers are members. Three or more officer party members in the same unit are a 'primary party organization' and 75 or more are a 'party committee'. Below the Party is the Komsomol to which about 80 percent of the enlisted and 20 percent of the officers belong. Membership is highly encouraged but again not automatic. Komsomol functions in the military are to aid in implementing party policies and preparing youth for later party membership.

Leadership: The Officer Corps

The Soviet officer is typically a well-educated career professional and member of the Party. Although Soviet public opinion data indicate that military officers do not rank high in the hierarchy of status in Soviet society, they are among the favored in that society. Officers are comparatively well paid, enjoy good perquisites and privileges, are favored in housing, and have access to special government stores. They are also politically loyal with much of the top command holding political as well as military rank. In 1979, for example, 21 officers were full members of the Party Central Committee and 15 more were candidate members. Overall, about

While the MPD is the Party's main instrument of indoctrination and verification, a second instrument for verification exists in the KGB. As the senior police and intelligence organization of the state, the KGB has a special branch to deal with the security and reliability of the military. KGB officers are assigned down to the regimental level and there are agents and informers at all levels in all services. While no favorable personnel action can occur without MPD approval, any KGB doubt about officer reliability can forever bar promotion and good postings.

Another important aspect of Party control

A Scud-B artillery rocket being raised to the firing position by the erector cradle on its MAZ-843 transporter/launcher vehicle. All the Warsaw Pact armies use the Scud missile but nuclear warheads are controlled by the Soviets.

6-8 percent of party membership is composed of serving officers. The Soviet military does not pursue its own political ends separate from and in competition with the Party but is an administrative arm of the Party. Against a background of broad and pragmatic policy consensus, William Odom notes, 'the Soviet system is dominated by military policy-making but not by marshals'. But the emphasis on party loyalty and activity has also produced officers who tend to be 'remote, bureaucratic and formalistic'.

The close connection between the officer corps and the state is not unique to the Soviet period of history. The old Russian elite was based primarily on a service aristocracy and the military was traditionally the closest to the crown. The early Bolsheviks inherited much of this military elite as some 50,000 Tsarist officers served their cause, including leading generals such as Brusilov, Kamenov, and Bouch-Bruevich. But the Tsarist officers were highly suspect to the Bolsheviks who used them only from dire necessity and watched them carefully with special political Commissars.

The early Bolshevik ideal was to have officers elected from the ranks with nothing to set them apart from their men in terms of rank, attire or privileges. But the same dire necessity that led to the use of the Tsarist officers led to a steady trend toward professionalization which reached its logical conclusion in 1935 when a rank structure from lieutenant to Marshal of the Soviet Union was instituted. The outward marks of the professional officer – rank, uniform, medals – were all in place when the corps received a body blow during Stalin's political purge of 1937. Commencing with the frame-ups of Marshal Tukhachevsky and other top officers, Stalin liquidated between 15,000-30,000 of his 75,000 officers, including three of five marshals, 57 of 85 corps commanders, and 110 of 195 division commanders. The poor Soviet showing in the Finnish War and early World War II can at least partly be related to the purge. So the purge to weed out the politically suspect was followed by a purge early in World War II to weed out the militarily incompetent.

Since World War II, the Soviets have made a

Presidents Carter and Brezhnev in Vienna at the signing of the SALT II Treaty in 1979. This treaty has never been ratified but its provisions have been generally observed.

Soviet military might on
show during the Moscow
May Day Parade.

major effort to improve officer quality and professionalism. There are about 500,000 serving officers equaling about 16 percent of the standing force (versus 11-13 percent in the West). These officers come from three sources. First and foremost are the 143 military colleges, each with an average enrollment of 1000. In addition to their military training, students also receive a degree in a technical subject or engineering. The Soviet military places strong emphasis on science and technical qualifications and all officers are required to have a specific technical skill. There are also officer training programs at every institution of higher education in which all male students must participate. Almost all male graduates receive a reserve officer's commission on graduation. Thus one important feature of the military mobilization system is that almost every male with a college degree can be called to active duty as a reserve officer. It is also possible to be commissioned from the ranks. For both soldiers and non-commissioned officers (NCOs), this requires at least a secondary education and passage of an examination.

For the already commissioned officer, there can be postings to one of 23 military academies which require a college-level degree for entrance and are roughly equivalent to graduate schools. The academies are given high priority in material support, student recruitment and faculty selection. Many officers with advanced degrees can be found in civilian universities and especially the USSR Academy of Sciences. The push to improve the educational level of the officer corps has not been easy, especially in finding qualified faculty. By 1980, however, the

Opposite: Two US Navy photographs of Soviet installations in Somalia in 1975. Foreign interventions are virtually impossible to conceal in an age of spy satellites and advanced electronics. However, no military satellite photographs have ever been released for publication.

Red Star could report that up to 80 percent of officers had the equivalent of a Bachelor of Science degree with the officers of the elite Strategic Rocket Forces holding the highest proportion of formal degrees.

The increasing educational level of the officer corps is but one of several signs that a professional military class is emerging. The ten Suvorov academies, originally founded to train military orphans in World War II, now are almost the exclusive province of sons of serving officers and are considered a good start for a military career. That sons of officers tend to follow in their fathers' footsteps, a tendency shared with the children of Party members and diplomats, is often mentioned in the Soviet military press. This revival of the traditional hereditary military service is viewed favorably by the Soviets who see it as increasing military professionalism as well as the morale and commitment of the officer corps. Thus the military appears to be joining a number of other hereditary castes in the classless Soviet society.

There is no 'up or out' policy for officers. An officer is promoted to the level of his competence in a positive application of the 'Peter Principle'. It is thus possible to spend an entire career from commissioning to mandatory retirement as a junior lieutenant on active duty in contrast to, say, the American army with its frequent rotations and emphasis on competitive evaluations. The Soviets see their personnel policy as providing leadership stability at lower levels and Richard Gabriel has suggested that there may indeed be important benefits for small unit cohesion and leadership.

The officer corps is a 'heavily bureaucratized and careerist organization' in which the main emphasis is on technical skills and the active expression of political loyalty and far less on command and leadership qualities. Success stems from conformity and sticking to the letter of plans, schedules and especially orders, all of which minimize personal responsibility for mistakes and failures. Data from emigrés gathered by Richard Gabriel suggest that the Soviet officer is reluctant to use initiative but instead emphasizes control and pleasing his superiors. In these characteristics, the officer corps simply mirrors the rest of Soviet society. The memory of the 230 generals executed or reduced to the rank of private in a penal battalion for disciplinary reasons, incompetence or failure during World War II is also a powerful reason why senior officers in particular are reluctant to delegate responsibility and prefer to do things 'by the book'.

The Soviet military promotes rigid discipline and conformity but also recognizes the need for individual officer initiative. While the officer must always act in strict obedience to his orders, there will surely be many cases in which his orders will not be received in the chaos of the modern battlefield. In such situations, the officer must then exercise what the Soviets term 'correct initiative' which is to estimate correctly what his orders would have been in that situation and then have the courage, skill and knowledge to act successfully on his estimate. The tenor of the continuing discussion about correct initiative in the military press indicates that few if any officers yet approach this ideal.

Below: An Ilyushin 38 May maritime patrol aircraft and an F-14 Tomcat from the USS *America* seen over the Indian Ocean in 1981.

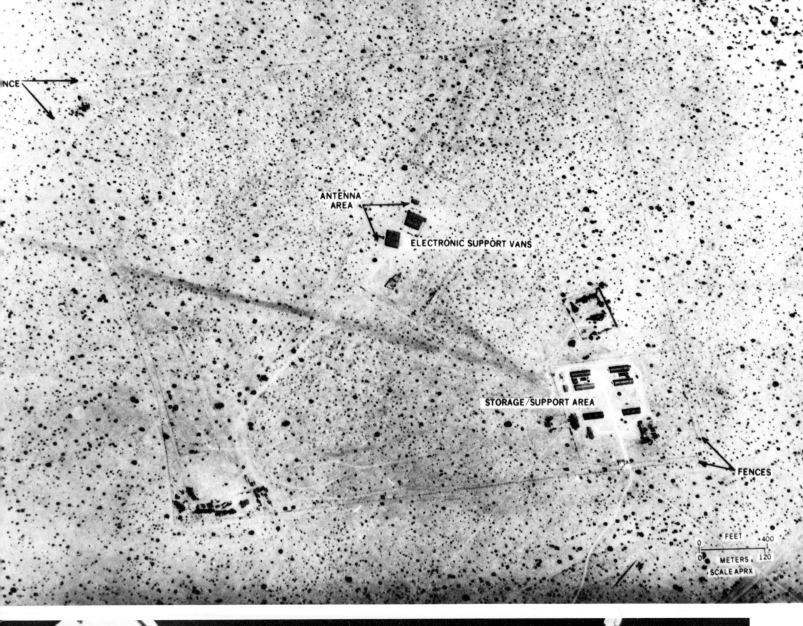

NCE

ANTENNA
AREA

ELECTRONIC SUPPORT VANS

STORAGE/SUPPORT AREA

FENCES

FEET   400
0
METERS   120
0
SCALE APRX

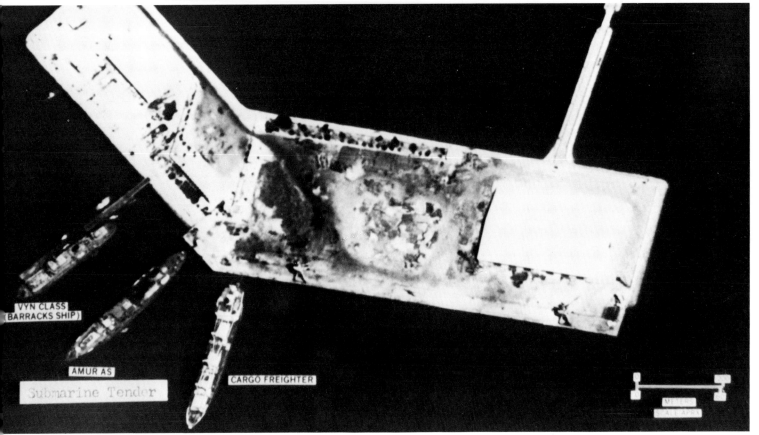

VYN CLASS
(BARRACKS SHIP)

AMUR AS

Submarine Tender

CARGO FREIGHTER

ARCTIC OCEAN

Greenland (Den.)

U.S.

Canada

Iceland

NORTH ATLANTIC OCEAN

Ireland United Kingdom Neth.

France

Monaco

Andorra Medi

Portugal Spain (45 Ship

United States

PACIFIC OCEAN

Morocco

Algeria

Western Sahara

Mauritania

Mali

U.S.

Mexico

Caribbean
(3-4 Ships, Average)

The Bahamas

Cuba

Dominican Republic

Haiti

Belize(U.K.) Jamaica

St. Lucia

Guatemala Honduras

St. Vincent and the Grenadines

Dominica

Barbados

Grenada

Cape Verde

Senegal
Gambia
Guinea-Bissau
Sierra Leone
Liberia

Upper Volta

Guinea

Ivory Coast

Ghana

Benin

Togo

Nig

Nicaragua

El Salvador

Costa Rica

Panama

Trinidad and Tobago

Venezuela

Guyana

Suriname

French Guiana (Fr.)

Sao Tome and Principe

Colombia

Ecuador

Equator Guine

Peru

Brazil

West Africa
(5-6 Ships, Average)

Bolivia

Paraguay

SOUTH ATLANTIC OCEAN

Chile

Uruguay

Argentina

MILITARY AND CIVILIAN ADVISORS
(Significant Presence)

	SOVIET	CUBAN	EAST GERMAN
LATIN AMERICA			
Cuba	12,000		
Nicaragua	50	3,200	
Peru	175	10	
SUB-SAHARAN AFRICA			
Angola	700	8,000	450
Congo	850	950	15
Ethiopia	2,400	5,900	550
Guinea	375	280	125
Mali	635		20
Madagascar	370	55	
Mozambique	500	1,000	100
Tanzania	300	95	15
MIDEAST AND NORTH AFRICA			
Algeria	8,500	170	250
Iraq	8,000	2,200	160
Libya	2,300	3,000	
North Yemen	475		5
South Yemen	2,500	800	325
Syria	4,000	5	210
ASIA			
Afghanistan	87,000	100	
India	1,550		

The Soviet record in Afghanistan, the sole opportunity they or anyone else have had to evaluate the effectiveness of the officer corps in combat since 1945, attests to the veracity of the criticisms in the military press. The planning for the invasion was done carefully and systematically and the smooth execution was watched with awe by Western observers. Once past the stage where a preplanned operation could be executed and unplanned initiative and innovative tactics became important, however, the Soviets quickly got low marks from Western observers for their inability to respond to situations not found in textbooks. As one observer noted, 'They are always slow to respond. Their morning attacks are always planned the night before and it sometimes takes them a day or two to move against the insurgents'. The Soviet command was quickly reduced to reporting exaggerated body counts to demonstrate to Moscow progress against the enemy. The consensus of Western analysts has been that the Soviets need a more flexible command structure to allow field officers more authority. Only slowly did the Soviets adapt their tactics to the peculiar exigencies of their Afghan campaign. By the time of the withdrawal in 1988, many would argue that they had still not got them right.

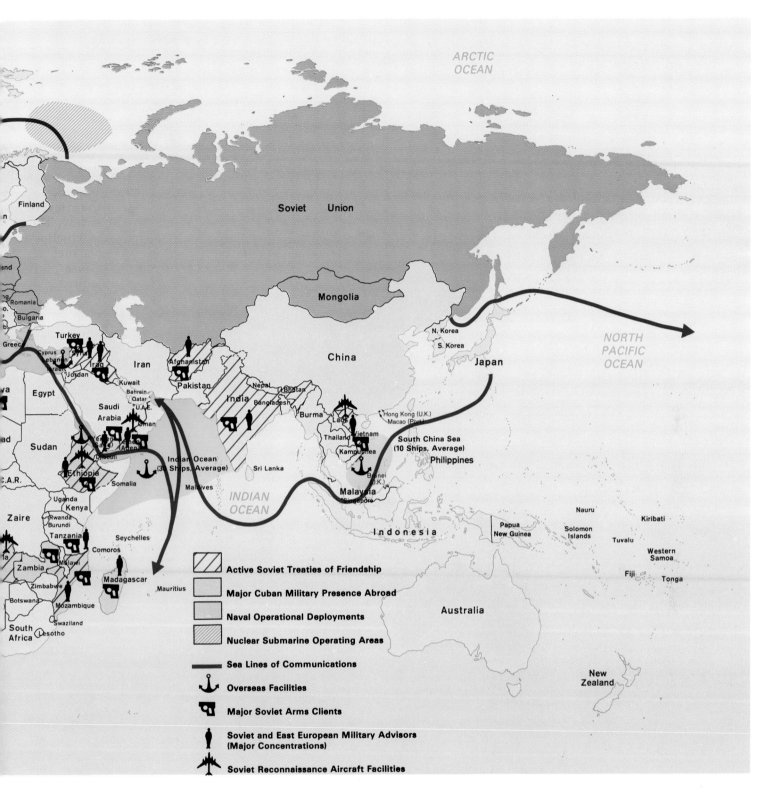

Above: Soviet power around the world.

The Ranks and NCOs

That the Soviet soldier is a stolid peasant, rugged and inured to hardship, is a decidedly dated western stereotype. Census data from 1970 show that only 38 percent of the population is engaged in agriculture and 'peasants' at best may constitute only 25 percent of the population. In view of the overall trend toward urbanization in Soviet society, these figures have undoubtedly decreased in the intervening years. Like the officer corps, where less than 15 percent may come from rural backgrounds, the ranks are predominantly urban since over 60 percent of the age 15-19 males were located in urban areas in the 1970 census. The ranks are also increasingly better educated and more sophisticated, a factor which in recent years has created pressures for improvements in living conditions and less stress on physical discipline and coercion in training.

The non-commissioned officers or NCOs are largely one term conscripts, perhaps as much as 95 percent in Richard Gabriel's estimate. The NCOs are temporary cadres and have the same attitudes toward service as the ranks. Since the NCOs are largely conscripts, they tend to want to do their service as easily as possible and are prone to avoid responsibility even more than

Above: Forger aircraft land on a carrier. Maintenance of such complicated machines may present problems for the average Soviet conscript. Technical tasks that would be performed by skilled enlisted men in Western services are often undertaken by Soviet officers because they alone have sufficient technical training.

Right: Mountain troops on exercise. Russian training traditionally takes account of extremes of terrain and climate.

Soviet society is multi-ethnic, with Russians comprising over 50 percent, Ukrainians almost 20 percent, Uzbeks and Belorussians about 4 percent and other nationalisties – Tatars, Kazakhs, Armenians, Jews, Germans, Georgians, Tadzhiks, Bashkirs, Moldavians, and others – 2 percent or less each. There are 102 national groups in the fifteen Soviet republics but Russians are considered the 'leading nation' and enjoy a 'qualitative hegemony' in Soviet political life and society. All nationalities are subject to military service and the ethnic composition of the military, especially the army, is probably fairly representative of society. The officer corps, on the other hand, is heavily Russian supplemented by other Slavs such as Ukrainians and Belorussians because good education and fluent Russian are required. The

high command is almost exclusively Slavs, mainly Russians. The price of a successful career for non-Russian officers is clearly voluntary Russification.

While the Soviet constitution makes a number of concessions, including language, to the non-Russian groups, the military does not. The state in fact uses military service as a major and intense instrument of Russification, especially through the forced use of Russian. The MPD sponsors an armed forces wide remedial program in Russian while ethnic soldiers with problems are assigned a Komsomol activist to assist them with their training. Next to the educational system, the armed forces are the most important and influential state agent for promoting bilingualism.

Since the civil war, the military has been trying to deal with the problems arising from the ethnic variety of its ranks. There has always been a heavy emphasis on Russification and ethnically mixed units even though the exigencies of World War II forced the creation of some purely ethnic units. Non-Russians often fought well but there were also mass defections and

officers. Thus the two primary characteristics of the NCOs, as described by Gabriel, are their temporary status and their poorly developed sense of professionalism and motivation. Up to a third of the total force may be NCOs versus 25 percent in the West, as the Soviets use numbers and overlap to compensate for inexperience and quality. Another important compensation is assigning officers to many jobs that Western armies typically assign to NCOs.

NCOs are selected from the ranks, sometimes after as little as a few months of service, and sent to NCO school for six weeks. They are sometimes selected by their draft boards on the basis of aptitude and preconscription training even before induction. Good performance brings rapid promotion and it is not atypical to make top sergeant during two years of service.

NCOs tend to occupy a somewhat anomalous position in that officers identify them with the conscripts while the conscripts see them as aloof and remote like officers. Emigrés report that neither officers nor conscripts identify the NCOs as 'good men to go into combat with'. Gabriel concludes that NCOs suffer from severe leadership and combat-related deficiencies and constitute a major institutional weakness of the Soviet military. The Soviets apparently agree because in 1971 they introduced the new senior NCO rank of *praporshchik*, roughly equivalent to the Western warrant officer, in an effort to create a cadre of 'wise old soldiers'. Western opinion differs as to how successful this innovation has been.

Afghan Moslem rebels pose with an assortment of weapons including an AK-47, left, and, man seated, a PPSh submachine gun, used by Soviet forces during World War II and after.

A young Afghan poses on the remains of a Russian tank destroyed in a camouflaged pit dug by resistance fighters.

Soviet troops mounted on their armored personnel carriers withdraw from Afghanistan.

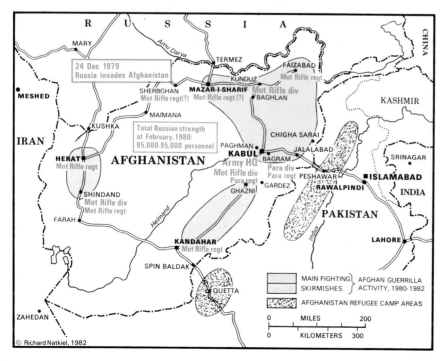

The Soviet deployment in Afghanistan between 1979 and 1982.

active service with the enemy. After the war, the Soviets quickly returned to mixed units and wrote a formal requirement for mixed units into the 1967 military law. *Red Star* reported in 1980 that the elite Tamanski division boasts 29 nationalities in its ranks. A main theme in military-political indoctrination is the 'friendship of the peoples' which stresses the growth of common features and disappearance of differences among the Soviet nationalities. Since the early 1970s, the Communist Party has acknowledged ethnic nationalism as a growing problem and subjected the military to a series of national integration indoctrination campaigns.

Some Western students see ethnicity as a problem for the military on the same scale as it seems to be in society. There is unquestionably some ethnic tension in the military, which the authorities take pains to minimize, but it is not major compared to other conflicts such as that between conscripts and regulars. The level of ethnic tension is probably a function of overall unit morale and tends more to exacerbate other problems, especially in low status units such as construction troops. Poor fluency in Russian, suggests Ellen Jones, is a far greater problem.

Morale and Discipline

Ivan endures a tough, regimented and spartan existence during his two year term of service because the Soviets believe that military life and training must approximate the rigors of war as much as possible to be truly effective. Barracks facilities have typically been rudimentary and only within the last several years has there been a conscious effort to improve conditions through renovation of old barracks and the introduction of such amenities as central heating and indoor plumbing. Diet typically consists of porridge, bread, cabbage, potatoes, fish and a little meat. The food is repetitive, poor quality, and usually poorly prepared, although elite units fare better than line units. The military is also not much more immune to food shortages than is civilian society. Emigrés report that vitamin deficiencies and related ailments are common. Since the soldier is paid 3-5

rubles monthly (about $10), stealing military supplies such as rope and gasoline to sell is common to get money for extra food and especially drink.

Service is further characterized by restriction to post. Leave is not automatic but granted only at the discretion of the commander. Leave is in fact seldom granted for fear of problems with the locals and consequent effects on the commander's career. It is not uncommon for a soldier to receive no leave during his entire two year hitch. Instead, the soldier can be released from service ten days early. Soldiers are almost never allowed off post without supervising officers.

Such conditions of service are clearly deleterious to morale. Former servicemen surveyed

Afghans cluster triumphantly atop a BTR APC.

Above: Units of the Baltic Fleet during the exercise 'Soyuz 81' which also involved East German forces in a display which some observers regarded as a rehearsal for a possible Soviet military intervention in Poland.

Right: Polish and East German units on maneuvers in Poland in August 1981. The effectiveness and reliability of Warsaw Pact forces are a cause for concern for the Soviet leadership.

by Gabriel reported fairly high rates of absence without leave, desertion, assault on officers, and suicide. Going AWOL is almost the soldiers' only chance for female companionship and drink. It is apparently ignored if brief and no trouble ensues. The stiff penalties for desertion, on the other hand, are enforced. If the deserter takes his weapon, he is likely to be shot on sight. It is also not unknown for officers to desert. Overall, however, desertion appears no more serious than in Western armies. Assaults on officers and NCOs apparently occur with fair frequency but there are no documented instances of killing. These attacks tend to be related to drunkeness and high levels of personal frustration. Emigrés and defectors suggest that there may be as high a rate of suicide in the military as in civilian society. The defector Alexei Myagkov reported 75 suicides during his three year stint as head of KGB surveillance of the 20th Guards Tank Army in Berlin. Attemp-

Poland's Premier, General Jaruzelski, must satisfy his Soviet masters that his government will not deviate from policies approved by Moscow and yet he must also retain some popular support in a country whose socialist economy seems to be moribund.

An armored personnel carrier in the streets of Warsaw shortly after martial law was declared in 1981.

Above: A Delta II class SSBN. This class of boat carries the SS-N-8 missile (16 tubes) which was the first two-stage Soviet SLBM.

Left: One of the four Kynda class ships, seen in the Mediterranean in 1968. In common with many Soviet designs the Kyndas carry two sets of most of the types of radar with which they are fitted. This may indicate a provision for battle damage or may simply be necessary because individual sets are not sufficiently reliable.

M1974 122mm self-propelled howitzers. The Soviets expect self-propelled artillery to operate in forward positions in the combat zone whereas the western practice is to treat such equipment as simply a more mobile form of artillery and to employ it accordingly.

The Mi-24 Hind-D carries a turret-mounted Gatling gun in the chin position and is more streamlined than earlier versions of the type. The pilot's position is above and behind the gunner's.

ted suicides are fairly frequent, apparently because soldiers use them to lay the groundwork for the Soviet equivalent of a Section 8 discharge.

Perhaps the most basic indicator of the morale of the forces is the high rate of alcohol consumption which mirrors that of the society at large. A Soviet magazine noted in 1976 that the forces are 'awash in a sea of vodka'. Defectors describe the widespread theft of equipment to sell or barter for vodka because of the cost and nonavailability of drink. Because drunkenness, sometimes on duty, by ranks and officers is so common, punishments are light and much is overlooked, although it is interesting to note that, since coming to power, Mikhail Gorbachev has pledged himself to cutting down alcoholism in Soviet society as a whole.

Rigid discipline is enforced because, as one military writer stated, 'Standards of discipline are increasing as the importance of the time factor increases. Complete readiness to repel a surprise attack and successful action to destroy the enemy are only possible with a high level of discipline and organization'. No deviance such as altering uniforms or wearing scarfs is permitted. Discipline demands precise and immediate obedience to all orders and regulations, and proper care of all government and military property. In the latter case, liability incurred during service can follow the hapless into civilian life through confiscation of property and earnings. Hooliganism, defined as any activity offensive to the authorities (interest in Western music, for example, or display of religious beliefs) can result in up to five years in jail or commitment to a psychiatric hospital.

Conformity is enforced by various pressures. There are cash awards and official letters to family and former employers are standard practice. The authorities have powerful levers over those with career or educational aspirations. Peer pressure is also widely employed. And in the end, there is always the 'discipline of the revolver'. In World War II, execution for disciplinary reasons was not seen as extraordinary while at least 100 soldiers were summarily shot by their officers during the 1968 invasion of Czechoslovakia.

Training and Motivation

The typical Soviet unit functions as a training as well as an operational unit. Up to 25 percent of its most experienced personnel are replaced with green conscripts twice a year. Conscripts are supposed to arrive with basic training courtesy of the DOSAAF but only about 50 percent do so. Sole exceptions are the elite Strategic Rocket Forces and airborne units which receive only personnel with pre-induction training. The unit must teach the manual of arms, drill, military regulations and courtesy, and infantry weapons before it can move on to more advanced training. Training requirements are high as the

COMPOSITION OF A MOTOR RIFLE DIVISION

Division Headquarters

Reconnaissance Battalion	Independent Tank Battalion *31 tanks, 1 APC*	Tank Regiment *95 tanks, 8 APC*	3 × Motor Rifle Rgmt. *31 tanks, 112 APC*	Artillery
		3 Tank Battalions 1 Motor Rifle Company	Each 3 Motor Rifle Battalions 1 Tank Battalion	

Artillery Regiment *54 guns, 9 Batteries* *6 Batteries of 122mm* *or 130mm guns* *3 Batteries of 152mm guns*	Anti-aircraft Regiment *24 ZSU-23-4, 4 Batteries*	Anti-tank Battalion *3 Batteries of 6 100mm guns* *& 3 ATGM*	Rocket-launcher Btn. *3 Batteries of 6 BM-21*	Observation Company	FROG Battalion *2 Batteries of* *2 launchers*

Divisional Troops include: Engineer, Signals, Medical, Maintenance, Transport and Chemical Defense Battalions

Total Strength: 1100 officers   219 main battle tanks
                10,400 men   19 light tanks
                             372 APC

COMPOSITION OF A TANK DIVISION

Division Headquarters

Reconnaissance Btn.	3 × Tank Regiment	Motor Rifle Regiment	Artillery	Support Services

Total Strength: 1000 officers   316 main battle tanks
                9700 men   19 light tanks
                            165 APC

Composition and equipment of component units as for components of Motor Rifle Division except
1. Tank Regiments have 3 × Motor Rifle Company
2. Artillery has no Anti-tank Battalion

---

complexity of the equipment has increased over the years. In addition to mastering one primary skill, the soldier is further required to learn two other related skills to reduce unit vulnerability to losses. The combat readiness of units, so important to the Soviets, is thus reduced in the early part of the semi-annual training cycle and peaks near the end.

Throughout his two years, the conscript is subjected to a rigorous training day which allows him 30 minutes of rest and 30 minutes of free time. Yet the free time is not really free because Soviet military pedagogues believe that conformity and morale are best served by keeping the soldier as busy as possible. As President Brezhnev stated the essence of this view in 1976, 'Free time is not time which is free of responsibility before society'. Training in general is made as rigorous and realistic as possible with heavy emphasis on field exercises and sheer task repetition.

As ideology tends to permeate all aspects of life in Soviet society and provides the basis on which all else is judged, it is not surprising that the Soviets stress ideology as the main element in troop motivation. In addition to constant political indoctrination, the military has taken two important motivational devices from the civilian sector in the 'socialist competition' and the collective. Whereas workers compete to meet production goals in the civilian socialist competition, the military pits unit against unit in military and task proficiency. The military press is replete with reports and discussions of these competitions, praising winners and castigating sub-par performances. Marshal Tolubko of the Strategic Rocket Forces, for example,

Above: Soldiers receive instruction in infantry firepower tactics.

wrote in 1981 that 'A powerful means of increasing mastery of combat skills on the part of our personnel is found to lie in socialist competition, which we hold under the banner of striving for the utmost in combat readiness and rigorous adherence to required military procedures . . .' He went on to note that 'our personnel initiatives are widespread under the slogans: No laggards here – Individual excellence today, unit excellence tomorrow – From a master in the crew to a crew of masters'.

The collective is the small social group to which every Soviet belongs either at school, job or residence. The leader is usually elected. In the military, the collective is typically based on the squad or platoon with the leader often not in the formal chain of command. Military collectives organize voluntary labor and socialist

Right: SA-6 Gainful low-to-medium altitude SAMs serve at divisional level with Soviet ground forces. They are carried on modified PT-76 chassis and can keep pace with a rapid advance.

competitions and activities to fill any free time. They are also used to reinforce mastery of combat skills and stress conformity and group support. After the soldier has mastered the required military skills, which can take up to two months, he takes the military oath – a formal promise of duty and loyalty to the collective – in a formal ceremony before his comrades. One soldier described his collective in these terms: '. . . we live together like blood brothers, we help each other in everything . . . everyone feels co-responsible, carries out his duties completely and does not malinger'. This epitome of the soldier as a loyal, obedient team player stems, as William Baxter has noted, from the Marxist conception of man as a collective rather than an individual being.

How Well Would Ivan Fight?

Socialist competitions and collectives notwithstanding, the observably poor state of motivation and productivity in civilian society is probably not an accurate reflection of the motivation and effectiveness of the Soviet soldier. History shows that Ivan can be very effective and motivated. It was after all the bayonets of the Imperial Russian Army that captured Napoleon and occupied Paris in 1814 to end French dominance

Left: Soviet military writings often discuss tactics for airborne assault as being practised in this training picture.

Main picture: A Tu-95 Bear in flight over the Pacific. This is an example of the Bear-D type with chin and belly fairings over radar and electronics equipment.

of continental Europe. And it was the then Red Army which broke the back of the Wehrmacht, the most formidable modern military machine the world has yet seen, to meet the Allies on the Elbe in 1945. There is no question that the Soviet soldier fought and fought well in World War II which was first and foremost a Soviet-German conflict in Europe.

But what of Ivan since 1945? The military clearly works hard to train him mentally, physically and ideologically and provides him with generally excellent and up-to-date equipment. But he experienced his first real postwar combat with the 1979 Christmas invasion and con-tinuing campaign in Afghanistan, previously being employed only against the unarmed populations in Hungary and Czechoslovakia. Since 1979, the Soviets have fought an increasingly bitter war against the Afghan guerrillas – a war that has reportedly cost the Soviets 13,310 soldiers and led to great strains among the men fighting there. Demoralization has been noted, not just among soldiers in Afghanistan but also among veterans returning home.

Western writers have questioned the motivation and effectiveness of the Soviet soldier, pointing to such problems as morale, discipline and alcohol, the gap between officers and men,

Two Soviet soldiers patrol a mountain road near Kabul. As this picture suggests reports of disillusioned conscripts may be exaggerated. The Soviet soldier may indeed be a formidable opponent.

the centralized and inflexible command structure, and the marked preference for rigid pre-planning versus operational flexibility. But morale and discipline problems are common to any peacetime force, especially one composed largely of temporary citizen soldiers. Under wartime conditions, these factors would undoubtedly be muted to a great extent. And rightly or wrongly, the Soviets firmly believe in their style of leadership and command. They may well be wrong in this belief but this will never be known until put to the test. The emphasis on the ideological basis of troop motivation, however, runs directly counter to the weight of western military sociology and combat experience. This experience has been that ideology is seldom important to the 'grunts' in the line who basically depend on the personal attachments of the immediate group for support and unit solidarity.

But evidence past and present suggests that Ivan would fight hard for the *rodina* – the Soviet motherland. As Hedrick Smith has written, 'The passionate patriotism of the Russians contains not only this deep and unwavering love of homeland . . . but a primeval sense of community, a clannish defensiveness toward outsiders and intolerance toward renegades within, of Victorian pride in national power and empire, of blinding ethnocentrism and of conviction of moral superiority'. Patriotic, well equipped, well trained and led by a cadre of professional military members of the Communist Party, the Soviet soldier would surely prove as tough and determined an adversary in the future as he has in the past.

INDEX

Page numbers in italics refer to illustrations

Aeroflot 111
Afghanistan 28, 77, 79, 80, 94, 96, 121, 136, 141, 193, 206, *209-11*, 219, *220*
Africa 9, 32
air defense 100, 104, 106, 109, 111, 113, 114, 127, 130, 132, 135
Air Force 25
  Frontal Aviation 25, 102, 104-6, 111-16, 119-22, 141
  Long Range Aviation 25, 102, 107-10, 111, 124-5
  Military Transport Aviation 25, 111, 126-7
  National Air Defense Forces (PVO Strany) 25, 111, 127, 130, 132, 135
air superiority 102, 111, 113, 115
conscription 193
history 101
in World War II 102, 104
jet development 104-7, 108
operational control 101
organization 102, 104, 111, 112-13, 124, 126-7, 130
reconnaissance 111, 122, 124, 138
strategic role of 101, 108, 111
tactical role 100, 101, 102, 104-7, 111, 122, 141
training 115
air refueling 109, 124, 125, 135
aircraft
  An-12 126, *129, 130*
  An-22 127, *132*
  I-15, I-16 101
  Il-2 *100*, 102
  Il-10 104, 105
  Il-18 124
  Il-28 105, 153
  Il-38 *173, 204*
  Il-76 126, *127, 128*
  M-4 Bison *108*, 108-9, 124
  MiG-15 105, 106
  MiG-17 106, 10?
  MiG-19 106
  MiG-21 *28, 104,* 106, *115,* 115-16, 122, 138, 140

MiG-23 115, 116, *117,* 119, *119, 120,* 132
MiG-25 122, 132, *134, 135,* 138
MiG-27 115, 116, *117,* 119-20, 175
MiG-29 116, 141
Pl-2 *101*
SB-2 101
Sikorsky Muromets 101
Su-7 106, *106,* 107, 109, 116, 119
Su-15 132, *133*
Su-17 115, 116, *116,* 119
Su-22 *114*
Su-24 115, 116, *117,* 120
Su-25 121
Su-27 116
Tu-4 108
Tu-16 108, *108,* 111, 124, 125, 153
Tu-22 Blinder 110, *110,* 124
Tu-22M Backfire 100, 125, *127*
Tu-28 125, 132, *133*
Tu-85 108
Tu-95 *2, 23, 99,* 108, 109, *112, 123,* 124, 138, *219*
Tu-126 *136*
Yak-25 106
Yak-28 106-7, *107,* 120, 122, 124, 132
Yak-36 *172*
aircraft, Western allies 52, 108, 116, 120, 121, 125
aircraft carriers 175
  Kiev class 144, *169,* 181, 188
  Minsk 172
Andropov, Yuri 21, *23, 24,* 25, 28
anti-aircraft weapons 68, 90, 111, 114
  M53 59 sp gun *93*
  S-60 57mm *66*
  ZSU-23-4 sp gun *15*
  see also missiles, surface-to-air
anti-ballistic missile defense (USSR) 45, *48, 50,* 52, 135
anti-ballistic missile defense (US) 43, 50, 52
anti-tank weapons 93
  AT-6 Spiral 122
  RPG-7 grenade launcher *73*
  SD-44 85mm gun *76*
  T-12 100mm gun *69*
  Sagger missile *18, 88*

Swatter missile 122
Arab-Israeli conflict 8, 136, 138
  1973 106, 125, 140-41
  1982 Lebanon 17
armored command vehicle BTR-50PU *192*
armored personnel carriers 90, 94
  BTR series *19, 68, 80-81,* 94, *193, 210*
armored scout car BRDM *67*
arms, export of 8-9, 17
Army 12, 25, 56-7, 62-5, 67-8, 70, 74, 77, 79-86, 88-90, 93-6
  and combined arms concept 77, 80, 94
  and conventional operations 77, 89
  conscription 83
  in World War I *56-8*
  in World War II 21, 56, *59, 63,* 64-5, 67, 93
  mobilization 77, 79, 82, 84, 193
  nuclear strategy and 74, 86, 88
  organization 25, 67-8, 70, 77, 79, 80-81, 85
  present deployment 79-80, 96
  rear services 81-2
  roles of 57, 65, 77, 81
  Stalin and 10, 62, 64
  strategy 68, 74, 81
  strength 84
  tactics 68, 85-6, 94
  training *19,* 86, 88, 90, 193, *194-5*
  transport 82-3
  weaponry 89-90, 93-4, 95
artillery 80, 86, 88, 90, 93-4
  ASU-57 assault gun *66*
  ASU-85 sp gun *86*
  D-30 122mm howitzer 77, *87*
  self propelled guns *75,* 94
assault rifles,
  Kalashnikov 55, 79, 92, 94-5, *96*
Austria 68

Baker, John 41, 42, 49
Bakes, Arthur 168
Basic Principles of Operational Arts and Tactics (Savkin) 84
Bathurst, Robert 148, 150

battlecruiser, *Kirov* class 144, 183, *186-7*
Baxter, William 218
Becquerel, Henri 33
Berdyaev, Nikolai 8
Berman, Robert 41, 42, 49, 112, 115
Bolsheviks, Bolshevism 8, 9, 59, 62, 148, 192, 201
breakthrough attack 85, 86, 93
Brest Litovsk Treaty 59
Brezhnev, Leonid 8, 16, 21, *23, 24,* 25, 28, 47, 74, 196, *201,* 217
Britain 9, 17, 32, 67, 68
Brown, General George 95
Budenny, Marshal S M *58,* 62

Carter, President 47, 50, *201*
Castro, Fidel 12
Chiang Kai-shek 8, 63
China 8, 11, 17, 48, 63, 84
  and Russia 15-16, 43, 57, 74, 77
  and the West 28
  goes nuclear 74
Churchill, Winston 11, *14*
civil defense 192, 194, 196
Civil War 8, 62, 84, 148
combined arms concept 77, 94, 100, 111, 141, 161, 176
Communist Party 21, 192, 196-8, 201, 210, 220
conscription 83, 192-4
cruisers 161
  Boris Chilikin 153
  Kara class *11, 176,* 181
  Kresta class *177,* 180, *180,* 181
  Kynda class 177, 180, *215*
  Sverdlov class *152,* 153
Cuba 8, 12, 80, 140
  missile crisis *36-7,* 38, 40, *41*
Curie, Pierre et Marie 33
Czechoslovakia 17, 18, 80
  1968 intervention 18, *20-21,* 32, 77, 80, 82-3, 84, 136, 141, 193, 219

Defense, Ministry of 21, 57, 161
defense spending 18-20
destroyers 161
  Kashin class *4, 157,*

159, 179, 180, 181
Kildin class 177
Kola class 153
Kotlin class *152,* 153, *155, 157, 159,* 177, *178,* 181
Krupny class 177, 181
Riga class *179*
Skoryy class 153, *179*
Sovremennyy class *28,* *177,* 184
Udaloy class 184, *189*
detente 25, 28
deterrence 49, 50, 88
DOSAAF (Voluntary Association for Army, Navy and Air Force) 193, 194, 216

East Germany 17, 18
echeloning 85
Egypt 12, 93, 106, 136, 138, 140
Eisenhower, President *15*
electronic countermeasures 116, 120, 122, 124, 125
Erickson, John 113
Ethiopia 141, 189
ethnic problems 208, 210
Europe, Eastern 57, 65, 68, 80, 84, 136
Europe, Western 28, 36, 42, 47, 49, 65, 84, 111, 112, 116, 124

Far East 36, 42, 47, 57, 63, 101, 111, 112, 124
Fermi, Enrico 33
Finnish War 1939-40 64
Five Year Plans 58, 63, 149
France 9, 17, 67, 68
'fronts' 25, 81
Friedman, Norman 162
frigates 181, *181, 183,* *196*
Frunze, M V 21, *58,* 62, 192
Fuchs, Klaus 33

Gabriel, Richard 204, 207, 208
Gagarin, Yuri 37
General Staff (Stavka) 21, 24, 57
Germany 10, 36, 62, 64-5, 101
Gorshkov, Adm S G 144, 153, 156, 157, 160, 161, 163, *172,* 175, 176, 188, 189
Grechko, Marshal 196
grenade launchers 55,

79, 93
GRU see Main Intelligence Directorate

Heiman, Leo 82
helicopter carrier (cruiser) Moskva 153, 158, 170, 175
helicopters 18, 85, 121-2
Ka-25 158, 163, 170, 180, 181, 183, 184, 197
Mi-4 121, 124
Mi-6/10 121, 121
Mi-8 12, 121, 122, 122
Mi-24 78, 95, 121, 122, 122, 216
Mi-26 121
Helix 189
Herzog, John 158
Hitler, Adolf 9, 10, 64
hovercraft 184, 184, 187
Hungary 17, 18, 68, 80
1956 intervention in 18, 80, 84, 219

India 12, 32, 107, 140
infantry combat vehicle BMP 18, 55, 68, 78, 79, 80, 94, 95
internal security 8, 9, 28
Iran 28, 140
Iraq 80, 125, 140
Isby, David 84, 86, 94
Israel 8, 17, 32, 106, 136, 138
Ivan IV, Tsar 58

Japan 28, 32, 57, 63, 64, 77, 84, 101
Johnson, President 32
Jones, Ellen 194, 211

KGB see State Security
Kahn, Herman 49
Kapitsa, Peter 33
Katyusha 'Stalin organ' 36
Keegan, John 9
Kennedy, President 38
Kosygin, Alexei 74
Komsomol 194, 196, 197, 198
Krylov, Marshal 50
Kutakhov, Marshal 111
Kutuzov, General 56
Khrushchev, Nikita 15, 15, 74, 164, 177
and Cuba 38, 40
and external security 11, 17
nuclear doctrine 14-15, 16, 70, 157, 176

Landing ships 182, 184, 186

Lebanon 17
Lenin, I V 9, 9, 59, 147
Libya 80, 140

MccGwire, Michael 144, 146, 149, 151, 156, 160, 163, 181
MacIntosh, Malcolm 77
MacNamara, Robert 42, 49
Main Intelligence Directorate (GRU) 24
Main Political Directorate 196-8, 208
Malinovsky, Marshal 68
Mao Tse-tung 15, 43
meeting engagement 85
Middle East 9, 32, 42, 107, 141
military power
and foreign goals 8, 28
and security 8
command structure 21, 24-5
competition with US 9, 11, 12, 17, 28
conventional weapons complement nuclear 100
doctrine, strategy 14, 28
function of 21, 196
garrison economy 18-20
in World War II 10
role in history 8
military service
conscription 83, 192-4
morale and discipline 211-12, 216, 219-20
NCOs and men 203, 207-8, 210
officer corps 67, 198, 201, 203-4, 206, 208
political context 196-7, 217, 220
Military Strategy (Sokolovsky) 21, 43
Milyutin, Dmitry 59
MIRV (multiple independently targeted re-entry vehicle) 45, 46, 46, 47, 165, 168
missile attack boats 155, 156, 160
missiles, air-to-air 115
AA-2 Atoll 114, 119
AA-3 Anab 132
AA-6 Acrid 134
AA-7 Apex 115, 116
AA-8 Ahpid 115, 116
AA-9 116
missiles, air-to-surface
AS-1 Kennel 32

AS-3 Kitchen 109
AS-4 Kitchen 125
AS-5 Kelt 124, 125
AS-6 Kingfisher 124, 125
AS-7 Kerry 116
AS-9 121
AS-10 116
missile, ASW
SS-N-14 180, 181, 184
missiles, anti-tank
AT-3 Sagger 88
AT-4 Spigot 88
missiles, ballistic 14, 32, 34, 42, 47, 49, 50, 70, 100
guidance systems 37, 50, 52
MIRV 45, 46, 46, 47, 165, 168
SS-3 36
SS-4 31, 36, 38, 42, 47
SS-5 36, 36, 38, 42, 47
SS-6 36, 37
SS-7 37, 40, 47
SS-8 32, 37, 40
SS-9 33, 40, 41, 42, 45
SS-11 40, 41, 42, 45, 47, 52
SS-12 Scaleboard 48, 93
SS-13 40, 48
SS-17 45, 46, 47
SS-18 45, 46, 52
SS-19 45, 46, 47, 52
SS-20 47, 47
SS-X-14 42
missiles, ballistic, US
Minuteman series 40, 41-2, 45, 46, 47
MX 44, 45, 46, 47
Pershing 47
missiles, cruise 47, 52, 111, 165, 177
SS-N-1 177
SS-N-2 181
SS-N-3 165, 167, 175, 177, 180
SS-N-7 167
SS-N-19 169, 183, 186
missiles, cruise, US 184
missiles, interceptor
Galosh 49, 50, 52
Griffon 50
missiles, interceptor, US 50
missiles, short-range, tactical
SS-1, SS-2 36
FROG (Free Rocket Over Ground) 38-9, 50, 89, 93
Scud 51, 81, 93, 97, 200
missiles, submarine launched 40, 47, 49, 50, 52, 159, 163
SS-N-4, SS-N-5 164

SS-N-6 44, 158, 165
SS-N-8 159, 165
SS-N-13 167
SS-N-15 168
SS-N-18 165, 168
missiles, submarine launched, US 52, 160
missiles, surface-to-air 68, 100, 106, 109, 111, 114, 127, 132, 136, 138, 141, 177
SA-2 104, 132, 140, 141
SA-3 Goa 105, 135, 138, 177
SA-4 138
SA-5 132, 135
SA-6 138, 218
SA-8, SA-9 137
SA-10 135, 141
SA-N-1 177, 180, 181
SA-N-3 181
SA-N-4 181, 183
SA-N-6 183, 184, 186
SA-N-7 184
missile, surface-to-surface
SS-N-12 184
mobilization 77, 79, 82, 84, 193
mutually assured destruction 49
Myagkov, Alexei 212, 216

Napoleon 8, 58, 218
nation in arms concept 192
NATO 11, 16, 17, 36, 43, 49, 57, 67, 77, 84, 88, 141, 159
Navy 25, 65, 111, 190-91
Baltic Sea fleet 25, 161, 198, 212
Black Sea fleet 25, 161, 187
Northern fleet 25, 161, 183, 187
Pacific fleet 25, 161, 183, 187
amphibious forces 184, 186-8
air forces 153, 161, 172-3, 175
conscription 193
Gorshkov and 153, 156-7, 163
history of 144-9
in World War II 149-50, 150-52
organization 161, 187
planning 158-60
roles of 157-8, 160-61, 175, 188
submarines in 162-9, 172

surface vessels 175-7, 180-84
tactics 162
Nixon, President 49
North Vietnam 74, 80, 140
nuclear reaction 33-4
nuclear war
concern with 43, 52, 86
doctrine of 14-15, 32, 49, 50
strategy in 50, 67, 70, 86, 88-9, 114
training for 43, 84

Odom, William 193, 201
Oppenheimer, J Robert 33

Pakistan 32
peaceful coexistence 15
Peru 140
Peter the Great 8, 58, 145
Poland 17, 18, 68, 77, 80, 84, 212-13
Politburo 21, 23
Polmar, Norman 157, 162

Reagan, President 47, 50
Record, Jeffrey 84, 89
Red Army 9, 56, 59, 62-5
Red Guards 7, 59
Red Star 32, 88, 89, 193, 204, 210
rocketry 36, 89
Rohwer, Jurgen 144, 146, 149
Romania 17, 18, 68
Roosevelt, F D 11, 14
Rosenbergs, the 33
Rotmistrov, Marshal 90
Rush, Myron 18
Russia, imperial 8, 56-7, 57-9
Russo-Japanese war 59, 146

SALT see Strategic Arms Limitation Talks
Savkin, V Y 84, 89-90
Scott, William and Harriet 14
Seaton, Albert 84
Seapower of the State (Gorshkov) 157
security 8, 9-12, 14-17, 28
Shaposhnikov, Marshal 65
Skirdo, M P 89
Smith, Hedrik 220
Sokolovsky, Marshal 21, 43
Soviets
air policy 135-6, 140-41

and China 15, 16, 43, 63, 74
and nuclear war 43, 52, 86, 88, 93
and Warsaw Pact 17-18, 57
as superpower 8, 17, 32, 43, 47
competition with US 9, 11, 12, 17, 28, 32, 34, 36-8, 40, 42, 65, 104, 144
defense spending 18-20
detente and 25, 28
export of arms 8-9, 17, 140, 141
foreign goals 8, 28, 140
garrison economy 18-20
in World War II 10, 56, 60, 84
industry 9, 18, 19-20, 63, 64, 65
inter-war German collaboration 62, 101
military command structure 21, 24-5
military doctrine 9, 11, 14, 15, 21, 25, 28, 49, 50, 57, 67, 70, 81, 84-6, 88-9, 104, 135-6, 144, 156, 159, 161, 192
naval policy 144, 145, 152-3, 156, 157-60
nuclear development 33, 34, 36-8, 40, 47, 57, 67, 70, 104-5
Vietnam and 74, 80, 140
Soyuz spacecraft 34-5
space race 9, 34, 34-5, 36-7
Spain 8, 63, 101
Stalin, J 9, 10, 11, 17, 101, 148, 152
and army 10, 62, 64, 67
and nuclear weapons 12, 33, 67, 70
in World War II 10-11, 14, 56, 64
purges 62, 64, 149, 201
START see Strategic Arms Reduction Talks
State Security, Committee on (KGB) 21, 83, 196, 198
Strategic Arms Limitation Talks 32, 43-4
SALT I 37, 40, 41, 44, 46, 47, 52, 168, 172
SALT II 47

Vladivostock Accord 44
Strategic Arms Reduction Talks 47, 52
strategic nuclear forces 8, 11-12, 14, 17, 50, 70
basic factor in future war 14, 16, 70
limitations 32, 40, 43-4, 47
Strategic Rocket Forces 25, 106, 124, 144, 188, 216
formation 14, 25, 34, 157
function 25, 34, 109, 110, 111, 164
missiles of 36-7, 160
'strategic triad' 34
Strokov, A A 14
submarines 124, 144, 148-9, 149, 153
submarines, SS
Bravo class 168
Foxtrot class 25, 143, 167, 168
Golf class 164, 164, 172
Kilo class 169
Quebec class 153
Tango class 172
Whiskey class 153,

164, 165, 165, 172
submarines, SSB
Zulu class 153, 164
submarines, SSBN 156, 157-8, 164-5, 188
Delta class 159, 165, 165, 168, 172, 215
Hotel class 164, 165
Typhoon class 166, 168
Yankee class 44, 158, 165, 167, 172
submarines, SSBN, US 52, 160, 164, 168
submarines, SSG
Juliett class 163, 167
submarines, SSGN
Charlie class 165, 167, 168
Echo class 162, 167, 169
Oscar class 169
submarines, SSN
Alfa class 166, 168-9
November class 163, 165
Victor class 28, 162, 167, 168, 196
submarines, SSN, NATO 159
Syria 17, 80, 93, 140

Tactical nuclear weapons 16, 68, 86, 89, 93, 106

tanks 1, 86, 89, 90
BLG-60 bridging tank 82
Joseph Stalin 67
KV 65, 67
T-34 16, 63, 65, 67, 93
T-54/T-55 series 93
T-55 20, 21, 69, 73, 74-5, 82
T-62 90-91, 93
T-64 10, 85, 93
T-64/T-72 series 93
T-72 96, 97, 194
T-80 93
tank, light
PT-76 19, 86
Teller, Edward 33
Third World 8, 12, 74
Tolubko, Marshal 217
'total war' 192
training 198-9, 203
military 19, 86, 88, 90, 193, 211, 216-18
political 196
Trans-Siberian Railroad 82
Trotsky, Leon 62
Tsiolkowski, Konstantin 36
Tukhachevsky, Marshal 58, 62, 201

United States 32, 43
and Cuban missile

crisis 38, 40
and space race 34, 35, 36
and USSR as superpower 8, 17, 32, 43
competition of USSR 9, 11, 12, 17, 28, 32, 34, 36-8, 40-42, 65, 144
defense policy 32, 34, 49, 50
forces in Europe 11, 67, 68
involvement in SEA 74
nuclear arsenal of 11, 12, 17
policy re USSR 28, 32, 43, 49
Soviet policy re 57, 77, 84
United States Department of Defense 19, 88, 125, 141
Ustinov, Dmitry 21, 28

Vasilevsky, Marshal 65
Vernadsky, V I 33
Voluntary Association for the Army, Navy and Air Forces see DOSAAF
Voroshilov, Marshal 58, 62

Warsaw Pact 17-18, 57, 95
aircraft of 115
forces of 82, 88, 93
membership 17
organization 18
Soviet General Staff Directorate for 24
weapons systems, quality of 20
West Germany 11, 16
White Russians 9, 62
Wolfe, Thomas 65, 109
women, and conscription 194
World War I 32, 56, 57, 59
World War II 10, 21, 32, 56, 59, 60, 63, 67, 93, 94, 102, 104, 150-52, 201, 219

Yakubovsky, Marshal 89
Yugoslavia 84

Zampolit 196, 197
Zavilov, I 32, 88
Zhukov, Marshal 63, 65, 68, 68

Acknowledgements

The author and publishers would like to thank Donald Sommerville who edited this book, Design 23 who designed it and Ron Watson who compiled the index. The majority of the pictures were supplied by the Public Affairs and Audiovisual services of the US Department of Defense, the US Navy, US Army and US Air Force. Production of this book would have been impossible without their kind assistance. In addition thanks are owed to the following individuals and agencies who also supplied illustrations.

AP: p 15.
Bison Picture Library: pp 10, 18-19 all four, 28 left, 30-31, 34-35 both inset, 42 both, 50, 54-55, 58 both lower, 70 top, 74 top, 74-75, 78 top, 79, 90 top two, 91 lower, 92 top, 93 top, 94, 95, 104 top, 105 both, 120 bottom, 158 bottom, 167 top, 168, 218 top, 219 top.
Chaz Bowyer: p 100 top.
Bundesarchiv: pp 102, 146 top.
Peter Endsleigh Castle: (artwork) pp 87 top, 91 top, 111.
Hoover Institute: pp 6-7, 8, 9 all three.
Robert Hunt Library: pp 56 bottom, 57, 68 top, 100 bottom.
Imperial War Museum, London: pp 14, 145 both, 146-147, 150 top, 151 top left.
Ministry of Defence, London: p 59.
NASA: pp 34-35 main picture.
Map p 210 © Richard Natkiel.
Novosti: pp 56 both top, 58 top, 60-61, 62-63, 65, 101, 148-149 all three, 150-151.
Popperfoto: p 211.
TASS: pp 52-53, 96 top, 97 bottom, 151 top right, 202-203.
Ullstein: pp 16, 17.
Wide World Photos: pp 20-21 all three, 23 inset, 24 both, 28 top, 201, 209, 210 top & center.